NOMAD
HEART

I0211579

NOMAD HEART

Adventures on and off the set

Ian Roberts

Jonathan Ball Publishers
Johannesburg & Cape Town

All rights reserved.
No part of this publication may be reproduced or transmitted, in any form or by any means, without prior permission from the publisher or copyright holder.

© Text: Ian Keith Roberts (2024)
© Cover images: Alet Pretorius (main images on front and back cover) and Barry Lucas (image of Ian on the set of *Arende*)
© Internal images: Ian Roberts, Jane Curtis, Barrie Hesse, Barry Lucas, Gallo Images
© Published edition: Jonathan Ball Publishers (2024)

Originally published in South Africa in 2024 by
JONATHAN BALL PUBLISHERS
A division of Media24 (Pty) Ltd
PO Box 33977
Jeppestown
2043

ISBN 978-1-77619-354-7
ebook ISBN 978-1-77619-355-4
audiobook ISBN 978-1-77619-445-2

Every effort has been made to trace the copyright holders and to obtain their permission for the use of copyright material. The publishers apologise for any errors or omissions and would be grateful to be notified of any corrections that should be incorporated in future editions of this book.

jonathanball.co.za
x.com/JonathanBallPub
facebook.com/JonathanBallPublishers

Cover by Sean Robertson
Design and typesetting by Johan Koortzen
Set in 11.5 pt on 15pt Adobe Garamond Pro

This book is dedicated to the Roberts family of Baddaford Citrus Estates: To my grandfather Daniel and my grandmother Gangie Isobel (McDonald); my father Llewellyn snr, my uncle Dan snr, my mother Lynn and my aunt Theo; my brother Llewellyn jnr, sisters Barrie and Jane and my cousins Dan jnr and Jonathan, Barbara and Sallyanne.

And then, of course, the Hunter-Gatherers: Pieter Trompetter, Djonni Kieghlaar, Pese and Kununu Piet.

Also to the staff at the Big House: Florence Duze, Mieta Piet, sis' Tyeniwe Vusani, sis' Nonkululeko Mselana and Thembekile Qeqe.

Lastly, to the one who left us too soon, Christopher.

Contents

1

We, the Hunter-Gatherers

I GREW UP WITH MANY scary things on the doorstep of my childhood home at Baddaford Citrus Estates in the foothills of the Katberg mountains of the rural Eastern Cape. Some kids grow up having to face far worse things, such as war and all its horrific brutalities. As a farmer's son, I was brought up in the supposedly idyllic world of orange orchards and irrigation furrows.

But, even as a small child, I knew that the ghosts of violence hung in the air. I couldn't see them, but I could feel them. In 1879, only eighty years before my birth, the Frontier Wars over the land came to an end, with the Kei River accepted as the boundary. I was to discover that possession of the piece of land now called Baddaford Citrus Estates, covered by the peaceful-looking orange trees my great-grandfather had planted in the early 1900s, had once been hotly contested by Xhosa pastoralist-warriors, British settlers and the Boers.

When I was a child, nobody ever told me about these conflicts. It has been said that Carl Jung, the Swiss psychiatrist and psychoanalyst, described how, after landing at the airports of certain countries, he could smell blood in the air – a fact that would make him cancel his visit and fly straight back home to Switzerland. It was as if this same smell hung in the air of the Eastern Cape world that surrounded me.

One evening, when I was about four years old, I was woken in the deep of the night by a violent hammering on our kitchen door. My father, Llewellyn, opened it to find a Xhosa woman on the doorstep. Her husband had sliced her open in a drunken frenzy. As my father drove her down the dirt road to the hospital, eight kilometres away in the town of Fort Beaufort, the poor woman's intestines had to be held in her stomach cavity by my mother. Luckily, the woman made a full recovery.

I also recall one Saturday afternoon when I watched a fight between a coloured man we called Lawiesh (his name was actually Louis), who was

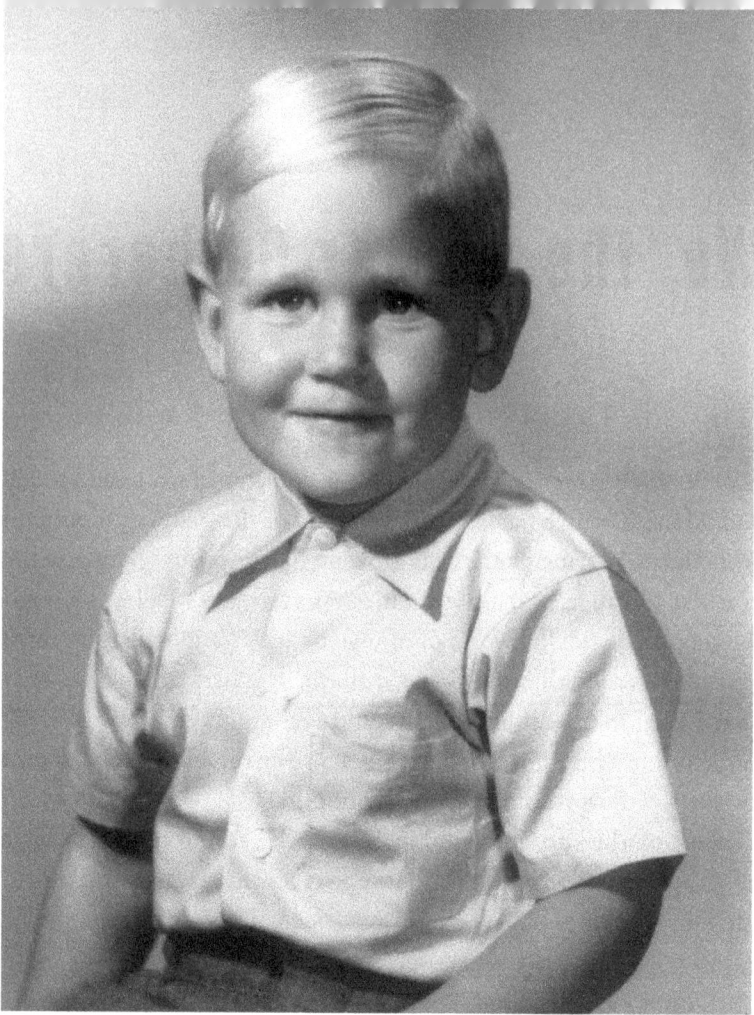

Best clothes, best hair, best smile. A photo of me as a young boy.

armed with a knife, and a Xhosa man called Mzwandile, who was armed with a *kierie* (a knobbed stick; *isigweba* in Xhosa). Their confrontation took place at the farm labourers' huts. Everybody had been drinking a lot of booze and their blood was hot for violence. The women screamed and wailed, while the winds of a brewing thunderstorm blasted the bushes, shaking them violently and whipping up clouds of dust, all adding to what seemed to me a frenzied madness. Fortunately for my innocent young eyes, Lawiesh was hit by such severe blows that he crumpled to the ground before he could stab and draw blood, and the fight ended. Still, I felt numbed by this vista of violence. If I had been given the choice right there and then, I might have liked, even as a delinquent, to have made like Jung and left that place for good.

My parents, Llewellyn and Lynn, outside St Andrew's College chapel
on their wedding day.

In the 1830s, my great-great-grandfather, Daniel Roberts, had the temerity and good faith to trek eastwards from the Albany district, where most of the 1820 Settlers had established themselves, generally as farmers. He set up a trading store on or near the banks of the Peddie River. He was also a lay preacher for the Wesleyan Church in the Grahamstown district. It was in this capacity that Daniel played a part in organising, and paying for, a son of the Xhosa chief Ngqika to travel by ship to Scotland to attend boarding school there.

In 1837, the Xhosa rose up and invaded the Cape Colony from the east. (If you ask me, the authorities in England should have been more honest with the 1820 Settlers, who were sent to a strange, dangerous land basically to act as a buffer between the Xhosa and the Cape Colony.) Early one morning, the house of my great-great-grandfather was surrounded by a horde of young warriors. While his trading store was being plundered and burnt, he was asked to send his wife and children away: unlike the Zulu under Dingane, the Xhosa never killed the women and children of the Settlers. The same cannot be said of Mzilikazi's impis, who, during their breakout from Zululand, wiped the eastern foothills of the Drakensberg clean of people.

(Recently, a journalist who was writing an article phoned me with a question: 'Mr Roberts, as an actor who was raised in an English family, how do you feel about having acted in so many TV series in the language of the oppressor?'

'Look, I've only acted in two TV series in Zulu,' I responded.

A pause followed.

'Excuse me? No, I'm talking about Afrikaans.'

'Yes of course, I know you are. But Afrikaans is not the only language of oppression. Zulu is too.')

But the Xhosa were not like this. With Daniel's young wife and small children having been sent to safety, the warriors told him they were going to kill him and burn his house.

'On whose orders am I to die?' Daniel asked, playing his last, desperate card.

This proved to be a perplexing question, as no one seemed sure. The raiding party hadn't been sent by the king. They were on their own mission of retribution against the settlers.

'Who is your king?' Daniel then asked.

They answered that his name was Ngqika.

'Well, then, you must first ask Nkosi Ngqika if Daniel Roberts is to be killed.'

Because Ngqika was not far away, a runner was sent. While they waited for the runner to return, the young warriors became impatient and began nicking Daniel's skin with their assegai points, saying, 'When the runner comes back and says the nkosi tells us to kill you, that is where I am going to sink my blade into your pale white skin.'

After a while, streaks of blood were running down his body. The runner came speeding back in great haste shouting, 'Yekani! Inkosi ithethile umthetho wayo!' (The king has spoken!)

My entry for the annual art competition at St Andrew's Preparatory School.

Ngqika's response was that if one hair on the head of Daniel Roberts was disturbed, he would have all the warriors killed.

Daniel was allowed to retreat to the shade of his house, while some warriors tried to put out the fire raging in his trading store. The truth was that the leader of the insurrection was a son of the king – and the same son whom Daniel Roberts had helped to go and study in Scotland! Yet he had returned from his studies still full of war.

This incident was mentioned to us children as an example of how uncertain the chances of survival were for the Roberts clan in those days. Several years ago, I went to the Albany Museum in Grahamstown (today Makhanda) and, under the guidance of the librarian, found an article in the *Grahamstown Journal* from 1837 that proved the story told to me by my parents was true and correct.

After this, Daniel decided to leave the frontier area and head westwards, and he became involved with a Wesleyan Church farming project near the settlement of Salem. Here, struggling Africans were given a place to settle and work on land bought by the Wesleyans, and it was here that Daniel built a church, which stands to this day.

It is my good fortune that the Roberts family survived the violence of the Frontier Wars. Life was slightly easier for my great-grandfather, Llewellyn James Roberts, who was an inventor-farmer. He was the first man in the world to construct a gate by *bending* steel tubing without weakening or disfiguring it. Having patented this technique, he made good money for a while building gates at his factory, located on a railway siding called Kroomie, between Fort Beaufort and Adelaide.

After buying the farm in 1903, he decided to build a house to his own design. The position of the house was dictated by where the blue granite boulders stopped rolling after he'd dynamited a cliff high up on the mountainside. The boulders were cut into building blocks by British stonemasons who had been commissioned by the Cape government to build a bridge over the Kat River at Fort Beaufort. The bridge has withstood many raging floods of the Kat River.

Llewellyn's house accommodated the steep slope of the hill and consisted of three storeys with no internal passageways. All the living areas radiated from a large central room, which was (and still is) called 'the Court', created by raising the middle of the corrugated-iron roof, with two rows of windows added to allow the sun in. Llewellyn built a grand stairway, with a curving wooden balustrade, leading from the top floor down into the Court, and the rooms were exquisitely wood-panelled.

Sadly, the house burnt down in the 1930s and the two young men who were staying there at the time could save only two things: a magnificent Steinway baby grand piano and a three-quarter-size billiard table. The fire had started because the gardener had left a paraffin lamp burning in the cellar. The blue granite walls, however, still stood gaunt but proud when the smoke cleared, and the house was rebuilt – less grandly finished than before but still magnificent. We called it 'the Big House' and this was where I grew up.

My great-grandfather Llewellyn died young, at the age of 54, a result of burns sustained in a freak accident near Douglas, a far-off town on the Vaal River, where he had been installing a pump. This pump, designed by an Englishman, HA Humphrey, had to be placed in a pit dug down to below the level of the river. The water in the vertical pipe, which served as cylinder, created a piston to compress a mixture of petrol and air. When the mixture was ignited, the explosion pushed the water upwards to irrigate the farmland above.

At some point the petrol caught fire, engulfing the pit in sudden and horrific heat. Llewellyn managed to scramble up the ladder but went back down into the inferno to help his two labourers escape. In doing so, he was so badly burnt that he had to drive to Kimberley, assisted by

The Big House at Baddaford Citrus Estates, home of the Roberts family.

his young daughter Helen, who had to change the gears for him. They managed to get to Kimberley but, sadly, Llewellyn died some days later in hospital. The labourer survived.

Many years later, in about 1993, I was staying in Douglas while shooting the third series of the SABC production *Arende*. On an off day, I went to visit the farm of distant relatives, the Jacksons, on the north bank of the Vaal River. Bruce Jackson and I got chatting over a cup of tea and I asked if they knew where my great-grandfather had been fatally burnt. They told me how to get there and I made my way down the river to a neighbouring farm.

On the red, barren earth, beneath some scrawny white-thorn trees, I found a circle of large stones about six metres in diameter that marked the place. Rains had washed the pit full of silt, almost completely filling it in. I stood looking at it, finding myself lost in imaginings of the calamity that had happened there eighty or so years before. Right beside the circle of stones sparkled the icy-blue waters of the Vaal River.

Llewellyn's son Daniel, my grandfather, had to take over the running of the farm at the age of 17. As a boy, he had been struck down with polio, which so badly withered one of his legs that he had to wear a metal calliper. He walked with difficulty using a walking stick and had a pronounced limp.

My grandfather was a quiet man. In his sixties, the polio seemed to get to him, and he also had a weakened heart. One day, he was gruff with me when I got in his way. I scampered out of the Big House very quickly. A little while later, my grandmother, Gangie, found me and said soothingly, 'My boy, you mustn't think that your grandfather means you ill. He is just not feeling well, please forgive him.'

But I could never have felt offended by my grandfather. He was like a god to me. He had a study into which I never, ever thought of venturing. It was dark and full of magical things – finely crafted bamboo trout rods and feathered flies, and on a table stood all the glass pipettes and flasks and things that were used to test the acidity and sugar levels of the oranges to see if they were ready for export.

Once, three of us were ordered to be outside our grandfather's study at 10 on a Monday morning. Our small band consisted of me, my eldeer

My father (left) and his twin brother, Dan.

brother Llewellyn and my cousin Dan (who, although he was christened Dan, had always been called Ronald, his second name, because there were so many Dans on the farm). Dan and I were born less than a month apart and both our families lived on Baddaford Citrus Estates. Our fathers were identical twins and both worked for my grandfather.

That morning, the three of us had been scrubbed clean by our mothers and were dressed in the best clothes we had. We even had our hair combed. We thought our grandfather had found out about some of the bad things we'd done, and that we were in for the high jump, but we couldn't work out what we'd done.

Eventually, our grandfather struggled down the stairs. Time seemed to stand still as he gazed down at us, leaning on his walking stick with the curved handle, the rubber-covered tip placed on the floor uncomfortably between my hastily polished shoes. At this moment we tried to think one last time what we might have done wrong, until eventually God spoke.

'Good morning, boys.'

'Good morning, Grampa,' we chimed.

Standing between the two Llewellyns – my father and my elder brother –
at Schoenmakerskop, where I'd just caught a bluefish.

I loved the ocean from the first time I experienced it. I'm on the far left
with my brother Llewellyn and sister Barrie next to me.

'Thank you, young fellows, for coming here. Please come into my office.' We followed him into the hallowed room.

Three chairs had been set out for us. We sat down and glanced at each other.

'Right, now today I am going to teach you boys how to tie trout-fishing knots.'

With great relief, we watched avidly as he demonstrated the knots to us. I still use one of the knots I learnt that day when I fish from the rocks into the sea.

'Always among the huts' could have been my second name, because that is where you were most likely to find me as a young boy. The huts were the houses of the farm labourers and their families, which were situated up the steep bushy hill behind the Big House. My affinity for the huts had much to do with the fact that my friends stayed there.

One of my first friends was George Piet, the eldest son of our cook, Mieta Piet. George was a highly emotional type of person and also a bit older than me. One fine winter's morning, I heard an altercation out behind the kitchen: my brother Llewellyn and George were fighting over some issue. Eventually, George laid into my brother with a *kierie*, hitting him violently across the back and on his legs.

This was the first time I became aware that living inside me was a mad red-haired Irishman, who feared nothing and no man (this was probably thanks to my mother's Irish heritage). I hurried upstairs to where my brother's .22 rifle was stored, and ran back out. George saw me coming, dashed through the fence and headed into the thick bush up the hill. I fired a bullet at his disappearing form and then chased after him into the bush, past the huts, swearing Xhosa obscenities that seriously insulted his bloodline. Thankfully, he managed to vanish.

So did our friendship.

After that, my comrades were Xhosa-speaking coloured boys more my own age. They were the descendants of Khoi soldiers who had been granted land by the British for helping them fight the Xhosa during the Frontier Wars. These men had been conscripted mostly from mission stations in the Cape, places such as Genadendal and Elim. Their lands were a bit further up the Kat Valley, at places such as Lower Blinkwater, Balfour and Hertzog.

One of my comrades was Pieter Trompetter – might his grandfather have been a trumpeter in the Cape colonial forces? Pieter was a scrawny boy like me, but he had a swollen midriff, which I was told was caused by a malady called kwashiorkor, the product of malnutrition. I never knew who Pieter's parents were and neither did he. He didn't seem to care much about them, or perhaps that was just because he had a remarkable ability to turn any situation into a humorous one. When people called him 'No-Roesu' (derived from *roes*, which means rust in Afrikaans) because some of his teeth were discoloured, he would say, 'Andikhathaleli! Solanki ndiyaphefumla!' which is a mixture of Xhosa and Afrikaans meaning, 'I don't care! As long as I am breathing!'

Pieter's other regular saying was: 'Khawubophe, man!' (How about rolling us a smoke, man!) And could he smoke! Tobacco was his first love, and perhaps his last. First prize for him was a smoke rolled from BB Best Blend, a pipe tobacco that had a little bit of Virginia mixed in. It was much milder than Boxer and much more smokeable than the black, viciously strong Katrivier blend, a dark and dubious pipe tobacco smoked only by old people. We preferred to roll our smokes in the brown paper used in shops in those days. Newspaper could also work.

Although we preferred tobacco, we also smoked *intsangu* (dagga) from early on. I remember getting back to St Andrew's College after a holiday and listening to 16-year-old Joburg and Cape Town boys boasting how they had smoked dope for the first time. *Welcome to the club*, I thought, *I've been smoking that stuff since I was ten years old!*

Pieter was being looked after by an old woman called Francis, who was the mother of Mieta Piet and the matriarch of the family. Mieta was a pale-skinned lady with almost Chinese eyes, a round face and the sparse black hair of the Khoi. She always oozed a sense of calm, and she became a second mother to me. Most importantly, Mieta was a magical cook: she could make anything taste good – even the carp we used to catch in the muddy Kat River.

My other two buddies, Pese and Kununu Piet, were children of Mieta and her partner Charlie Manie, with Pese the older of the two. His nickname was 'uFoh-Foh', mainly because he was tall and thin, and the wind could blow him around in a 'foh-foh' kind of way (derived from the sound we thought the wind made when it blew on him and fluffed through his loosely fitting clothes). Kununu was called 'Kaai' and I have no idea why. I was never called Ian and had different nicknames over the years. One of my earliest names was 'uMobza' because I was always looking for petrol for my motorbikes and go-kart, and in those days the Mobil petrol tankers, with the flying white horse painted on their bright-blue sides, were very popular. When I grew older, I was nicknamed 'uBhurkwala', which means 'young boy who has been circumcised and is about to be accepted among the ranks of men'.

My other friend was Djonni Kieghlaar, whose parents were James and Katie, two elderly coloured folks. I can still remember the night they cooked up a big pot of prickly pears on the fire. I was told that they were making prickly pear wine, which they would distil to make a powerful *turksvyblits* (prickly pear moonshine). They looked like alchemists as they stirred the gummy liquid in their giant pots, with halos of pungent steam and smoke wafting about their heads.

Once, when we were repairing the wire cars that we used to push around the dirt tracks on the farm, I offered Djonni the use of a pair of pliers my father had lent me with the firm instruction to give them back to him: 'Remember, those are *elastic* pliers, my boy!'

Djonni responded with a haughty smile. 'Hayi, suka wena. Andifuni tanga mna' (Bugger off, I don't need pliers).

He proudly held up his hands, which were far stouter than mine. 'Nazi tanga ezami!' (These are my pliers!)

To prove it, he bent a tough piece of galvanised wire with his fingers without any hassle. I was soon to learn that those tough fingers could also play a mean rhythm guitar. Given that we roamed around freely on the farm and also starting camping together in the wild, when I look back now, I think of our little group as the Hunter-Gatherers – a concept I would encounter in social anthropology, one of my subjects at Rhodes University. At night, we would sometimes walk from the Big House, where my grandparents lived, to the Cottage, home to my parents and their four children – my elder sister Barrie, my elder brother Llewellyn, me and my younger sister Jane – about a kilometre away along a track through the bush.

Now, the thing about the bushes in that part of the Eastern Cape is that they are extremely dense. Different hardy (and often thorny) plants form thickets, as if to keep each other company, creating an impenetrable

The Roberts siblings from left to right: Jane, me, Llewellyn and Barrie circa 1960.

tangled mass of spiky bush. At night, they took on a threatening aspect when the dense black shadows beneath them looked very scary.

As we set out into the dark, we were the epitome of bravery. Soon, however, one of us would begin to recall the stories of *oohili* – dark beings of the netherworld. Then came the scary descriptions of *izithunzela*, taller devils who could run very fast. No matter how fast you were, they would catch you and carry you off into the dark shadows and you would never be seen again. We were truly scared of these enigmatic entities, which were part of Xhosa folklore.

About 150 metres from the lighted security of the Big House, the track took a dip into a gully where a stream ran after the rains. It was always somewhere in the bottom of that dip that the shadows under the bushes would become blacker than the blackest ink. One of us would begin to walk almost imperceptibly faster, and, even though it was very dark, the others would notice and we would all begin to play catch-up. We knew only too well that the one who straggled would be caught first by the *izithunzela*, which always came up from behind. About halfway between the Big House and the Cottage stood the thickest clumps of bushes, with the blackest pools of shadow underneath.

'That is why *oohili* are so short,' said Pese in a breathy whisper. 'They can easily stand upright underneath these thorny bushes and watch us!'

He was edging ahead of us and we struggled to catch up without showing our fear by running. We had our own name for these ghosts – *oogcumm-gcumm* – because we believed their hairy feet would make a sound like *gcumm, gcumm, gcumm* as they ran to grab you in their powerful claws and drag you into their lair.

As we walked faster and faster it was just a matter of time until Pese would turn back and 'see' something creeping up on us and whisper under his breath, 'Ooo Thixo! Nasi isithunzela sivele ngaphantsi kwalela hlathi! Nasi emva kwam! I yoooooh!' (Oh my God, there is *isithunzela* underneath that bush there! Here it is just behind me!)

'I-yoooooh, ek skrik my amper dood!' (I-yooooh, I will die of fright!), Djonni Kieghlaar would shout, and that was more than we could bear. The dam wall of our bravery would burst and we'd run screaming with blind terror towards the single light that burnt several hundred metres away at the Cottage.

Other spooky things sustained our fear. Once, a baboon reportedly began climbing onto the roofs of the labourers' houses in the dead of night and dragging a chain over the corrugated iron. Of course, we Hunter-Gatherers knew that the baboon had been sent as *utokoloshe* – a creature that would bring the evil spells cast on the inhabitants of the house by a bad sangoma.

My uncle Dan decided to spend a night hiding in thick bush with a .303 rifle, so that if he saw such a baboon, he could kill it. I waited expectantly for the shot to echo through the night. But, after hearing nothing, I eventually fell asleep. In the morning, my uncle yawned as he told us he had watched the staff houses right through the night but had seen absolutely no sign of anything clambering over the roofs, let alone a baboon.

A Mfengu man called Nani lived on a remote piece of open veld deep on the hilly farm Argyle, which my grandfather had also bought. Nani was a great carpenter, and I would often watch in fascination as he cooked up his own glue in a pot on a Primus stove. When I got in the way, he scolded me and shoved me away, but I would always return to watch his every move with the old-fashioned awls and saws. I also noticed that he used no screws or nails, just wooden pegs. Watching grey-haired Nani weave his magic was the beginning of my love of working with my hands.

After Nani died, his family buried him in a fine grave with a carved granite headstone. Later, they all moved away and his house fell to the ground. Years later, I set out to find it. It took me at least an hour to cut through dense clumps of prickly pear and tightly woven branches of tambookie thorn bushes, with their hooked thorns. There, surrounded by the sounds of the wild, I paid my respects to Nani.

It was mostly thanks to my friendship with the other Hunter-Gatherers that I learnt to speak Xhosa from an early age. By the time I turned six, I was completely fluent in the language. However, at times I felt like an alien child who was unwelcome in the homes of the workers. Once, Jane Gqirhana, the woman who ran the farm's roadside kiosk, said to me, 'Asiyithandi ukuthi wena uman' ukujikeleze apha ngaphakathi kwethu – asikwazi ukuhleba' (We do not like it when you move around here among us, because we cannot speak about people behind their backs).

The practice of *ukuhleba* always disturbed me. In English, *ukuhleba* could be taken to mean 'gossip', but for us boys the word had a darker meaning. It usually meant to speak ill of people behind their backs or even to conspire against them. The only people on the farm who could not understand Xhosa were my folks.

When there were major functions at the Big House (for example, when family members got married there), I used to spend most of the time in the kitchen. I preferred to help Mieta and the other servants with kitchen chores rather than have to deal with the pressures that came with being someone's cousin or great-grandson.

Even so, I was not black enough to be included in the ranks of the Xhosa *ukuhleba.* The separation was too wide, the racism too thickly embedded. Maybe that's why I could relate so easily to the coloured kids, because they were also marginalised by *ukuhleba.* They were called *amaLawu* by the Xhosa workers on the farm, just as whites were called *abeLungu.* The singular of this word – *umLungu* – refers to the white foam or scum that comes off the sea in a storm. I always wondered what secret things were spoken about the white and coloured people that we were not permitted to hear.

One day, the Hunter-Gatherers were busy tending one of the small vegetable gardens we always planted at special places on the farm when my father drove up in his bakkie.

'Good morning, boys, and what are you chaps busy doing?' he asked with a smiling face.

In such a situation I would always be the spokesman. 'We are just lungisaing onse garden, Dad' (We are just sorting out our garden, Dad).

'Oh, a garden, hey? That's good. And what have you planted there?'

'I-boontjies, nama-ertjies, silima nama-pumpkins also' (Beans, peas and we plant pumpkins also).

'Oh, so you haven't planted any flowers, then? That would make your mother happy.'

'Nee, no flowers. Pese uthi ons kannie ama-flowers eat nie, Dad' (Pese says we can't eat flowers, Dad).

I remember Dad laughing and shaking his head good-humouredly as he drove off. I think he was secretly impressed by the new language – a strange mix of Xhosa, English and Afrikaans – that we Hunter-Gatherers had created. My dad liked things like that. Just because he was the one who held things together on the farm didn't mean he didn't like it when the mould was broken a bit. Few people knew this, but Llewellyn MacDonald Roberts also had a crazy red-haired Irishman inside him who sometimes liked to go, 'Hwa-ar, hwa-ar! Avast, ye landlubbers!'

2

The magic the adults didn't see

THE FIRST SCHOOL I WENT to was the Holy Rosary Convent in Fort Beaufort, where we were taught by nuns. My first teacher was Sister De Ricci, a tall, attractive woman. She found the strange kind of English I spoke unacceptable, so the nuns made me do some extra English classes. It did not take long before I spoke English well enough for them. They were Italian anyway, so their standards couldn't have been all that high.

I remember a few things from this school. There was one boy who was so turned on by Sister De Ricci that he used to masturbate while she was trying to teach us arithmetic. This would cause his desk to shake and squeak. I found him and his actions moronic and rude. Afrikaans has the best word to describe his behaviour: walglik (repulsive). He was much older than the rest of us and had obviously been held back because he was too dumb, or too obsessed with his sexuality, to pass.

I also recall at some point being accused of breaking the laws of the convent and ordered to report to the Mother Superior, whose office was up a stairway. I refused to go because I felt I was innocent. So the prefects and some helpers came and grabbed me and started to usher me towards the stairs. One of these boys was the masturbator; I was so disgusted that he was laying his filthy hands on me that I began to fight like a madman.

Scrawny as I was, these bigger boys really struggled to hold me. As they were dragging me towards the dreaded stairway, I managed to grab onto a lamp-post. In those days, lamp-posts were made mostly out of thick steel with cast-iron trimmings. Once I had my arms around the post, there was no way those prefects were going to pull me off. I was also screaming with terror. That is another thing: I have always had an incredibly powerful voice. Eventually, the prefects gave up and let me go and the head boy had

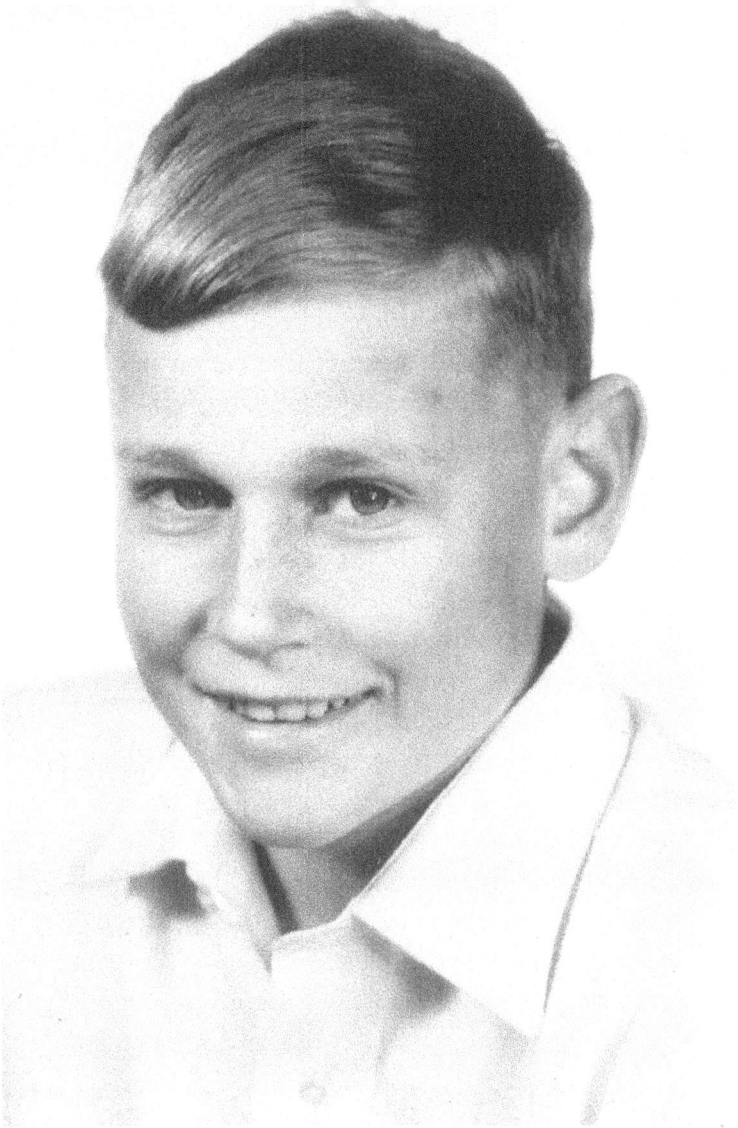

All cleaned up and hair combed for primary school.

to climb the stairs, his ears ringing, to tell the Mother Superior that if she wanted to see 'that boy' Roberts, then she would have to take her holiness downstairs herself. She decided not to. As I wiped away my tears, I knew my outrage had been justified.

After a year or so at the convent, in 1960, I was carted off in my father's Ford Consul to become a boarder at St Andrew's Preparatory School in Grahamstown. I was seven years old at the time. The school was reached by driving 80 kilometres over a rough dirt road that was very hilly and seriously tested the suspension of any vehicle.

That I did not become clinically schizophrenic over the next couple of years is something of a miracle. I had become so ensconced – through my wilful curiosity – in the African world of the farm that I found the new world of a strictly rule-driven Anglican church school an immensely cold and alienating place to live for three months (the length of each term).

We slept in dormitories with a row of iron beds down each wall and open floor in between (old Oregon pine, polished over the years by many a boy's bare foot or grey sock). I was told I had to wear a clean shirt every day. What? That meant seven different shirts for a week. On the farm, the Hunter-Gatherers and I purposely wore the same shirt for as long as possible because that meant we could recognise each other at a distance.

A prefect slept near the doorway to keep an eye on us. Breakfast, lunch and supper were eaten in a dining hall where we sat at long tables. If we broke the rules, we would get a thrashing with a cane called Benjy. No wonder I am very seldom late, even to this day.

At St Andrew's prep school, the average day went as follows: first, wake up, shower and get dressed (you were lucky if you found an unoccupied toilet). After breakfast in the hall at your table of thirty, go to the classroom to learn Latin, arithmetic, history. Then there was a break, followed by geography and physical science. After lunch, go down to the sports field. Then go back to the house to shower, with supper followed by prep time doing homework. Finally, it was off to bed and lights out. Now, all boys must sleep, but what if you are a night owl who likes to prowl? You were allowed to go and have a pee, but that was it.

I would often lie awake, listening to the different types of snoring from the other boys, most of whom would quickly fall asleep. Sometimes, thankfully, I could listen to a steam train huffing and puffing into the cold night air as it laboured up the steep tracks near the school, heading out of Grahamstown into the dark night of the wide world. I was envious of that train. Although it ran on tracks, it was free.

On the farm, the average day had a completely different rhythm: wake up, don't even think of washing your face, put on exactly the same clothes as yesterday and the day before and the day before that, wander downstairs past the dining-room table towards the kitchen, grab any bacon rinds or half a piece of toast your father might have neglected to eat, and scoff an egg given to you by Mieta. Then go outside, find Pieter Trompetter and Kununu and Pese Piet – easily recognisable by the clothes they wore – who might be sitting at a small fire warming themselves and boiling some sweet tea in an empty jam tin. Have a sip of the tea while listening to the humorous banter that seemed to circle about us like the smoke from our fires. Often, someone would get up from beside the fire and tell a story or do comedic mimicry of characters on the farm. My taste for acting started during these early years of my life.

It was only after I entered St Andrew's Preparatory School that I heard there were such things as professional actors or that acting was a career. Up until then, and because of my Hunter-Gatherer friends, I had assumed that everyone was an actor. It was only after I took part in various dramatic projects, under the encouragement and guidance of the school's enigmatic and exceptional headmaster, Griff Mullins, that I realised most boys didn't want to go near the stage. This extraordinary man, with his great love for the dramatic arts, had decreed that the school hall be opened every Saturday afternoon to allow scholars the opportunity to do any performance they wanted to conjure up on the stage, for anyone who was interested enough to watch it, while everyone else was playing cricket or rugby. There couldn't have been many other prep schools in the world in the early 1960s where such an unusual project would have been allowed, and indeed encouraged by the headmaster.

It was because of this that I, at the age of ten, together with my cousin Dan, wrote and produced my first play, a whodunnit detective story. The leading role was played by another schoolboy called PG 'Piggy' Southey, a bespectacled and – to us – suitably Sherlock Holmes-type character. Together with a few other boys, I acted in the play, while Dan was the director.

I don't know of any other instance where boys at our school wrote a play, or why Dan and I chose to do so, so I can only attribute it to one of those shafts of inspiration that have come to me throughout my life. For me, acting and writing were a natural progression from the impromptu comic performances in the flickering light of the campfire on the farm. If all dramatic art is about storytelling, then the campfire was where I began to learn, but I owe my ability to script a story to the influence of the St Andrew's prep school classroom.

I remember one curious incident from my early childhood. It was during the school holidays. I was back at home from boarding school when I had a sort of vision: I saw myself standing on a stage somewhere, and before me were many people cheering and clapping their hands. My mother saw the strange expression on my face and asked me what I was thinking about. I tried to explain to her what I had seen.

'What on earth are you talking about, my boy?' she asked, intrigued. 'That is very strange indeed.'

My mother, who was born Lynn McWilliams, was of Irish descent. The Irish are a people not overly disturbed by ephemeral things, so luckily my parents never took me to Port Elizabeth to see the nearest shrink. Perhaps they thought my vision was merely a delusion of grandeur. Little did I know that this vision would materialise years later when I received the DALRO best actor award in 1987.

The first time I was taken camping on the farm was when I was about four years old. One afternoon, my father led the family up through the huts behind the Big House and we began climbing the steep, rocky path up the mountain. We struggled through the thick undergrowth and up onto the plateau, past the dark brooding cliffs from which my great-grandfather dynamited the stones used to build the house.

What I remember most about that climb was that my corduroy dungarees were impossible to take off and that I needed to do a number two in the bush. Eventually, I had to ask somebody (my mother?) to help me. By then, everybody knew I was desperate for a toilet. Feeling imprisoned every time I wore the dungarees, I grew to hate them and used to deliberately scrape them across any rock I could find to reduce them to tatters as soon as I could. It did not take long before I was free of them forever.

Once we reached the bushy plateau, my father put up a tent and taught us how to start a fire using only one match. For this, he painstakingly packed small sticks and bits of dried grass into an arch. He told us he had learnt this trick while fighting the Desert Fox – German Field Marshal Erwin Rommel – in North Africa during the Second World War. As the fire took hold from his single match, I remember staring at it, mesmerised by my dad's genius.

We spent a night on top of the plateau, but after my sister Barrie mistakenly drank some paraffin out of what she thought was a water bottle, we had to hurry down the mountain. She was made to drink milk to neutralise the paraffin. The camping trip was over. But I had had my first taste of what it was like out there in the bush. Deep down, I knew I wanted more.

The next time, I was lucky to be invited by my brother Llewellyn to go and camp with him and his friends in a green canvas tent purchased by my father. The dark nights were scary, and, to my alarm, I seemed to always be the one pushed to the edge of the tent by the bigger boys. One night, I was terrified when I heard a rasping sound on the other side of the canvas, right near my head. The others were fast asleep, so I eased up the tent flap to find myself looking straight into the face of a surprised cow, which, thus frightened, moved off immediately.

After that, my brother and his friends lost interest in camping and we Hunter-Gatherers took over the green tent. Every time I got back from boarding school, I would ask my father for a tractor and trailer to take us up into the bush. There we would pitch the tent and stay for at least three weeks, until I would have to go home to prepare to go back to boarding school and civilisation. We would take with us a pocket of potatoes, a bag of mielie meal, a supply of coffee, tea, Klim milk powder and sugar, together with a few bottles of cooking oil and some salt and pepper. We were proud Hunter-Gatherers and would eat whatever we managed to shoot, which were mostly dassies, sometimes a wood pigeon or guinea fowl or a long-eared *hasie* (African hare; *imvundla* in Xhosa). We weren't very good hunters. We only killed something every now and then. It was more like we were playing bush games.

If we discovered a hare hiding under a bush, Djonni Kieghlaar would start calling out in a soothing tone, 'Ho-looo! Ho-loooo! Ho-looo!' setting up the chant. We would all freeze where we were standing and join in, 'Ho-looo! Haw-loooore, Haw-LoreWAH!' This was supposed to mesmerise the hare into not immediately running for its life. The African hare can move astoundingly fast.

The chant gave us time to get our knobkieries ready. When the hare had decided it had had enough of our discordant noise and broke cover, we would hurl our sticks to try and take it down. We seldom managed to kill one, though. It would have been far easier to shoot one, but that wasn't as much of a challenge and no fun. When the hare escaped, we would dance around in the sun laughing at each other's inaccurate stick-throwing. What we enjoyed most was the rave of the hunt.

Once, when travelling into the bush on a trailer pulled by a Massey Ferguson tractor, we stopped at the huts on Argyle, the neighbouring farm, which also belonged to my family. This was the first time I came up close and face to face with a baboon. One of the farm workers had raised the animal after its mother had been killed. He had named her Kees, an informal Afrikaans word for baboon. From the first moment, Kees took a liking to me, and, as we rode off to the camping grounds, she clung to me so tightly and screeched so loudly when her owner tried to pull her away that he simply gave up and waved us off. That was how Kees came to go camping with us.

It was astounding how easily the baboon fitted in with camp life. When it came to food, Kees would eat whatever we were eating. She would even sip tea. She could sleep anywhere – curled up in a corner of the tent or on top of the wooden structure where we put our food to protect it from insects and animals.

On our frequent hunting trips, she would move along quietly through the bush with us, her new tribe. She would observe everything quietly, eating wild fruits or a scorpion if she could find one. Around midday, when we usually got tired of walking, we would find a tree that gave enough shade and go to sleep. In the bush one is always wary of being caught unawares, and you are most vulnerable when you are asleep, but with Kees around, we could relax completely.

The little baboon would climb to the top of the tree and keep a lookout. Sometimes she would grunt a soft alarm. Next thing, she would point in a certain direction with her muzzle. We would most often need binoculars to see what she was seeing – a distant farm worker checking for holes in the fencing or a group of goats.

Kees needed nothing from anybody, but she loved Wilson's toffees. If I went to Chummy Moss's store on my Sachs 50 moped and came back with a packet of Wilson's toffees, I would hide them by placing them under my arm and zipping up my jacket. Back at the camp, and before I could even get off the bike, Kees would jump onto my lap and look intently at me with those ancient red-brown eyes of hers and make a soft grunting sound – she always knew when I was hiding something. I would pretend to have nothing, and then she would begin prodding my jacket, her incredibly sensitive hearing noting any crackling sound that would indicate 'packet of sweets'. Eventually, she would isolate it and grunt at me. I could only laugh in acknowledgement of her genius, take out the packet and give her a toffee.

Kees took us on as her tribe. Such a sense of belonging remains eternally intangible but is very real to those who have experienced it in the wild. It's like the fireside, that holiest of holies, where the sense of togetherness leads to a deep and sure contentment.

A strange incident happened when the rains at long last returned, breaking the terrible drought of the 1960s. (Many orange trees had become so dry that they turned black from the high sulphur content in the borehole water that my father, in desperation, used to irrigate them).

The long furrow that carried water down to the farm from a weir up the valley had begun leaking precious water back into the Kat River. I went with my father and a team of labourers to fix it.

At one point, my father was feeling under the muddy water with his hand for the hole when a worker called Ndenzile thrust downward with his spade and split my dad's index finger in two, longways. He pulled his hand out of the muddy water: it was a bloody mess.

My father said nothing and merely walked back to his Austin bakkie. I had to help him change gears so he could drive home. Of course, Ndenzile was terribly apologetic, but all the while I kept wondering why the hell he had chosen to thrust his spade into the mud just at the moment when my father's hand was in there. My father's finger had to be amputated just before the first knuckle.

When asked about the accident, my father's answer to a group of well-wishers sipping tea in the Court was: 'It was a mistake. It was raining, there was thunder and lightning. We were rushing to fix the leaking furrow and the water was muddy brown.'

But I was not so sure. I watched the adults sipping tea, knowing they were ignorant of so much that was going down on the farm. We Hunter-Gatherers knew that Ndenzile was not as he appeared on the surface; he had secret agendas. We had seen him coming out of the bush on Argyle that was off limits to farm workers, and we suspected that he was using snares to poach. We had even heard rumours that he had a gun. But I kept my mouth shut and ate pecan-nut biscuits instead.

One day a short while later, I was standing on the front lawn of the Cottage when I saw Ndenzile coming through the gate and into our yard. I decided to confront him. Why I did this, I am not too sure. I think I was trying to keep him away from our house because I did not like or trust him. Ndenzile was a powerful young man and he could have beaten me to a pulp if he'd managed to catch me, but I refused to let him get close to our house. My mother's Corgi felt the same way I did and barked wildly at him as the two of us kept him from walking up to the house.

At this point, my mother happened to return from town. I was pleased to see her, thinking she could help me send this bad guy away.

Instead she shouted at me. 'What on earth do you think you're doing, Ian?'

She told me to stop my nonsense and tried to shoo her dog away, but we both refused. She ended up slapping me. I had to retreat into the house, nursing a hurtful loss of face, while Ndenzile – whose name means 'I did it' – crossed our yard with impunity. From then on, the man remained a dangerous presence on the radar of Pese, Kununu, Pieter Trompetter, Djonni Kieghlaar and me. We were watching and listening. Sooner or later, we would become aware of anything that went down on Baddaford Farm.

Take, for example, the curious case of a man called Enzwathi, who had worked for many years in the nursery that supplied the farm (and many other farms in the district) with new citrus trees. The nursery was my uncle Dan's department. The workers were mostly women, and I always found it a calm and pleasant part of the farm.

For some years, my father and my uncle had tried to promote labourers to supervisory or management positions to run a section of the farm. So my uncle promoted Enzwathi to nursery manager. Enzwathi was about fifty years old and well respected. In any case, he had been the unstated boss of the nursery for some time. His salary went up accordingly.

But we Hunter-Gatherers knew that trouble would soon start to brew. Bhuti Enzwathi now had to officially tell other Xhosa people what to do. In effect, he had become an *umLungu* – a white boss. We knew that, in the eyes of the other workers, he would be 'making himself grand'. BIG mistake!

After a while we noticed that Enzwathi, who was paler than most Xhosas and quite heavy, was beginning to lose weight. Whenever we Hunter-

Gatherers passed the nursery, we noticed how skinny he was becoming. Moreover, he had a permanently worried expression on his face, which also seemed to become darker. We were way ahead of the shoeshine in the matter of the deterioration of Enzwathi. 'Waye thakhathwa' – he was being bewitched. Or he was bewitching himself for having had the temerity to think he could stand out from the crowd and be counted.

Sure enough, before long Enzwathi approached my uncle with a request: he wanted to be demoted. Enzwathi was adamant, despite my uncle's best efforts to dissuade him. Here was a man living in fear of his life. We Hunter-Gatherers knew that, for Enzwathi, this was truly a matter of life or death. Eventually my uncle, although he did not believe in 'that kind of stuff', gave in and demoted him. In fact, he shifted Enzwathi clear out of the nursery and sent him up to the roadside kiosk, where he could sit out of sight in the shade, sorting avocado pears by size and packaging them.

Although his salary had been halved, the man began to regain his weight and his happy disposition. He had stepped down and thus managed to detox any bad spells that had been cast on him and his family for being so bold as to become part of management.

Thereafter my uncle returned to managing the nursery. He could nurse orange, naartjie and grapefruit seeds to life, but he could not induce a Xhosa worker to become a manager. This frustrated my uncle immensely. To him, it felt like a kind of failure.

My wild imagination didn't leave it there. Where does this leave my father and my uncle, the main managers on the farm? I wondered. Were they not therefore the most exposed to this witchcraft that had so easily rendered the good Enzwathi into a gibbering half-man? And what about their families? In other words, what about me?

These things filled my young mind with wild thoughts about potential threats and danger.

While there was no discrimination among the Hunter-Gatherers, it was impossible to escape the apartheid politics of the day. No matter how many newspaper photos of politicians we smoked in our rolled BB cigarettes, politics kept entering our world. It seemed to settle over us like the dust of the seemingly endless drought.

When it came to deciding whether to give civil rights to black South Africans, I believe the National Party represented a people who had fought for political autonomy, trekking into a dangerous hinterland to free themselves of English rule. I felt that they feared black rule and had seen what had taken place in the Congo and other parts of Africa during decolonisation. It is never advisable to make decisions when one is driven by fear and apprehension, because such decisions often turn out to be bad ones.

My sister Barrie left South Africa as soon as she could. Years later, she told me she simply could not deal with the disparity between the haves and the have-nots. I, however, never thought of leaving the country. While I had a privileged upbringing, I was also more directly engaged in the daily lives of my less-privileged friends on the farm. We Hunter-Gatherers shared everything, even our clothes and the lice in our hair and our powerful wood-smoke smell. So, unlike most of my friends at St Andrew's, I not only spent a lot of time with people of other races but also learnt a lot about traditional African beliefs and ways.

Once, when I was back home during a winter holiday, a small child went missing from a labourer's house at the Vlei, one of the staff living areas, situated on the far side of the three dams my grandfather had built. We searched the surrounding area and the dams, holding hands to form a human chain and stumbling through the ice-cold, murky waters. We used our feet to search along the muddy bottom for a little body, but without success.

My father phoned the police, who arrived in their big Ford F250 pickup. They searched with their tracker dogs but found nothing. Their conclusion was that the child must have been taken by a wild animal such as a jackal or a lynx, or perhaps had fallen into the nearby furrow, to be washed away by the muddy water. For the police, the case was closed. For my dad too. But not for us.

Members of the Zionist Church – called 'AmaZion' – came over one weekend and danced non-stop to their drumbeats till someone would fall to the ground in a trance and speak of things that cannot be seen with the eyes. Still, none of them could 'see' where the child was. Then, even though it went against his better judgement, my father, on request, put up the money to send a deputation to the powerful sangoma – *ugqhira* to me and my friends but 'the witch doctor' around the breakfast table at home – who lived high in the mountains of the Kat Valley.

Eventually, for the right amount of money, the enigmatic sangoma 'saw' what had happened and shared his vision with a group of labourers and us Hunter-Gatherers, who hung around on the edges of the group: He claimed that the child had been taken by a withered old woman called Thokiki, who happened to be the mother of Meni, a friend of ours, and another old *magogo*, NoSawuthi. They had arrived flying on a carpet and had landed and snatched the child, he said. The two women had then taken the child off to a remote place, where they had killed her and cooked her for *muthi* (traditional medicines).

We Hunter-Gatherers were ready to believe the sangoma, even though the implications of the seer's readings meant no good for the well-being of Thokiki and NoSawuthi, who now occupied the dangerous status of witches. I went to my father, who was drinking his 11 am cup of tea, and told him the whole saga. He just smiled at me and said, 'That's a good story, my boy, but, you know, I don't believe in all that kind of stuff.'

I was completely taken aback by his lack of interest in what the sangoma had discovered. How could he simply disregard it? Soon after, he carted me back to boarding school. There I heard about Jesus and the forgiveness of sins and Lazarus rising from the dead, but I simply couldn't believe it. That all came from some old book, whereas I was completely embroiled in the African beliefs and traditions that I experienced at first hand. The African belief system made far more combustible fuel for the fires of my vibrant imagination.

After about a month back at boarding school, my father visited me and told me that the decomposed remains of the poor toddler had been found. She had not been used for *muthi* at all. The little one had apparently become entangled in the density of a *wag-'n-bietjiebos* ('wait-a-while' bush, with its sharp and powerful hooked thorns) some distance from her house, and the parents had not heard her crying. Finally, the case could be closed. Thokiki and NoSawuthi were asked for their forgiveness by the people on the farm and were able to live out their old age not as witches but as normal old ladies.

In the year I turned 12, a massive thunderbolt hit the farm. Shortly before, the municipality of Fort Beaufort had sent a bulldozer to heap up sand along the Kat River so that lorries could carry it to town for some building project. One morning, I went with a friend and my first cousin Christopher Roberts to play in the sand as it toppled down the slope of the mound. Then, as we were waiting at the top edge of the mound for the bulldozer to bring the next lot of sand, for some inexplicable reason my little cousin suddenly ran down to the oncoming wave of sand and began crawling before it, as if trying to 'ride it' back up the slope towards us.

I screamed at him to come back, but the thunderous sound of the straining bulldozer engine drowned out my normally loud voice. My friend and I watched as the heavy, moist, curling sand suddenly enveloped Christopher and buried him as the bulldozer roared on inexorably towards us.

I stood transfixed and speechless, completely helpless in the face of this horror. We ran down screaming at the driver, who stopped the bulldozer. We all started digging desperately, but there was simply too much sand.

So I ran. I was searching desperately for help – a parent driving past in a bakkie, a gang of workers, men with shovels who might be working close by – but the world was deserted. I can still remember that desperate run, spit dribbling out of my mouth, my eyes not seeing from being filled with tears, not caring that I smashed my bare feet so that my blood ran on the gravel and dust in the road, saying over and over to myself, 'This is a terrible day, this is a terrible day, this is a terrible day, this is a terrible day, this is a terrible day.'

I ran up the steep hill to the Big House and found one of the grown-ups – I think it was my mother. Within minutes, they had uncovered Christopher's body at the site and raced with him to the hospital in town. But dear Christopher was gone for ever. It was a blow deep, deep down in my gut that I still feel to this day. My heart beats faster even now at the memory of it. I used to lie in my bed in the dormitory at St Andrew's College, unable to sleep and thinking it would be better to die right there and get out of that place and go to meet Christopher on the other side of human life. But always the morning would come.

After Christopher's death, that place of sand along the Kat River was taboo to us Hunter-Gatherers.

Many years later, after I moved back to the Kat Valley, I decided to challenge the taboo. At midnight I drove my Land Rover to that place on the banks of the Kat River where the tragedy had happened. I set up a small table and lit four incense sticks I had brought along. I sat down on a folding stool, trying to empty my mind so that I could be receptive to anything that might manifest out of the dark. It was autumn and a gentle but chilly breeze wafted down the valley along the river, causing me to wrap myself in a small blanket against the cold.

I allowed the memories of Christopher and that terrible day to come back from whence I had banished them, hoping for some sign. But all that came back to me was an enduring sense of timelessness. Insects resumed their night noises and presently I began to hear, for the first time, an insect I had been told about by Pese Piet and Pieter Trompetter (who by this time were both sadly also deceased) in our Hunter-Gatherer days. They called this creature *uFonyowli*. Often, in the flickering light of the campfire, they would describe how *uFonyowli* started up. In the dead of night, the insect would make a 'Foh, foh, foh' sound that steadily became louder and louder, which, according to Pese, Kununu and Pieter, was the sound of the insect inflating itself with more and more air. So much so, they told me, that it would eventually explode with a loud 'dwah!' sound. And then the night would be silent again.

Now, as I sat there, *uFonyowli* started up, its strange sound emanating from the dark shadow beneath a bush directly in front of me. I was mesmerised by the 'Foh, foh' sound that began in a low tone and volume and then built up, just as they had described it. But this *Fonyowli* never exploded. Its sound just grew to fever pitch and then stopped. After a while, it started up again.

I sat listening, swathed in the smell and the smoke of the incense sticks, doing my best to tell *uFonyowli* I was sorry I had not moved quickly enough all those years back, and that I wished I could have prevented Christopher from running down towards the cascading sand in front of the bulldozer.

Yet no ghosts appeared. No revelation came either.

However, I did become aware of an increasing sense of 'It's okay' – an inexplicable feeling of warmth even though the night was cold. When the incense sticks burnt out and the insect went quiet, I packed up my stuff and drove home, at about 1.30 am. I didn't know what, if anything, I had achieved, but I felt somehow relieved. Sometimes achieving what appears to be nothing can make a person feel strangely contented.

Some years later, after my mother had passed, I was standing in the dark, looking out over the Bushmans River at Kenton-on-Sea, when *uFonyowli* started up in the bush in front of our family's holiday cottage. I was astounded, as it was the first time in many, many years that I had stood on that piece of lawn overlooking the river and heard one. It would also be the last time. As I listened to its strange, archaic, oboe-like sound, it was as if *uFonyowli* was talking on behalf of the God of the universe, saying that things were fine. I swear I could feel the turning of the Earth as it spun through space.

3

Dancing around the fire

FOR MOST OF MY CHILDHOOD, I lived torn between two worlds: on the farm I disappeared into the magical world of the bush and the familiarity of my friends, while at St Andrew's I had to face the reality of routine and the path set out for me by my parents. After completing primary school, the natural progression was to enrol for high school at St Andrew's College in 1966. I became a boarder at Upper House, one of six residences for students at the college and the one where most of the farmers preferred their sons to be.

At the end of each holiday, after I had spent weeks camping in the wild with the other Hunter-Gatherers, I had to scrub myself squeaky clean and be deloused by my mother before I could be sent back to St Andrew's. We knew that we lived with lice in our hair, but we never cared. I honestly never really noticed them! Dassies, hadedas and hares scratched themselves, so why shouldn't we? They never bothered us. However, arriving with lice at St Andrew's College would have caused absolute bedlam.

Luckily, my mother had a foolproof technique for completely ridding my head of lice – paraffin. You see, bugs such as lice, ticks and fleas breathe through small holes in their undersides. Paraffin has exactly the right consistency to clog those breathing holes and suffocate the buggers. I would sit in the Court as paraffin was combed into my hair by my mother. My sisters Barrie and Jane thought this 'gross' and 'disgusting', but I didn't mind. If living in the bush meant I had lice, then too bad. It was just an occupational hazard.

My mother would always ask, 'Now, my boy, what would you like for your last lunch at home?'

'Boerewors and mashed potatoes with green peas, please!'

When I got back to Upper House at St Andrew's College, I would listen to the stories about how some of the richer Joburg boys had gone to the

My mother, Lynn, with Llewellyn (left), Barrie (right)
and me seated on my mom's lap.

Alps to ski or to New York to watch Broadway shows. I felt sorry for them because they had flown in Boeing airliners. I imagined them sitting cramped up for so long in an aluminium cigar and having to be clean and dressed in clothes smelling of washing powder every day. Yuck. To me, they spoke of life in a claustrophobic suburban prison. Why do that when you could be free in the African bush?

We Hunter-Gatherers had a much better life and only needed new clothes every once in a while. Once, my dear mother took me shopping for some new clothes at the OK Bazaars in Port Elizabeth – a visit to the big city and a special occasion for a *plaasjapie* (country bumpkin). She was perplexed when I insisted on a green shirt, which was an unusual colour for a shirt back then – and still is.

'Gawd mawd, my boy, why on earth would you want such a peculiar colour shirt?'

'For camouflage, Ma,' I said quietly, slightly worried that the pretty blonde salesgirl would think I was a bit of a wuss for my choice.

When I was about 14 or 15, Simon Upfill-Brown, a boarder friend from

St Andrew's, decided to come and camp with us in the bush for the holidays instead of going back to Johannesburg. He was quickly introduced to some of our bush adventures. For example, when we happened to discover a wild cow with a calf out in the bush, we would always try our best to catch it so we could milk it. Of course, we were familiar with the trick of allowing the calf to come close so that the cow would *hlisa*, or let down her treasure into her udders. This milk we would first drink fresh, but when it went sour, its pungent curds were even better.

Simon was involved in one cow incident. He made a name for himself when the cow started chasing him, and he ran through the bush at such a speed that he managed to leave the enraged cow behind and escape. From that moment, he became one with us. Pese, Kununu, Pieter Trompetter and Djonni Kieghlaar immediately dubbed him 'Jowbeg' (Johannesburg). To gain a nickname in this way was a great honour. It rose above the things we were taught in history class at St Andrew's about how some pale-faced Englishman was tapped on the shoulder with a sword by the Queen to become a knight.

Simon had brought with him something that only rich kids like him could have: an Asahi Pentax 35 mm reflex camera with interchangeable lenses. For the first and last time, our crazy bush existence was caught on film.

Many times, in the flickering light of the campfire, Pese or Kununu would begin to mimic Jowbeg's desperate run for safety from the angry wild cow and we would laugh till we fell to the ground, and then simply stay there, flat on our backs, laughing at the bright stars.

Pese was a magician on a guitar. My father had driven me all the way to Port Elizabeth, where the nearest music shop was. There, in Bothner's, he bought me my first guitar – a beautiful mid-sized steel-string Ibanez guitar that was made in Japan and always smelled of cedarwood. That guitar got played to death. Out of its battered cedarwood sides, Pese could conjure rhythms interspersed with off-beat slaps of mind-boggling speed, which always got our feet moving. I did my best to copy his rhythms, and to this day I still try to copy them, but I can never quite recreate that wrist speed and pristine slapping of Pese's strumming.

We would all dance. One night, Simon's dancing became so wild, Djonni Kieghlaar and Kununu began to shout their encouragement for him to dance even wilder: 'Eyitsa! Jowbeg! Bri bri mntanam uyagula!' (Smart! Jowberg! Bright, bright! Your dance is far out, man!)

When he had too much sweet Jerepigo wine, Djonni would sometimes become strangely maudlin and shout, 'Ek vra jou Mobza! Wat is 'n huis sonder moeder?' (I ask you, Ian! What is a house without a mother?) I never could answer because I had always had a mother.

Around 2003, I had a role in the movie *King Solomon's Mines* with Patrick Swayze; it was shot on location in South Africa and at that point we were shooting near Grahamstown. One night I drove into town to a club where a friend's band was playing. Amazingly, Simon 'Jowbeg' was there; he had emigrated to America many years earlier but happened to be visiting Grahamstown. The band began playing a song I loved; since none of the girls wanted to dance, I went and danced wildly to the song on my own.

When I came off the dance floor, Simon was looking at me with his head cocked to one side and a strange expression on his face. I got the sense that he couldn't understand why the heck I would have wanted to go and dance on my own. Let me just say that when people emigrate from South Africa, many leave behind not only the bush but also their sense of humour.

The late South African ethnomusicologist, composer and folk singer Andrew Tracey, who spent many years travelling around southern Africa studying and recording African music, once came to give a talk in Fort Beaufort. Afterwards, he tested people by asking them to beat out on a drum any rhythm they wanted. He would listen for a while and then say where their musical heritage lay – say Eastern Europe, northern Germany or whatever. When I hit the drum, he held up his hands immediately and said, 'African!'

I started playing the guitar at the age of seven at St Andrew's prep school, where some of the older boys had guitars. My cousin Dan and I were enthralled and thankful to be given the chance to play. We learnt three-chord songs like 'Barbara Ann' by the Beach Boys, and soon both of us were given our own guitars by our fathers.

Listening to and playing music has always been as natural to me as eating a meal or taking a drink of water. My mother used to say to me: 'You know, my boy, you are the only one of my children who inherited the Womersleys' talent for music. Your father's family, the Robertses, know nothing about music. The MacDonalds and the McWilliamses are all completely tone-deaf, but your great-grandfather Womersley used to play the organ in the cathedral in Port Elizabeth.'

My mother's mother, Edith Eileen Womersley, had been a soprano opera singer and later became a singing coach in Port Elizabeth. One of my mother's parting gifts to me was a rolled-up scroll of Edith's acceptance as a coach in a London music academy.

I, on the other hand, was thrown out of the St Andrew's prep choir by Mrs Kirby, who told me emphatically, in front of all the other boys, that I was a 'puller' of notes. Apparently, I never came in on C because I would 'pull' the note of B up to C, and that was utterly unacceptable. A short while later, I got Mrs Kirby back after my brother ran up to the preparatory school from the college down the road, jubilantly carrying *Beatles for Sale*, which had just been released. I knew how to break into Mrs Kirby's choir room, where we played the LP on her sophisticated radiogram.

Thanks to Pese and Djonni Kieghlaar, the Hunter-Gatherers formed a band when we were about nine years old. I had been given a small Hohner student piano accordion by an aunt after my mother had told her I had musical talent. Pese, Djonni and I formed a trio and began to play songs on request at the weekend gatherings at the huts. These were called 'tea meetings', although tea played a very small role. For every tune we played, two cents would be tossed into a bowl. Now, when I was ten years old, a gallon of petrol cost 25 cents. My father made the mistake of asking me what I wanted for my tenth birthday, whereafter – being a man of his word – he built a go-kart for me. I also bought a Sachs 50 cc moped. So, for every 12 songs we Hunter-Gatherers played at the tea meetings, we could buy a gallon of petrol, and that was gold. We measured the success of our band in petrol, which explains why my nickname at this time became 'uMobza'.

The Hunter-Gatherers could play three numbers. The most popular – the hit everyone loved to dance to – was a song called 'Stekelina'. Many years later I discovered that this had been an American hit song in the 1960s, but then it was called 'Stagger Lee'. The Xhosa workers had changed the title according to their way of speaking. 'Stekelina' earned us more two-cent coins than any other number.

Then there was 'Pata Pata', a hit song by Miriam Makeba, which we cooked up in our own way. The third number we played was a medley of Afrikaans folk songs like 'Hasie, hoekom is jou stert so kort' and 'Jou kombers en my matras en daar lê die ding', and so on. We would play as long as the two-cent pieces kept being tossed into the bowl, and that would sometimes mean the entire afternoon. People would dance around us, kicking up more and more dust from the cow-dung floor.

Therefore, it would not be wrong to say my professional music career began around the age of ten. In later years, I became stupid and for long lived by the maxim that playing music for money is an insult to music. It took a while before I let go of that silly idea. Thanks to the genius of my cousin Dan and the writer and songwriter Rian Malan – the forces behind the creation of the band Die Radio Kalahari Orkes – I now get great pleasure playing music for people *and* earning money for it.

At the time, Dan was also very much into music, but in a different way to me. Like me, he had learnt to play and sing 'Barbara Ann' at age nine. But soon he developed a great liking for the music of Frank Zappa and Jimi Hendrix. His father, my uncle Dan, put up a large wooden zozo hut for him where he used to play the weird beast that was his electric guitar, so that the windows of the hut would shudder. Given how scarce electric guitars were in the area where we lived, Uncle Dan actually had to build the guitar for him. Dan junior even had an amplifier! He formed his own band at St Andrew's College – something that was virtually unheard of at the time.

My wild Hunter-Gatherer comrades and I couldn't play electric guitars because we were out there in the bush with no power points. When out camping, we would make our music in the flickering firelight, and when the wild dancing started, anything was possible. Quite often, someone would send an enamel plate spinning into the dark bush as an extension of the dance.

Some talents make it to expression; others, although potentially great, never do. A young man called Bomvana is an example of the impact that different cultural pressures can have on a talented individual. Bomvana made himself a violin out of a five-litre oil can strung with nylon fishing line. He lived on a neighbouring farm, but when he heard that there was live music happening at Baddaford, he came all the way to visit. Another motivation for walking the four-kilometre distance was to get some resin from the old cedar trees that grew at the Big House.

On that two-stringed instrument, Bomvana was nothing short of a genius. After listening attentively to a song on the radio just once, he could play the melody perfectly. He played at a few tea meetings with us but then suddenly vanished from the scene.

Some years later, I got back from boarding school to find Bomvana visiting again, but his face was now painted red and he had no violin. He had 'gone to the mountain' (undergone initiation), where older men would tell the boys how they should behave when they became men. Bomvana had now become *ikrwala*, a circumcised adolescent who was preparing to be accepted back into society as a fully fledged *indoda*, a real man who has turned his back on the things of his youth. Unfortunately, his violin was seen as a 'thing of his youth' and we never heard the sweet sound of Bomvana's violin again.

It was only many years later that I realised how unusual my childhood had been, not simply for the stark contrast between my carefree life on the farm and the structured routine at St Andrew's. During my hunter-gathering, bush-camping days, it was assumed that I was the unelected chief of the little tribe of my friends – Pieter Trompetter, Pese and Kununu Piet and Djonni Kieghlaar. In all our escapades on the farm, what I said was mostly what was done.

This was not some scheming plot of my own construction but rather the situation I had been born into. I was the son of the 'lord of the manor', but as a boy I was mostly not aware and did not care about the details of these relationships of power. These were the things of the adults, another nation who lived mostly on Mars or the moon.

As young boys, we Hunter-Gatherers hadn't been very conscious of race or class differences, but the fact that I was away at St Andrew's College for three months at a time created the potential for the difference between me and the other Hunter-Gatherers to become more stark. The greater my exposure to the world beyond Baddaford, the more I became aware of the inequalities that threatened to separate us, and it became part of my own loss of innocence.

Somehow, we didn't succumb to the apartheid mind-set and remained friends. When Prime Minister Hendrik Verwoerd was murdered in parliament in 1966, I happened to be up among the huts. I was quite surprised by

Jane Gqhirana's open and loud vocal jubilation as she carted her broad form past me over the rocky path to her home, after closing the roadside kiosk for the day. Our little group managed to distance ourselves from these matters of politics because, I suppose, we felt it had nothing to do with us. We were too busy making the most of our youthful energy, and these things would only have gotten in the way.

An example of how we used this youthful energy was in our scheme to make money picking pecan nuts. My father – who seemed keen to promote a sense of enterprise among us – would offer us an amount of money for every flour bag of pecans delivered to the roadside kiosk. The best and biggest trees were 15 kilometres up the Kat Valley on a small farm called Picardy that my father and uncle had bought.

Pieter Trompetter, Kununu and I would start our pecan-nut expeditions in the early morning. We set off on my Sachs moped on petrol and then, when it was warm enough, switched to power paraffin to save money. The Sachs had an elongated, curved petrol tank that went downwards from the handlebars, much like a woman's bicycle, and this is where the large single folded bag was placed, on top of which Kununu (the lightest of us all) would sit.

Pieter would sit on another bag on the rear carrier, and thus we would ride up the valley. At Picardy, we would spend the day climbing like the agile monkeys we were to the highest parts of the pecan trees and send the nuts tumbling to the ground. In the afternoon, the giant bag, now filled with nuts, would be placed in the Sachs's curved belly again. Kununu would climb on top, and we would power-paraffin back down the valley with our bounty – sometimes racing the steam train that was also returning to Fort Beaufort.

The driver of the train was a guy called Freddy Botha, and when we were on the dirt road that ran alongside the tracks, he would always hoot to say the race was on. Freddy later told me that the image of a 50 cc *help-my-trap* (help-me-pedal) moped with a big bag and three boys on it flying at full speed down the dirt road racing his train was quite a sight. We made a lot of money in this way.

At boarding school, I was a keen rugby player and so I was happy when a rugby field was created and grassed at the farm school, with sets of poles at each end. A team was founded on the farm, mainly at the instigation of the coloured labourers: they called themselves the 'Never Despairs'. Rugby boots and jerseys were bought, and on Saturday afternoons they played against teams from neighbouring farms. Saturdays were also halfway through the weekend's boozing. I ended up watching only a few games, because I didn't like the booze-driven unruly behaviour among opposing supporters on the touchlines. Often, there were disputes about the correctness of the referee's decisions, and pitch invasions were common.

One day tragedy struck: the referee, a tall, dignified, grey-haired worker called Verandah, who was from our farm, became involved in a dispute on the field. In the fracas, he was stabbed to death. I was full of despair and disgust. We Hunter-Gatherers were shocked: you don't knife old men to death; you listen to them because maybe they have something to teach you. After that, the rugby games of the Never Despairs petered out and weeds started to grow over the neglected field.

In a way, all these things played their part in my coming to terms with the disparities of my youth on the farm and as a boarder at St Andrew's prep school and St Andrew's College. School was indeed a very different world, but it also taught me several important life lessons. Something happened that had a lasting effect on me: I was badly injured playing rugby for the St Andrew's second team in a match against Gill College from Somerset East. All the tendons in my right ankle were torn through. It took some time before I could walk again, at first using crutches.

One day, the art master, the Reverend Donald McCleod, came to visit me while I was recuperating in the sanatorium. At my request he was kind enough to bring me paints and art paper. I began painting scenes of tropical islands with small, coved beaches and coconut palms, exotic birds and flowers. When the Reverend came to visit again, he was astounded: 'These are wonderful paintings, Roberts. Wherever do you find these images?'

'I don't know, sir … they just come to me,' was all I could say.

This was in the days before computers and smartphones, so my painting these scenes in such detail was proof of the power of my imagination.

When I was fit again, I made an important switch: I decided to give up rugby and become an oarsman in the school's rowing club. This was a break with tradition because the Robertses played rugby; both my father and uncle had played rugby for Eastern Province – twins playing together for a provincial team, with my uncle as captain sometimes. In 1949, Uncle

Dan had played flank for Eastern Province against the visiting All Blacks. But I have always had an affinity with water and I decided I wanted to row.

I was in my element when I travelled out to Settlers Dam for the first time. I simply loved rowing. The rowing club was small, and the rowers belonged to another kind of tribe, which was a portent of things to come. Actors do too. Sometimes one must be genuinely thankful for rugby injuries, or accidents in general, for that matter, because they can bring about valuable changes.

Before I knew it, I was in my last year at school. Another incident brought the mad red-haired Irishman in me to the fore. One night, three of us had bunked out of residence to attend a party where my cousin's band was playing. To change from our unattractive grey school clothes into our best civvies, we used a derelict vehicle that stood in the playground of a nearby kindergarten.

At the party, we not only danced with pretty girls but also committed the horrible sins of drinking alcohol and smoking cigarettes. We got a late-night lift in a friend's VW Beetle, but the boy who was sent to retrieve our school clothes said he couldn't find them, so we assumed someone had stolen them. Who did find them, though, the following Monday morning, was the lady who ran the kindergarten, which was called Stepping Stones. We were caught out, but we made up a story that we had gone downtown to watch a movie.

For about a week our lie held, but then, late one night, one of our group, Lee 'Harra' Harding, broke down and told the truth. Now we were in deep trouble. The next day the head boy, Gerry Catherine, who was normally a nice guy who smiled a lot, came up to me stern-faced: he was obviously bearing dire news.

'I'm sorry, pal, but you and Harra Harding and Pete Key have all been expelled.'

The mad red-haired Irishman who sometimes uses my mouth responded.

'Gerry, I want you to go back to the headmaster right now.'

I was as surprised as Gerry at hearing these words. All I could think about was how to break this shocking news to my parents. If I was expelled, it would heap mounds of shame on the Roberts name.

'What did you say?' Gerry asked.

'Go back and tell him I want a meeting with him, now. Please, Gerry. Hurry!'

Shortly afterwards, I faced the headmaster in his impressive office. I, or rather the Irishman, told him he could not expel me from St Andrew's because there had been at least 25 other schoolboys at that party. If he expelled us, then he had to expel everyone.

The headmaster was cornered. Hissing with anger, he told me that if I got all 25 boys to his office the following Monday morning, he would have to rescind his decision. On that Monday, 25 boys presented themselves to him. These brave lads saved us from being expelled, but we didn't get off scot-free.

The headmaster, who was also an ordained Anglican priest, thrashed me so hard with a cane that when I returned to painting a still life for my matric art exam, my shoe filled with blood that had run down my leg from the cuts. The art master, Rene Schalker, noticed blood on the floor and inquired why I was messing red paint. I explained to him it was from the hiding.

At his request I lowered my trousers, revealing the mess. 'Bloody barbarian!' he roared as he hitched up his academic gown and stormed off to the headmaster's office. Now, Rene was a big man. I heard later that he had stormed into the headmaster's office, grabbed him by the jacket and hoisted him out from behind his desk, pushing him up against the wall before alarmed staff members managed to pull him off. 'You're not a priest! You're a bloody barbarian!' he shouted as they dragged him away.

4

A rolling stone

WHEN PEOPLE BEGIN TELLING ARMY stories, my eyes glaze over and my ears grow dim. Like most men of my generation, I, too, had to go to the army after I finished high school. However, my army experiences were anything but usual. In my year in the army – 1971 – nobody shot at me. I became a sharpshooter, but I didn't shoot at anybody. However, in many ways the army was an important training camp for life.

I was posted to 1 Signal Regiment at Voortrekkerhoogte (Voortrekker Heights), near Pretoria; I had asked to be sent to the navy, so of course they posted me as far away from the sea as they could. If the army taught me anything truly valuable, also for my eventual career as an actor, it was how to see a gap and take it. Ten years at boarding school and many camping trips in the African bush had also taught me something: don't sit like a plum pudding near the icebox in the fridge and hope somebody is going to eat you so that you can get out of there. Rather start decomposing so that they take you out of there and throw you on the dump. Then at least you can dance free with the flies.

It was inspection morning for 1 Signal Regiment. There were eight of us two-stripe corporals who had attained our rank through blood, sweat and tears at Signal School. One of them was Corporal Pikkie de Lange, who had his own sense of time (his nickname, Pikkie, means 'little one', yet his surname, De Lange, means 'the long one').

'I'z just going quick-quick to the kitchen to get some chow. You want something?' Pikkie, who had quite a crunchy accent, asked me on his way out.

'Ja, bring me some toast with marmalade, please, man!'

I made final adjustments to my bed and wiped the windowsill down. I thought maybe Pikkie would miss the inspection, but he returned just as the bungalow next door reverberated with Staff Sergeant Marais's booming

'Aandag!' (Attention!) as he and Major Smit entered. Pikkie was breathing heavily from the exertion of walking normally, which was fast for him.

'Herezit, Ikey! Here's your sarmies!' He proudly held out two sandwiches of brown bread.

Unfortunately, the bungalow next door was full of *kop toe* (overly committed) soldiers, so it was always spick and span and passed inspection quickly. I knew the time was short before we were 'aandag'd' for inspection. I grabbed the sarmies and felt by their weight that Pikkie had spread ridiculous amounts of marmalade between the slices of bread. But I had no time to comment on this because, from my place near the door, I could see Staff Marais and Major Smit exiting the next-door bungalow and marching grimly towards us, as if they knew they were now heading for the bungalow of bad soldiers.

'Ag, thanks, Pikkie,' I said, for which Pikkie gave me a broad smile and hurried towards his bed, leaving me with *die gebakte pere* (holding the baby). My mind raced. There was no dustbin and I couldn't force the sandwiches down my throat, so I turned and placed them carefully under the laboriously cleaned grey rug on the floor next to my bed. This was a relatively safe place, because when one had achieved *ouman* (senior) status in the last months of training, inspections became increasingly slack: it was highly unlikely that Major Smit would bother to check for dust by running his finger over the green-painted cupboard that stood against the wall on the far side of the rug.

The officers entered sharply and stood gazing round at us. Although soldiers being inspected should keep their eyes unwaveringly to the front, I had developed a technique of squinting sidewise that enabled me to check out what the major was doing. On this morning he appeared unusually malevolent, as if he was already scheming on a way to take us down.

Then, for some inexplicable reason, he turned to his right and stepped straight onto my rug. The hairs rose on the back of my neck. The major was lackadaisically running his finger over my cupboard's green-painted top when suddenly his finger stopped moving. His eyes showed increasing confusion as he felt his feet sliding sideways, as if an earthquake was shifting the bungalow floor. He looked down with alarm to see the soles of his highly polished army-issue shoes being consumed by marmalade, the way a slug envelops its meal with slimy secretions from its body.

'Wat de fok …' said the major, who never swore. 'Stafsersant, sê my asseblief, wat de fok is dit dié?' (What the fuck? Staff Sergeant, pray tell, what the fuck is this?)

Staff Marais gawked at the major's gooey shoes. He bent down, scooped some of the marmalade with his finger, sniffed it loudly, and then tasted it warily.

'Fokkit, dis bliksemse djêm, Majoor!' (Dammit, its bloody jam, Major!)

Now, Major Smit was a good guy, mild-mannered, slow to chide and quick to bless, and we signallers liked him. But I could see he was getting ugly mad, like a puff adder that has had its tail stood on. Major Smit now stood in the centre of the bungalow and gazed at us with murderous intent. He lifted his eyes to the heavens, as if asking his God for help in dealing with this bunch of reprobates posing as non-commissioned officers in his squadron. Of course, God held himself distant and, anyway, the major's gaze could only go as far as the ceiling. But this was far enough.

Let me explain. In the army, mere signallers were not allowed to consume alcoholic beverages of any sort. That privilege was reserved for commissioned officers. So all the intakes who had gone before us in that bungalow had merely tossed their empty booze bottles up through a gaping hole in the ceiling at the far end of the bungalow. So grandly had they broken the rules that, straining under the weight of the ever-increasing load of bottles and cans, the ceiling had developed a dangerous sag. Major Smit, being wise, had tolerated this in the past, but now he wanted war. He looked down at his marmalade-coated shoes and then at Staff Sergeant Marais.

'Stafsersant Marais …'

'Ja, Majoor?' said Staff Marais, struggling to keep from smiling.

'Wat de fok gaan aan met die plafon?' (What the fuck is going on with the ceiling?)

'Nee, ek weet nie, Majoor' (I don't know, Major).

'Nou gaan kyk 'n bietjie in daardie donderse gat in!' (Go look into that bloody hole!)

As Marais made his way towards the far corner of the bungalow, we signalmen knew that, even though the likes of corporals Netherington, Solomon and Van der Merwe never drank a drop of booze, the shit was about to hit our fan: we were going to carry the consequences of ten years of illegal boozing.

Staff Marais pulled a trunk below the hole and climbed onto it to peer into the gloomy cosmos of the past.

'Jirre Jesus, Majoor!' What Jesus had to do with this situation, none of us knew.

'Wat sien jy, man?' (What do you see, man?)

'Drankbottels, Majoor! Dis die ene vieslike vuil klomp drank bottels en kanne en alles!' (Booze bottles, Major! It's a collection of filthy, grimy booze bottles, cans and all!)

Major Smit had reached breaking point. The way the ceiling was sagging meant that the boozing had been going on throughout his entire command. On top of that, his shoes were full of Koo marmalade. One should be careful of making decisions in anger; his next order to Staff Sergeant Marais turned out to be a big mistake.

'Trek die fokken ding af!' (Pull it down!), he shouted, so angry he could hardly pronounce the words.

Staff Sergeant Marais was a good rugby player, but he wasn't a fly half's arse. Or a fullback, or a scrum half or centre. He was more like a front rank or a hooker, otherwise he wouldn't have carried out the major's absurd order so blindly. But, as he pulled at the corner where the hole was, the entire tired ceiling gave way in one crashing inverted volcano of dust-caked empty bottles, cigarette packets and cans.

I was no longer using my squint-eye technique but looking directly at the major as a Mainstay bottle bounced off his impeccably coiffed dark hair, followed by numerous other beer bottles and cans, all of them raising a dark cloud of filthy dust. All that one could see of Major Smit's face was the whites of his two blazing eyes. Fortunately, he didn't try to wipe his face; that would have made things much worse.

'ORDERS!' He hissed loudly. 'Die hele fokken lot van julle!' (The whole fucking lot of you!)

He turned on his heel and was gone. Staff Marais looked even more ridiculously grime-blasted. He stopped and turned towards us.

'Julle fokken etters is kniediep innie kak. Orders 12 uur! Noú gaan julle kak!' (You fuckers are knee-deep in shit. Orders at 12! Now you're going to suffer!) And then he was gone.

I felt sorry for some members of our group. They were law-abiding young men: big Godfrey Solomon, a mild-mannered Jewish boy from Joburg,

ST. ANDREW'S COLLEGE
UPPER HOUSE — BOXING, 1970

STANDING – (L. TO R.): H. TURPIN, E. PRINGLE, M. DOBROWSKY, N. PAGDEN, A. GADD, R. ARMITAGE.
SITTING – (L. TO R.): E. DOBROWSKY, R. AUSTIN, I. ROBERTS (CAPTAIN), G. LEVEY, P. HIRD.
FRONT ROW – (L. TO R.): M. NEWBERY, C. TROLLIP.

The boxing champions of the inter-house competition.
I'm in the middle of the middle row.

didn't deserve this. Neither did the magician Netherington or clever Van der Merwe, who had got seven As in matric.

We were marched into the major's office by Staff Marais and stood at attention facing the major, who sat behind his desk. By now, he was much cleaner and calmer. We were asked one by one whether we had anything to say in our defence. I think someone asked for forgiveness. Staff Marais was hovering behind us, and if we did anything untoward, he would punch us hard in the kidneys.

When Pikkie de Lange was asked, he began to giggle. Despite numerous punches from Staff Marais, he couldn't stop. To Pikkie, getting stripes and losing stripes was all the same. We were all stripped of our rank during a parade in front of the entire 1 Signal Regiment. Staff Marais took great delight in ripping the stripes off our arms one by one and stamping them violently into the parade-ground dirt. After the whole regiment was dismissed, we had to go back onto the parade ground to dig them out again and take them back to the store – after all, they were army property!

In the end, the most violent thing I did in the army happened in the gym. Every afternoon, after having been marched stupid up and down the parade ground, we were allowed to go and exercise. In the centre of the large gym a boxing ring had been erected, because one of our intake was the Southern Transvaal light heavyweight champion. He used to do training sessions every day in which he would generally destroy all three sparring partners fed to him by his coach, who was also his father.

Thereafter, he had a habit of grabbing the top rope of the ring with his gloves and shouting loudly, so that his voice echoed off the corrugated-iron walls, 'Is daar niemand in hierdie fokken kamp wat my kan aanvat nie?' (Is there no one in this fucking camp who can take me on?)

I found this increasingly irritating. I had been taught the basics of boxing early on at St Andrew's prep school by Chum Sutherland, the PT master. Later, I had gone on to become the boxing captain of Upper House, where my coach was a big, well-set boxer called Beadle. When we finished training in preparation for my first inter-house competition, he told me to hit him with my best shot.

I was a scrawny boy with knees so knobbly the Xhosa farm workers often called me *Madolo* (Kneecaps) and Beadle was a giant by comparison. Still, the notion of laying into him with my best punch disturbed me.

'Where must I hit you, Beadle?'

'Here,' he stuck out his jaw and tapped it tauntingly.

I let rip with my right glove, using all my might. The punch shattered Beadle's composure, sending him staggering backwards.

'Jeez-zus, Roberts! That was some shot you gave me!' He rubbed his jaw as if to put it back in place.

When, in my first fight in front of the entire school, I was beaten stupid and bloodied after two rounds against a powerful opponent, I wanted to give up. Beadle was rubbing my stomach as I sat defeated on my stool in the pause before the third and final round.

'Roberts, this boy is hammering you. You're going to lose on points if he doesn't knock you out.'

'I know. I'm finished, sir.'

'Nonsense, Roberts! Now, do you remember that punch you gave me the other day?'

I nodded my head as I spat out blood from my cut lips.

'My jaw is *still* sore, Roberts. So just line the curly-haired tit up and hit him with that right hand.'

When the third round started, this was exactly what I did. My opponent was so staggered by that punch that the fight was stopped on a knockout.

I was amazed that no soldier in the thousand-strong 1 Signal Regiment ever answered the challenge from the loud-mouthed Southern Transvaal champion. That was until one day, when the mad red-haired Irishman chose to shout back at him on my behalf and, might I add, without my permission.

'Ja, ek sal jou aanvat!' (Yes, I'll take you on!), the Irishman said loudly, who now took to speaking Afrikaans, the language of the army.

The gym went deathly quiet as everyone turned to see which moron had decided to get beaten up. I walked to the ring. The champion's father/coach bound up my hands and put the gloves on for me while asking me where I came from and whether I could box. I told him I had boxed at school. He smiled as his son danced around.

In two rounds of sparring, I felt the speed and power of the champion as he tagged me with punches. But in the third round, I connected with my right-hand punch. I saw his eyes immediately narrow as he realised that he was fighting a man who had seriously tagged him. Thank heavens his father/coach saw this too and called off the fight. Boxing fitness is a very specific fitness and I was getting tired. This was the sum total of the fighting I did in the army, but one thing was sure: the champion never, ever shouted out a challenge to anybody in that gym again.

Many years later, I bought a fortune cookie that contained the following saying: 'Person who walk in other people footstep, leave no track.' If there's one thing the army taught me, it was to take a gap and make my own tracks.

After being discharged from the army at the end of 1971, I decided to go down to the coast with Alan Mohle, a friend I had made in 1 Signal Regiment. We were going to drink the army out of us until our back pay (about R350 each) was finished. This was a good sum of money at the time. We would be joined by his brother Garth.

We pitched our tent illegally in a forest reserve high above the beach. Our drinking project was centred on the Morgan Bay Hotel bar, whose extensive shelves, we were pleased to find out, supported the many exotic-looking bottles of what was spoken of as the biggest variety of liqueurs in the southern hemisphere. Every morning, excluding Sundays, we would be waiting outside the bar door. The barman dubbed us the 'Three Musketeers'.

One morning, while we were studying the girls in their bikinis on the beach below with binoculars, a game guard arrived on his horse and told us we were camping illegally in a state-owned forest reserve. He was an elderly and distinguished Xhosa man and I spoke to him in his language.

'Hawu, mhlekazi. Kuzofuneka imali engakanani ukuthi awusibonanga, bhuti?' (Tell me, sir, how much money will it cost for you to become blind?)

He pointed to his left eye. 'Kwileli mehlo, izaba lishumi' (For this eye, it will be ten rand).

He pointed to his right eye. 'Leli mehlo iza biza nayo lishumi ukulivala' (And to close this eye, it will also be ten rand).

We paid the R20 and kept our magnificent illegal campsite. Garth hitch-hiked back to Brakpan holding a flour bag containing a puff adder we had caught. After that, we became the Two Musketeers and it took Alan and me three weeks to drink up all our army back pay.

On the last night, when we had spent the last of our money buying beers and vodka and tequila at the bottle store, we were sitting around a large fire we'd built in front of the main rondavel of our friend Charlie Battle's camp. About midnight, a guy arrived to join the party, bringing a cake tin full of very good dagga from the Transkei. L-o-o-ng 'slow-boat' zols were rolled out of newspapers and passed around the twenty or so young men and girls who had arrived for the jol, until the entire tin was smoked up. Again, like the Hunter-Gatherers, we smoked the faces of politicians on the front page and the lithe-bodied sportsmen on the back. One guy became so stoned, he had to be restrained from jumping off the nearby cliffs of Cape Morgan into the night sea. Some people would call that night's reverie utter madness. But this was the effect the army had on us.

A period of my life had come to an end. Since I didn't yet know what I wanted to become in life, I returned to Baddaford for a few weeks and ended up working with my father and uncle for a year.

My brother Llewellyn, as the first-born son, was to inherit the farm. One day my father said, 'You are going to have to go and find your own way out there, my boy.' The time had come for me to leave the farm and fireside of my youth, and to try to become a man.

On my mother's advice, I set my sights on the big city of Port Elizabeth (today Gqeberha) and used one of her family connections to get a job as an apprentice quantity surveyor for LTA Construction. For six months, I worked on the site of the new library building of the University of Port Elizabeth (now Nelson Mandela University). After about a year at LTA Construction, I resigned and became the manager of Foamaglass Products, a fibreglass factory in the industrial area of North End. The owner's name was Grumpy Paine, and he was both of those things, including being a distant, uncaring kind of person to work for. I had about eight Xhosa guys who supposedly worked under me, but we were all in the shit together. All day long, we would mould fibreglass with paint brushes to make electrical terminal boxes, after which we tried to clean ourselves with acetone.

After a while, my dad took it upon himself to drive the 200 kilometres to PE to come and inspect my place of employment. He arrived there unannounced and found it not only an awful mess but a 'bloody health hazard'. After working there for six months, I resigned, feeling sad that those hard-working Xhosa guys did not also have fathers who could come and save them from working in hell.

Unemployed and broke but enjoying my freedom, one day I was strolling down PE's main street when I saw a signboard on the pavement that said, 'Get Rich Quick!' So I walked into the building and up the stairs and found myself sitting among about ten other hopefuls, listening to a Canadian man tell us how we were going to sell books and magazine subscriptions door to door and get rich. The company was called Global Readers' Services.

We hit the road, selling in towns and cities like Kimberley, Bloemfontein and Kroonstad, all the way to Joburg, and I did well, eventually becoming their top salesman. But I didn't like bullshitting innocent people into taking out subscriptions. After I came close to getting beaten up by an irate father and his buddies in Roosevelt Park in Joburg, while trying to clinch a magazine subscription deal with his attractive daughter, I resigned. Global Readers' Services then ripped me off, giving me almost none of the money due to me. That was a tough pill to swallow because I had been committed and had worked really hard.

So I went farming again. During this time, I got to know my father very well. He was a meticulously honest man and, as my mother always said, 'He never said a bad word about anyone.' I could never lay claim to these qualities and was probably always a bit of an enigma to him, but we farmed well together. He would tell me what to do and I would just go out and do it. I was good with my hands and now also had the experience from working with glass fibre. I could weld with brass or steel, take engines apart and replace piston rings and bearings and get them going again. Perhaps it was in my genes, given that my great-grandfather had invented and built numerous farming tools.

After another two-month stint back on the farm and almost a year of being a (hard-working) rolling stone, my mother started nudging me towards going to study. After my national service, my parents had sent me to a vocational guidance institution in Johannesburg. After three days of testing, they had told me I should become an architect or go into advertising. They gave me a thick wad of papers in an envelope to take to my parents, but the party on the train back down south was so good that I lost the envelope somewhere between Johannesburg and the Eastern Cape. My mother felt I would waste my potential or get bored as a farmer, so she arranged for me to go for an interview with the dean of the highly regarded Faculty of Architecture at the University of Port Elizabeth.

However, on arrival in Port Elizabeth, I met up with my cousin Dan, who had just enrolled in a photography course at CATE, the state-funded College for Advanced Technical Education (later PE Technikon). It was the first full-time photographic course in South Africa. This attracted me and, after failing to make the architecture interview, I phoned my father to tell him I'd decided to study photography instead. The long-suffering citrus farmer gave me the go-ahead: he would pay the fees.

Although I failed to complete the three years it took to get a diploma in photography, CATE was a meeting place of fascinating people and a hotbed of new experiences. I am eternally grateful to my cousin and to Michael Bouttal, the man who created the course.

In 1973, while I was studying photography, I found myself on the same path as a fellow student named Rob Pollock, whom we nicknamed Bugs owing to his pronounced front teeth. We were on a kind of delinquent danger-seeking mission, which was quite common among white youths in 1973 in South Africa. The hippie movement only really arrived in South Africa in the early 1970s, when people began smoking dope and taking drugs. But Rob and I had more specific campaigns against life. He was secretly mourning the passing of his father, and I was secretly mourning the loss of my first love to a harmonica-blowing pharmacy student at Rhodes University.

It was not as if you could tell your friend something heavy has been slapped on you by the universe and that it's upsetting you. *Talk* about it? *Voetsek! Hamba!* Let's just go out there and *do* something about it, like getting drunk or stoned or both, and push against the walls of our South African universe in the intense hope that something might give. Bugs's mother thought I was a bad influence on her son, and my mother thought Bugs was a bad influence on me. Nobody understood us, least of all ourselves, and neither did we really want to.

One day we were hanging out with a friend who lived in a room below street level that felt much like a dungeon. He had a very good sound system; the best Rob and I had were cheap Tedelex tape players in our cars. It was around 11 o'clock in the morning, and we had just bust the second bong, when the owner of the dungeon put on Frank Zappa's 'Billy the Mountain'. I can only speak for myself, because we were already pretty stoned, but Frank Zappa blew my hair back. I became completely absorbed by the wildly imaginative story of Billy the Mountain, who had a tree growing out of his shoulder that was his wife, Ethel. I felt as if I was being reborn into a new world, where trees were like mothers and mountains had people's names and could speak in sonorous voices.

Frank Zappa became our new hero. And why not? Our country's politics were pretty fucked-up, with apartheid playing a leading role in the farce, and our prime minister was the brandy-swigging BJ Vorster. I had already had to endure the indoctrination around the *swart gevaar* (black peril) and the *rooi gevaar* (red peril, or communist threat).

I have never been interested in or liked politics and have never felt much common ground with politicians. To lose oneself in the whacky world of Frank Zappa and the Mothers of Invention was just what we needed, and that was what Rob and I were giving our day to. We were going to smoke zol till we got to a place where we couldn't smoke any longer and lose ourselves in crazy stories.

Many years later, I was lucky to make a more immediate connection with (the by then late) Frank Zappa. I was acting as the baddy in a B- or C-grade action movie in which Dolph Lundgren was playing a somnambulant, extremely soft-spoken 'good' tough guy. (In the 1980s, if you were a white South African male, you were generally always cast as the Nazi.) We shot much of the movie deep in the belly of a defunct waterpark south of Johannesburg that the Lerner brothers, Avi and Davy, were using as a cheap, low-grade movie studio.

The director was a vertically challenged first-timer from Hawaii called Keanu, and the leading lady, let me call her Cassandra, was American. I was astounded to discover that Cassandra's boyfriend and chaperone was none other than Dweezil Zappa, so I got to meet the Great Man in the flesh after all, even if it was via his son. On the shoot, I discovered that friendly Dweezil was not like his father; he was just an average guy and his girlfriend a tall, attractive girl with quite a large nose.

In this particular movie, I had the dubious pleasure of having to slap Cassandra in a stunt style. I had successfully done many stunt punches and slaps over the years, and this one should have been straightforward, but Keanu was dithering, changing camera angles and lenses gratuitously. It was the kind of thing less confident directors always do. When we got to take 17, I misjudged the distance between my swinging right hand and the tip of Cassandra's nose. There was, unfortunately, a resounding connection and the lady went down, with blood streaming everywhere.

She was taken away to her caravan by the medics. When I went there to apologise, Dweezil was inside holding her hand. I felt very bad, having made such an ass of myself before Frank Zappa's son and his girlfriend. She sat there with bloodstained, rolled-up tissues sticking out of her swollen nostrils.

'I am so sorry, Cassandra,' I said gently. 'Please forgive me.'

'Forgive *you*, Eeeyan? No way, man!' she shouted so loudly that the plugs in her nostrils shuddered. 'It's that fucking Keanu! That asshole's gotta come in here on his knees and apologise! Seventeen takes? What – is he *blind*?'

I love how intolerant American actors are of inadequate directors – unlike South Africans. I was merely grateful that we were still friends, me and Frank's boy Dweezil, and his girl with the bloody nose.

After two years at the technikon, I got my certificate in photography, but I couldn't stay another year for the diploma because I had sparked a few head-on collisions with the lecturers. The mad red-haired Irishman inside me was having fun.

Apart from conflicts with my lecturers, I knew I was never going to be content with making a living out of photography, so I took a job as the manager of an upmarket clothing store in the brand-new Constantia Centre in PE's North End. After about a year of opening the shop door and putting the change in the till every morning, I happened to see an advertisement in *The Herald* for auditions for a play. It was *What the Butler Saw* by Joe Orton and it was going to be produced by the PE amateur dramatic society. The director was Roy Sargeant, the head of the Rhodes University drama department.

That small newspaper advert was calling me ... it was as if it had my name on it. By then I had realised that I was not destined to be a clothing-store manager for the rest of my life. I was still smarting over my rejection by my first love, Louise, for a pharmacy student at Rhodes University.

And so it was with feelings of inadequacy that I read about the audition, while leaning on a smelly dustbin on the pavement outside the shop. Alongside me stood Shorty, the hunchback Xhosa salesman. 'Ufundani mnumzana?' (What are you reading about, respected one?), asked Shorty as he stared at the passing traffic. It was while I was trying to explain to him, in Xhosa, that 'they were looking for players for a show' that I began to think: 'The hell with her for finding a pharmacy student more attractive than me. I am going to show her what I'm about. The army hammered all my acting from school out of me: I've forgotten it. So now I am going to go to these auditions and get it back. I'm going to become a famous actor, and I'll show her! The hell with it all – and this dustbin stinks!'

On the day of the auditions, I sat right at the back of the hall, too unsure whether I should go and put my name down. I sat watching until all the other wannabes had done their thing. Eventually, in the late afternoon, it was just the director, his secretary and me. I was still sitting at the back.

'Excuse me, have you come to audition?' asked the good lady.

'Ja, well ... uhm, I suppose so.'

I suspect that by then Professor Sargeant had seen enough auditions for the day. He sighed.

'Can you do a cockney accent?' he asked as he started packing his papers into his briefcase. I had heard the other attempts at cockney and I assumed they had not been good.

'Yes,' I said without a moment's hesitation. I had never done a cockney accent before, but somewhere in my ancient past some of my forefathers must have spoken that way. The secretary brought me the script. By some miracle, pure cockney came out of my mouth. I don't know who was more astounded – me or Roy Sargeant. He decided to cast me in the leading role of the butler.

Unfortunately, rehearsals never got under way and the play fell through owing to some problem, but my interest had been aroused. It was then that I decided to take my father's offer – 'I've had a good year with the citrus, Ian, so I'm putting this money away in the bank in case you ever find out what you want to be' – and study towards a university degree. There had been a lot of misdirected helter-skelter, but I now knew that I wanted to become an actor. I wanted to study speech and drama.

When young people ask me, bright-eyed with innocence, how to go about becoming an actor, I always say: 'Go get a job.' To get somewhere in acting, you have to experience the nitty-gritty of how people survive. When the great German film director Werner Herzog was asked whether he would consider starting a film school, he said that if he did start one, 'you would only be allowed to fill out an application form after you have walked alone on foot, let's say from Madrid to Kiev, a distance of about five thousand kilometres. While walking, write. Write about your experiences and give me your notebooks. I would be able to tell who had really walked the distance and who had not.'[1]

You'll have a better chance at acting the role of a door-to-door sales-man if you have tried to be one yourself in the real world. How, unless you get to know one, could you understand that the laughter dancing out at you from a warrior's cold, blue eyes could mean either that you are allowed to share in his joke or that it is the dangerous prelude to your imminent destruction?

The time I spent working at different places and trying a range of things after I left the army at the end of 1971 was not wasted. It gave me precious insights into how ordinary people manage to survive and progress, often

1   See https://www.imdb.com/name/nm0001348/quotes/.

in trying situations. These years also made me realise that studying towards a degree at university was a privilege and a luxury. It's only once you have gained experience of the world that you are ready to appreciate this truth and, more importantly, put it to good use.

5

My first steps into acting

WHEN I ENROLLED AT RHODES University in early 1976 to do a BA in speech and drama, I was already 24 years old. Most of the students in my class were 18 or 19. Initially, I struggled to make the transformation from a clothing-store manager to a speech and drama student, or, as the rugger buggers at Rhodes called it, 'Screech and Trauma'.

When I walked down the stairs into the movement room for my first movement class, I was dressed in Pep Stores rugby shorts and a T-shirt. The girls and boys who were already there were warming up against the bank of mirrors that covered one wall, all of them wearing leotards. These people were almost naked, I thought, and they were doing leg-stretching warm-ups that threatened to reveal all. When the movement lecturer, Gary Gordon, also wearing a tight-fitting leotard, came prancing down the other steps calling out, 'Hello my lovelies!' I had seen enough.

I turned on my heels and began walking up the stairs to get the heck out of there. I was heading towards the first available tickey box, from which I would phone my father to tell him I had made a big mistake. Just as I was about to exit, Gary called out sharply, 'Excuse me! And where do you think you're going?' in a playful and taunting way, which turned me off even more. As I hovered on the last step before stepping into the beckoning freedom of the street, something made me turn to look down at him.

'Uhm, look, sorry man, but I'm in the wrong place.'

'Oh no, you're not! Come back down here and do the class. After that, you can leave if you want to.'

In the end, it was Gary whom saved my career in Screech and Trauma. Many years later, I met him for a cup of coffee in Grahamstown so that I could look him in the eye and thank him for that.

Professor Roy Sargeant, whom I had first met at the auditions for *What the Butler Saw*, ran a very thorough drama school. Apart from learning techniques of breath control, movement and posture, students could find out about all aspects of the entertainment world, the only exception being scriptwriting. We were lucky to be able to act in live theatre productions on stage and to take part in three-camera video shoots, both in front of and behind the cameras. Because we were required to do productions, we learnt how to take criticism and how to use it to better our performances, instead of feeling inadequate. It really was a fantastic school.

But, as with all things wonderful, there was a downside. Almost from day one, invitations appeared on my door in residence: 'You are invited to a party at the dean of the faculty's house.' I knew that most of the people at these gatherings were under Sargeant's influence, and at that point I didn't feel like getting into that group of mostly gay people. So I always made some excuse and stayed away. It wasn't that I was uncomfortable with people who were gay; I stayed away because I wanted to remain autonomous and not fall into any group, or be under any specific person's influence, especially that of the dean of the faculty.

One day, about halfway through my first year, I was walking down New Street after a matinee performance of *Romeo and Juliet*, in which I was play-ing one of the rapier-wielding Capulet ruffians. One of the other Capulet ruffians, a student named Virgil, called out to me from across the street to join him in busting a pipe of dagga. We hit the pipe hard, but what he had failed to tell me was that a drug called Mandrax had been mixed with the dope. It was what they called a 'white pipe' and it was much more powerful than straight dope.

At that time, I was struggling with many things on an emotional level. I used to get strange tingling sensations down my back when I tried to do dance classes or voice training. I felt like a fish out of water, and a strong voice within me was saying, 'Get the hell out of this place. What you are doing is ridiculous.' But I kept denying this voice and went back for more.

This dichotomy between my heart's feeling and my mind's desires was in-exorably building up nervous tension. The theatre was a strange, alien world and it threatened to overwhelm me. I also heeded my father's warning – 'If you fail once, you're on your own' – and decided to clean up my act so I could have the best chance of passing at the end of the year. I gave up smoking cigarettes and dagga and drinking booze – all in one day. It has been said that giving up tobacco is more difficult than giving up heroin. Finding myself suddenly without my normal crutches for survival in the pressured student environment, I became depressed and, unbeknown to me, rather fragile.

As I walked down New Street past the police station after smoking the white pipe, I was suddenly launched into the whirlpool of an emotional breakdown. I entered what had overnight become the cold abyss of the pointlessness of life. If I had lived in the daylight before, my life now became a nightmare in a dark and frightening world. In philosophy lectures I had heard of the existential vacuum in which one can become convinced that there is no point to life. Another phrase that stuck with me was the French philosopher and playwright Jean-Paul Sartre's insight that 'hell is other people'.

That evening, I somehow ended up at a party thrown by the dean of the social sciences faculty. I tried to mingle, even though I wasn't feeling very well. When I saw the dean, the flesh on his face started falling away as his head morphed into a skull. I was high as a kite and starting to hallucinate. I felt my own head desperately as the faces of people around me sloughed away to reveal their skulls. When Prof Sargeant's skull asked me if I was okay because I was very pale, I could take it no more and ran out of the party to go and hide in some bushes.

How I continued over the next few weeks I have no idea, but I somehow managed to keep putting one foot in front of the other and to stay mutely and dumbly alive. On the advice of the only person I could tolerate being near to, my friend David Newman, who was studying fine art, I went to church in the grand Grahamstown Cathedral. If religion, with my confirmation and the taking of communion and the notion of forgiveness, had helped me before at boarding school, I now found no solace there.

In desperation, I went to St Andrew's College to visit David Hogge, a teacher who I'd taken a liking to because his first word to us, during our first English lesson, was the unsayable 'fuck'. ('Yes, you heard me right. Fuck. We are going to be studying *Lady Chatterley's Lover*, so I thought it would be better to get the word out of the way right from the start.') I found him alone in his house and agreed to drink one of his home-brewed beers. When I told him of my paranoid state, I prayed that his head would not turn into a skull. Maybe it was the beer, but his face stayed flesh as he said,

'I'm very sorry to hear this, Ian, but you know, some things we can teach you and other things you have to learn by yourself.'

I returned to the world of what I called 'the small things' and, unable to endure any kind of emotional interaction at all, withdrew into myself. The survival technique I eventually discovered was to walk out into the mountains around Grahamstown. I did this every single day after lectures, eventually beginning to jog the same route every evening. The bush and the birds and wild animals on Mountain Drive saved me, kept me sane.

At that time, an acquaintance who was studying fine art, Penny Siopis (who today is a well-known artist), told me that, in Greek culture, there was a word for what happens when a young man falls into the abyss. It was a huge comfort when I realised I was not alone. When I meet young men these days who I can see are experiencing that terrible, empty, dark night of the soul, I say to them, 'Don't worry. You are not alone. I've been there. You will be okay.' It was in this frazzled state that I slowly, day by day, became aware of a higher power, a kind of ordering force that exists in the world.

One day, when wandering in my zombie state, feeling like there was no point to life, I came upon a Fiat 500 that I knew must have been abandoned because of the long grass growing around it. Although it was deserted, I thought the little car must have an owner, so I left it alone. But I was to return to it later.

At the end of my first year at Rhodes, I felt such a failure and a wreck that I did not want to face my parents for the usual year-end Christmas gathering. I phoned home to apologise that I would not be returning to Baddaford for the holidays. My father wanted to know where I would be.

'I'm in Umtata, Dad, in the Transkei,' I answered.

'What the heck are you doing there? They're expecting trouble there with all this independence bulldust. Come home, everybody is here for Christmas.'

'I can't,' I said, not knowing how to explain what was going through my mind and my heart.

'Why not?'

'Because I just can't face you, Dad. I can't face anybody in my family. I feel such a failure.'

Such was the extent of my emotional debilitation. I could tolerate strangers, but family? No.

My friend from photography school, Rob Pollock, had set up a studio in Umtata and I designed and painted a sign for him. Then I got a job as a barman at the Holiday Inn, where I worked with a Xhosa guy called Headman. We wore blue-and-white-striped shirts and black trousers, with black bow ties, and ran the place every afternoon and deep into the night. For this we got a small salary but, more importantly, we could enjoy lunch and dinner on the hotel's tab. I never drank behind any bar I served in, so I made much money by appearing to have a drink when some kind patron bought me one. I just replaced the schnapps in the bottle with water and pocketed the cash.

In many ways, 1976 was a watershed year for South Africa. It was the year of the Soweto student uprising against the use of Afrikaans as a medium of instruction. The National Party government was increasingly condemned and ostracised internationally for apartheid. Later that year, independence was given to the Transkei, the first of ten so-called homelands created by the apartheid state as part of its policy of separate development.

On 26 October, power was to be transferred from BJ Vorster to Kaiser Matanzima, who was to become the prime minister (later president) of the 'independent' Transkei. Rumours spread that there would be widespread rioting in Umtata, the capital, and that all white-owned businesses were to be looted and burnt. People boarded up their shop windows, barred the doors and got out of town, but a group of friends, including Rob and I, did exactly the opposite. We went to the Umtata stadium to witness this curiosity of politics at first hand. We took our seats, armed with bottles of Jack Daniel's and Schweppes ginger ale, and a few pre-rolled zols – none of which I partook of.

We watched as Vorster's entourage arrived first, in six gleaming Mercedes-Benzes, escorted by heavily armed security forces running alongside on foot. The prime minister's party took their places of honour in the grandstand. Then Matanzima's cavalcade arrived, also comprising many gleaming Mercedes-Benzes. But then one of Matanzima's vehicles broke down and had to be parked to one side on the pitch, smoke billowing out of its engine – sadly symbolic of what was to become of the scheme to make South Africa a confederation of self-governing states.

That evening, I was back at the Holiday Inn when Vorster arrived. Everyone gathered at the entrance to catch a glimpse of the prime minister. As he walked past me, our eyes met. His were bright blue like mine and I felt the power in his: he had the kind of eyes that, should they linger long enough on you, would see right through you. The South African envoy to the Transkei was staying in the hotel's luxury suite, and his two young daughters used to come and chat with me. One night they invited me to their room after I'd closed the bar and I took some Babychams along. We talked and laughed and had innocent fun. That was the first and last drink I had on that holiday.

During the time I worked at the Holiday Inn bar, I met a few wild characters, including a guy called Jakes van Rheede van Oudtshoorn. He was the flight instructor at the local airfield. He also took tourists for flips in his Cessna for pocket money.

Jakes once invited me to accompany him on a chartered flight to the nearby town of Lusikisiki. After we had dropped off the single passenger, Jakes turned the Cessna around to return to Umtata. We were still gaining speed when a fence suddenly loomed up in front of us. 'Oh shit!' said Jakes as he pulled back on the stick and the little plane rose over the fence, just clearing it. 'Some tit has just put that there!' he shouted. 'There was no fence there a month ago. But this is the Transkei – anything is possible.'

We got off the ground and were climbing into a clear sky. When we cleared the cliffs of the magnificent and wild Umzimvubu Valley, the sea lay glistening in the distance in the hazy early-morning light. Suddenly, Jakes put the little plane into an almost vertical dive. I saw dark granite cliffs flashing by as we dropped at high speed towards the forest floor. Jakes laughed at my mortified expression as he pulled the Cessna out of the dive and we flew down the valley, following the green slither of the Umzimvubu River.

After Jakes did some heavy drinking at the (now defunct) Cape Hermes hotel, we decided to again go flying along the Wild Coast. Jakes, who was solidly drunk, flew the plane so low over the ocean that it seemed to me that the landing gear was almost touching the water. We were so far into the trough between the swells that all we could see was their monstrous shifting sides. Jakes had a smile on his face like a fighter pilot manoeuvring his plane to shoot down an opponent. I gave up thinking of the danger because the whole situation had become too ridiculous for fear.

Eventually we reached the Umtata River and Jakes flew the small plane over the wild surf of the river mouth. But while we had been gallivanting between the swells over the ocean, a giant bank of clouds had moved in over the land. We flew up the river as far as we could go until the cloud covered the cliffs on both sides, thereby trapping us.

'Okay, Boet, here we go, wish us luck!' Jakes said, pulling the stick back, and the plane began to climb. We quickly became enveloped in a world of dense cloud and thunderstorms. Lightning flashed white light on Jakes's face as he unfolded a basic map on his lap. The thunder roared so loudly that it caused the flimsy Plexiglass windows to shudder as my pilot looked from the Cessna's compass to his wristwatch and then back again to the map on his lap.

Suddenly, we broke through the storm into a beautiful, pristinely sunlit world above the clouds. Twenty-four minutes later, Jakes spoke. 'Right, this is it. Hullo or goodbye, Boet.'

He pushed the stick forward and we began to descend in an intense nosedive. Grey rain clouds swept past the windshield, interspersed with lighter cloud at high speed, and I couldn't help thinking that this might be my last day on earth. But then a miracle happened: when we broke through the clouds, we were exactly where we had to be: 300 feet above the approach to the Umtata Flying Club's landing strip. Jakes did a perfect landing, and as we taxied through the rain and sleet to the hanger, the engine began to cough and splutter. As he switched it off, Jakes finally decided to speak again.

'That was quite close. The bloody petrol just ran out.'

He tapped the fuel gauge; the needle was indeed on empty. Then he looked at me, shrugged and laughed. When I climbed down from the Cessna, I patted her wet aluminium flanks with deep gratitude for her lovely toughness, and in thanks to the engineers in America who had designed and built her.

I did not know it then, but that death-defying flight with Jakes set off a sea of change in me. A visit to the edge of death teaches a person stuck in the setting cement of an existential vacuum to regain a sense of the value of life. But for me it was not like a light going on instantly. It was more like the beginning of a slow, creeping sunrise.

It was an emotionally stronger drama student who returned to university for his second year. On my return, I found the little Fiat still standing there, now even more overgrown. I decided it was really abandoned, so I began fixing it. I felt like Robert M Pirsig in *Zen and the Art of Motorcycle Maintenance*, which I had read some time before. As I lost myself in working with my hands with borrowed spanners and dirty oil, I slowly became content again. I could look at myself in a mirror and say, 'You're okay.'

When I enrolled at Rhodes, I chose Xhosa as my second major. Although I received 100 per cent for my oral exam, I failed the subject owing to my hopeless grammar capability. This put me in a dire situation: my father had warned me that he would only pay for three years of studies. 'You fail once, my boy, and you're on your own,' he had said.

So I searched desperately for a two-year major and was relieved to find a subject called social anthropology. This was quite ironic, because in social anthropology I learnt many things about the Xhosa that I never would have discovered otherwise. A new dean of the faculty had just taken up his post – an inspirational professor from the University of Cape Town (UCT) called Michael Whisson. I became so intrigued by his lectures that, for the first time, I indulged in the luxury of spending an entire day at the Rhodes Library studying social anthropology.

It was in my social anthropology lectures that I learnt about the theory of the limited good. This was based on the results of a study done in a number of small towns in Mexico: researchers wanted to establish why no one in those communities ever seemed to progress. It was discovered that the community believed there was only a limited good available to them. If someone opened a furniture store and became wealthy, the others would feel he was taking too much of the limited good and then he would be 'taken down'.

It was as if a light bulb had exploded in my head. For the first time, I understood the situation among the labourers on Baddaford Citrus Estates. In the eyes of the other labourers, men like Enzwathi, who had accepted a promotion, were taking from their limited good. That was reason enough for him to be targeted by those who cast malicious spells, something Enzwathi feared and which meant that he was too scared to remain in his position.

Years later, on the set of a movie in a game reserve outside Eshowe, I sat around a fire with the musician Johnny Clegg and we discussed the theory of the limited good, a topic we had both studied in social anthropology. We contrasted this mind-set with the Jewish way of thinking about competition. Instead of taking an achiever down, Jews encourage them to do better, because 'the better they are, the better I can be' – an outlook that promotes progress.

I spent so much time in the library researching social anthropology that I almost failed the written speech and drama exams at the end of my third year. In line with Werner Herzog's requirements for would-be students at his film school, if I ever opened an acting school, I would insist on the applicants' having made at least some attempt at studying social anthropology.

A few weeks into my second year, I started to notice a certain vindictive attitude from Roy Sargeant towards me. For example, I went from playing Othello in that year's Shakespeare production to playing the third soldier from the left. It felt as if I was being systematically humiliated in front of the entire drama school, because the casting was put up on a large notice board for all to see.

When I did the lighting for the honours students' production of Samuel Beckett's *Waiting for Godot*, I thought I had done a good job. Yet when my mark went up on the notice board, it was FF. I decided I had to confront Sargeant about this and decided to use some acting smoke and mirrors in the process. I phoned his secretary and, putting on a thick Afrikaans accent, told her I was a Mr Koekemoer from Port Elizabeth who wanted to come and present the latest theatre lighting system to the head of the department.

The secretary scheduled an appointment for 10 am on a Wednesday morning. I put on my best clothing, which was a very ugly maroon-coloured bellbottom-trousered suit.

'Ian? What are *you* doing here?' she said, surprised, when I rocked up at the dean's office. 'I am expecting a Mr Koekemoer from PE.'

'That's me,' I answered in my best Afrikaans-accented English, 'Frikkie Koekemoer of Bay Lighting in *lewende lywe* [real life] and I'm here to see Professor Sargeant wif dis new lighting system.'

She let me through. After I entered Sargeant's office, I told him I had ten points I wanted to make, but on condition that he not speak until I finished. Sargeant was quick-witted and I knew he would quickly counter any accusation I made. He agreed. If I had been a theatre critic, his show as dean of the department would never have made it past opening night. At one point he became red-faced with anger, but he had agreed to silence and he stuck to his word.

I told him I had come to Rhodes because of my respect for him, but that his treatment of me had made me lose that respect. I then listed the specific situations in which I felt he had victimised me.

'Okay, that's all I've got to say,' I said. 'The floor's yours.'

He stared at me for a while, then leant back in his chair, folded his hands behind his head and said, 'I have nothing to say …'

I have always thought the measure of a man lies in his ability to take and deal with criticism. None of us are perfect. I must give Sargeant his due because he reacted like a big man to my attack. Thereafter his attitude towards me changed completely and he began to help me wherever he could. Later, he even engineered some roles for me out in the tough world of show business.

After a few weeks of tinkering, the 500 cc four-cylinder engine of the little Fiat sprang into life again. Although it was unlicensed, I began to drive around in the magnificent little car. I had now progressed from a bicycle to a car. The reason it had been abandoned was that it had blown a cylinder head gasket and used to overheat unless you stopped at intervals and replenished the water in the radiator. For me, this was simply a case of carrying water in the boot, which was in the front like other rear-engine cars. I undertook trips as far as my hometown of Fort Beaufort, eighty kilometres away. That little Fiat added to a new confidence that was growing in me.

At the end of my second year, I took a holiday job on a farm called Cranford that had recently been bought by my father and uncle. The idea was that I would grow Virginia tobacco. I did everything from scratch, including preparing the soil for the seed beds by fumigating it. Together with the staff, I planted out the small plants in rows, day in, day out. Eventually I had 60 hectares of magnificent plants, growing at a rate you could almost see if you looked closely enough on a hot December day. I slept on the floor of an abandoned rondavel on the neighbouring farm, Picardy.

For some strange reason, I had brought only one book with me: the New Testament. Every evening I made my own food and read a bit before falling asleep from exhaustion. Every morning at six, I would walk three kilometres through the crisp, cool morning air to Cranford and get the work going. The days were blisteringly hot, and in the evenings some of the African staff and I would often lie in the rapids of the Kat River to cool down.

One day calamity struck: the big six-cylinder Deutz diesel engine that pumped water from the river onto the farm broke, leaving the entire tobacco crop vulnerable. Then, just as I was dealing with this threat to my crop, the tractor driver placed the tines that were intended to remove weeds *onto* the rows of tobacco instead of *in between* the rows, destroying hundreds of metres of prime tobacco. Shortly after that, I discovered that the labourers had picked off the broad bottom leaves of every plant instead of the top leaves and flowers, thereby damaging an entire hectare of prime Virginia leaves.

When my uncle Dan arrived in answer to my desperate telephone call for help, I burst into tears. He put his arm consolingly round my shoulders, 'It's okay, Ernie, we'll get this all sorted out quick quick.'

He called me Ernie because, in his view, I was always so earnest about everything I did. He then proceeded to sort out all the problems one by one until only one was left – the broken pump. Even for that he had a solution. 'I'll phone Kenny Quinn at Mitchell Ford and he'll fetch it and fix it,' he said.

'But the tobacco needs water by tomorrow or it's going to wither up and die! All this work gone!' I shouted, throwing all the drama-school emotions at my uncle.

He looked at me with eyes that, over the years, had become two dark slits thanks to the merciless glare of the sun. He gazed towards the Western horizon from whence the rains came. 'I wouldn't worry about it if I were you, Ernie ...'

'Why the hell not?'

He took his gaze away from the horizon and clapped his eye-slits on me. 'Because I think it's going to rain tomorrow.'

I staggered under the outrageous audacity of his statement. I couldn't speak. Three months! *Three months* under the blistering sun had made the idea of rain an ever more distant impossibility to me. And to think that the rains would come exactly when I needed them to save my tobacco crop? I began to laugh at his ridiculous idea, but he kept his gaze on me. I realised that he was serious.

The very next day it rained. Long and solid. The tobacco remained wet until the repaired Deutz was brought back.

In the last weeks before I was to return to university, I stood among the fully grown tobacco plants with my eyes riveted to the massive cloud banks that were approaching. One thing a tobacco plant cannot survive is hail. Hail is always represented by a greeny-blue tint on the underside of the clouds and, to my horror, this was what I was seeing.

I started striding towards the northernmost boundary of the farm, where the last rows of tobacco stood against the fence on the edge of the Kat River. I turned and faced the oncoming storm and began to talk with God. I had done this a couple of times in my life, but mostly when bound up in fear. This time I was in a rage.

I began by asking God to spare the result of my three months' hard labour under the blistering sun. Then, as the storm drew closer, I began to demand that God make the storm pass.

When the clouds began hurling down rain and ice, it was with such fury that I ran for cover in a small shed. After the storm had moved on up the valley, I ventured out to see the damage. I was amazed to find that God had listened: Only the leaves of the last rows of tobacco plants had a few holes in them from the hail. I later heard that, beyond Cranford Farm, all the tobacco for 30 kilometres up the valley had been destroyed.

As taxing as these experiences were, I was incredibly fortunate to have had them. Ten years later, I would play the role of a farmer who shouts at God in the play *Die Koggelaar* by Pieter Fourie. For that performance I won the DALRO award for best actor in Afrikaans theatre for 1987.

By 1978, my third year at Rhodes, I had regained my confidence without resorting to my usual feel-good kicks of boozing and smoking cigarettes and dope. I had begun to see the world a little differently. I had also learnt to take note of those people who went through life in a quiet manner, who chased their desires without the noise.

That year I decided to make my own movie. I was doing a filler subject – visual communication – to make up the credits I needed for a Bachelor of Arts degree. I asked the lecturer in charge if I could deliver a movie instead of writing the final exam, and she agreed.

I hitch-hiked to PE and borrowed two Super 8 sound movie cameras from Basil Thornhill, the wonderfully unusual camera store owner who had helped all of us photography students whenever we were in need of equipment. I bought a pile of film cartridges and set about filming the process leading up to the Rhodes Rag, a project run by the students to raise money for charities. I asked the help of my friends Carl Becker and a distant cousin, James Whyle, and we began filming the fundraising stunts and events around campus. I also acquired an editing desk with money I had earned as a bartender and began editing the pieces together. I used the ceiling beams to hang the different clips of film from for easy reference, and soon a forest of clips dangled from above.

At the time, I was staying on the second floor of a block that was directly across the street from the police station in New Street. Sometimes, I could hear the sounds of suspects getting beaten up by the cops while I was busy cutting scene after scene deep into the night. One night, I had actually been so bold as to invite a pretty blonde-haired girl to spend the night with me. In the early hours of the morning, we were lying in bed chatting when we heard heavy boots clomping across the floor leading to my door. The next moment, three burly men unceremoniously barged in, pointing their flashlights in our faces.

'Sergeant Blignaut from the security police! Watse kak movie maak jy hier, meneertjie?' (What shit movie are you making, sonny?) 'What is all this nonsense hanging from the roof? Is dit propaganda vir die fokken ANC?' (Is this propaganda for the fucking ANC?)

'No ways, man, what the hell?' I shouted. 'I'm just making a documentary film about Rhodes Rag!'

He held up his hand to shut me up. 'Don't worry. We will soon see.'

They began going through the strips of film, shining their torches through the frames. They checked all the papers on my desk, rifled through my

LPs, pulled every piece of whatever out of the cupboards and promptly left, leaving a big mess and not bothering to close the door behind them. The girl and I looked at each other, astounded.

When the editing was done, it was a one-and-a-half-hour feature-length movie. I rented two Super 8 sound projectors, also from Basil Thornhill, and showed it for three packed nights at one of the raked lecture rooms. We charged students a fee at the door to help pay for the projectors. More importantly, I passed visual communication.

Unfortunately, I had become so distracted by my Rag film that – to my horror – I discovered that I had been denied the right to write my social anthropology final papers. I put on my best clothes and went to see Professor Whisson at the department to ask for leniency. He refused, saying that I had failed to deliver three important essays during the year, which was unacceptable, and that I could therefore not write the final exams.

'If you don't allow me to write, Prof, it will mean that I'll have to come back next year.'

'Precisely! Applications open next February.'

The professor's neck was red with anger and his breathing was quick. The crazy red-haired Irishman chose that particular moment to speak through my mouth.

'You have no right to do this to me …'

'No right? What's that you say?'

'Well, sorry, sir, it wasn't really me–'

'I can assure you, as dean of this faculty I have every bloody right, young man. You may leave my office right now and I'll see you next year!'

'Sir, I don't have enough money to come back next year. I'll have to go out and work. *Please* reconsider, Professor,' I begged.

Whisson glared at me long and belligerently. Then, suddenly, his breathing eased and his neck started to lose its crimson hue. I was surprised by what he said next.

'Let's have a whisky.'

He turned to where his whisky bottle stood on the bookcase and poured us each a double, topping it off with soda and ice from his little fridge in the corner of the office. He handed me my drink.

'Cheers!'

We clinked our glasses and, even though I didn't like whisky, I took a deep sip.

'Congratulations, young man. You have succeeded where all others have failed. You have changed my mind. Have those three essays on my desk on Monday morning. I will study them, and if they are good enough, you will have my blessing and can write your final papers.'

That was the Friday. Monday was two days and two nights away. The red-haired Irishman had a big mouth, but he was useless at writing essays. I needed help. I asked my friend Christine Buirski to help me. She wrote one essay and her friend wrote another. All I had to do was copy them in my handwriting. The third essay I wrote myself.

Some years later, I drove to Grahamstown to collect Professor Whisson, who was due to be a guest at the Fort Beaufort Speakers' Club. As we were driving, he said he had wanted to congratulate me on my papers in the final exams. What he said next made me feel very good: I had come first out of that year's finalists in social anthropology.

Recently, I fished out that Rag film and played it on my ageing Super 8 sound projector. I wanted to get a sense of what we university students were all about back then. I was struck by one pervading quality: innocence. Despite our youthful exuberance, most of us lacked confidence. We were searching for the meaning of life and, in the process, sometimes made idiots of ourselves. We all seemed to want to become someone or something that ultimately would bring an end to our innocence.

6

The young actor

IN 1978, TOWARDS THE END of our final year as drama students, we were invited to audition before talent scouts from the various performing arts boards around the country, who were looking for fresh talent to join their actors' ensembles. At the time, each of the four provinces had its own performing arts board that was funded by the state. For example, the Cape Province had the Cape Performing Arts Board (Capab) and in the north was the Performing Arts Council of the Transvaal (PACT). Sadly, South African artists have since been robbed of this remarkable system, which fostered the performing arts and supported upcoming talent.

I was given the chance to perform before this very distinguished-looking and important audience in the Rhodes Theatre. A short while later, I heard that I had been hired by director and playwright Pieter Fourie, who was also the head of Capab Drama at the Nico Malan Theatre Centre (today Artscape) in Cape Town. I had landed a full-time job as an actor! There was no time to waste, as I had to report for rehearsals for my first play – *The Merchant of Venice* – at Maynardville Open-Air Theatre.

Earlier that year, I had taken out a student loan from Barclays Bank (at only four per cent interest) and bought a VW Kombi that had been converted into a camper by Westfalia in Germany. It had a back seat that ingeniously folded out into a double bed and brilliantly designed louvre windows, backed by mosquito gauze, that could be opened to the precise level one wanted. And at its heart, which was at the rear, it had a magnificent 1 600 cc air-cooled engine coupled to a superbly slick gearbox. It had roof racks where one could strap surfboards, firewood and other accoutrements.

I drove down to Cape Town in the Kombi with my young cousin Jonathan Roberts, stopping at Plettenberg Bay to camp. There I had a close encounter with a shark, and to this day I will not swim at Robberg Beach!

My first experience as a professional actor is remembered for all the wrong

Running wild at one of my favourite places: the beach.

reasons. One night, one of the soldiers of the court was being played by Gavin Heyward, who had also been at Rhodes University. There was a scene in which all the soldiers stood alongside each other on a sort of parapet. Out of the corner of my eye, I saw Gavin – who was drunk or stoned, or both – begin to sway dangerously forwards and then backwards until he did a belly flop and crashed to the floor of the stage. The audience thought this was part of the scene and clapped as the unconscious Gavin was dragged offstage by the rest of us soldiers.

During the first half of the play, it began to drizzle softly. At the interval, a deputation of senior actors went to ask the producers to stop the performance because the stage was too wet and the conditions too trying for the actors. However, the two lady producers refused, obviously not wanting to cancel and lose money by refunding tickets.

Then, in the middle of a scene after the interval, the stick-on moustache of another actor, Johan Esterhuizen, came loose on one side, hanging in a transverse hairline across his mouth. Johan, a man with a fiery persona and a quick temper that could erupt with outrage at minor provocation, was already struggling to come to terms with Shakespearean English. He was busy with a speech and had to keep straightening his slipping moustache, but every time it slid down again, blocking his mouth with the sticky soppiness of melted mastics.

Seconds later, he stopped in mid-sentence, shouting: 'Ag nee, fok dit!' (Argghh, fuck this!) The rest of the drenched cast stood rooted to the stage, while the audience, together with the ghost of the Bard, struggled to come to terms with this bombastic intrusion in Afrikaans. Johan ripped his moustache off and hurled it with such violence that water splashed up as it hit the sodden stage. Shouting more expletives, he grabbed his cloak, water streaming off it as he swung it round his shoulders, and stormed offstage. The audience, by now all sitting under umbrellas, managed to applaud his performance and then finally the play was called off.

The next two productions mounted by Capab were *The Relapse*, a camp 17th-century comedy of high style and costly wardrobes, written by John Vanbrugh, and *Death of a Salesman* by Arthur Miller. The leading role in both pieces was played by Michael Atkinson, who managed the roles expertly even though they were two completely different characters.

In *Death of a Salesman*, there was a scene where my character, Happy Loman, had to weep upon hearing of his father's death. I simply couldn't get myself to cry, even though Michael had shown me how he could weep on cue. I went to White's Pharmacy, which specialised in homeopathic medicines, and asked the chemist if he had anything that I could use to make myself weep. He gave me a little bottle of ammonia, and during the next performance, I rubbed it in my eyes. Well, Happy Loman did some extreme weeping in that scene. In fact, the tears kept flowing until the curtain came down and I could run to the dressing room to wash out my eyes.

The other thing was that Paul Slabolepszy, who was playing my brother Biff, and I had to open the show from our bedroom. Problem was, Paul had begun doing transcendental meditation and had also become a vegetarian. Every night, as we lay in the dark waiting for the curtain to go up, he would let rip with the most diverse array of pungent farts. Of course, he would apologise after every outburst, but it added a comic aspect to the opening of the play that Arthur Miller surely never intended.

The plays went on tour to the Opera House in Port Elizabeth. At this point in my young life, I had an interesting experience … increasingly, I started to find the gay men in the play more and more attractive. They were highly charming people, and some of them were also very sophisticated in the way they charmed me!

We were staying in the grand old King Edward Hotel on top of the hill. As I sat in the bar after a show, I began to think that even the barman, Frikkie, was attractive. I thought to myself that if it turned out I was gay, I did not really care. So what if I find this barman attractive? Still, I felt I needed to talk to someone about this.

The only person I trusted with this information was fellow cast member Mary Dreyer. I had gotten to know her and her husband well over the rehearsal periods, sometimes visiting them at their home in Hout Bay. I decided to call her room and ask to speak to her.

'Ian, it's 11 o'clock,' Mary said sleepily when she picked up the phone.

'It's very important, Mary. Please may I come and talk to you?'

'Okay, okay!'

I made my way to her room and resolved to ask her straight away whether she thought I was gay. I knocked and she opened the door. Mary was wearing an exquisite pale negligée; she stood with one hand on the door and looked at me with her bright brown eyes from under her dark hair.

'Yes, Mr Roberts?'

My eyes travelled down from her eyes over her body and I felt my manhood responding immediately.

'Uhmmm, it's okay, Mary. I think I've got my answer. Thanks very much, I'm going back to the bar!'

'Oh no you're not. You've woken me up. Now you better come and have a cup of coffee with me.'

And from that night on, I never again pondered over whether I was straight or gay.

Capab also did school tours, when the new actors would take performances of set works to government schools in the Cape hinterland. In the winter of 1980, Susan Gehr, Adri van der Merwe, Marthinus Basson and I headed northwards out of Cape Town in a pristine red-and-white-painted 2.1-litre automatic VW Kombi.

The performances were taxing and sometimes had to be done twice in a morning before difficult audiences. Even so, I have fond remembrances of the trip. We were driving around in a fantastic touring vehicle, all expenses paid. Every day, our youthful energy and voracious sense of adventure were gifted with the sight of new horizons of a truly fascinating countryside. Who could ask for more? I took my Canon 514 XLR Super 8 sound movie camera and a tripod along and shot a rough movie of the trip.

We ended the tour in Grahamstown with a performance at the schools festival at the Settlers Monument, as a prelude to the main National Arts Festival. We performed our school version of *Macbeth* in the afternoon, with the audience seated on three sides of the stage. At this point, we thought we were bulletproof, having been toughened by many daylight performances at all kinds of schools under a range of conditions. However, nothing could have prepared us for what would happen that day …

In the front row, we noticed Professor Roy Sargeant and Michael Atkinson, accompanied by a number of acolytes. Even though Marthinus, Susan and Adri had not studied at Rhodes, they knew our performances were about to be severely scrutinised. Initially, things went fairly well and we were managing to entertain, until Marthinus got to a short speech in which he was supposed to say something like the following: 'Banquo hath helped himself homeward on his horse …'

Now, Marthinus's home language was Afrikaans and Shakespearean English was not his forte. This meant that the line came out as follows: 'Panquo hath pelped pimpself pomeward on pis porse.' Shakespeare would have understood: 'The player is merely drunk on too much of the honeybee's mead and all his "aitches" he merely "pee'd",' he might've said with an understanding smile.

Not so Roy Sargeant and Michael Atkinson. They rose from their seats and walked out of the arena. Their acolytes followed and the rest of the audience began to whisper and shuffle their feet. It felt as if they too wanted to leave. We cut them short and ended the performance anyway. I have always wondered what Sargeant and Atkinson said to each other when they got outside. Perhaps nothing. Maybe they were shocked speechless by our terrible performances and our wrecking of Shakespeare.

One evening, I arrived at a party of UCT drama students in Vredehoek. These students had been our opposition at the annual intervarsity competitions at the National Arts Festival. I knew who they were and they knew who I was. I had seen the work that they had done, and I had respect for their talent – the old rivalry was gone now. I found the party buzzing and the atmosphere electric. They all seemed to share a hunger to make it big.

I recognised one particularly unusual person – Richard Grant, fresh out of UCT's drama department and at that time directing the play *Metamorphosis*. Today he is the famous Swaziland-born actor better known as Richard E Grant. He was standing with his back against a wall, ranting about the inadequate performance of an actor in a play he was directing at the famous, but now defunct, Space Theatre in Long Street. Richard sounded desperate and on the verge of cancelling the production of *Metamorphosis*.

In time, I would come to know Richard as given to melodrama even in ordinary worldly dealings. He didn't smoke zol or drink alcohol and thus lived close to his nerves and their concordant emotions.

Destiny has chosen certain moments in my life to make me do unexpected things, that is, unexpected from my point of view. Then there's the matter of the mad red-haired Irishman who often chooses to use my mouth to speak without my permission. That is probably why I turned to Richard and said, 'I'll play that role for you.'

The only thing missing in this preposterous proposal was an Irish accent. As mentioned, Richard's face was always extremely expressive and I could see the cogs spinning behind the gleam of his bright eyes.

'You will do what?'

'Uhm, I said if you want, Richard, I will come and play that role for you.'

'You will?!'

'Yes, but on one condition: you have to make it okay with the guy who's not swinging it.'

'Ooooh fuck! That's amaaaaazing!' Richard exclaimed excitedly. 'I'll speak to him and phone you tomorrow.'

When Richard called the next day, he said the other actor was highly pissed off but had agreed to leave, and please could I come to the Space as soon as possible to start rehearsals. The next moment, I was thrust into the production and trying to play catch-up. *Metamorphosis* is based on a

THEATRE

'Metamorphosis'

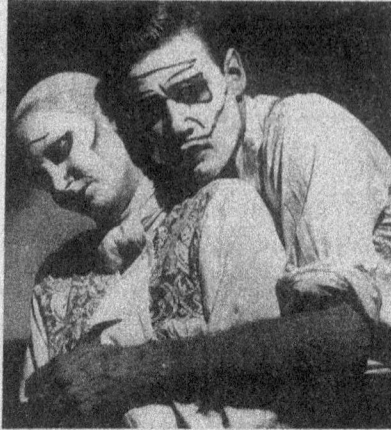

METAMORPHOSIS, a play by Steven Berkoff based on the story by Franz Kafka, with Henry Goodman, Hilary Jones, Fiona Ramsay, Ian Roberts, Charles Whaley, Chas Unwin and Michael O'Brien. Directed by Richard Grant and Michael O'Brien. At The People's Space, Long Street.

STEVEN BERKOFF's play sticks very closely to the letter and spirit of Franz Kafka's symbolical narrative. It has been described as one of the most dreadful stories ever written and it remains so even today. It's terror has not been minimized in any way by the shocks and horrors of science fiction. In fact, with modern society in the sort of chaos which makes it difficult for people to find meaning in their lives, it is more relevant than ever.

Kafka was concerned with moral and spiritual problems: man's struggle to find his real self and true vocation in accordance with divine law. Most people find nothing at all except isolation and rejection. Kafka, because he was an invalid and had Jewish blood, felt doubly isolated from the community and probably saw the problem more starkly than anyone else. He certainly illuminated it with unequalled imaginative power.

Reading the story and seeing the play are two different experiences. In the very first sentence of the story Gregor Samsa wakes up one morning to find that he has been transformed into a giant insect. By an act of imagination the reader immediately identifies with his predicament and becomes totally absorbed by the horror of it all.

But to see the same thing on the stage with Henry Goodman brilliantly miming the part of the insect is not so imaginatively convincing. There are too many distracting pitfalls in conveying the insect image. The insect is there before us all the time. Goodman creeps, crawls, grovels, hides under the sofa, climbs on the ceiling, squeaks, squelches, scrapes his feelers, secretes a great of saliva and succeeds in looking progressively wretched until in the end he lies on his back with his feet up and dies of starvation.

He did all this marvellously well with a strange muffled power which unfortunately succeed in shifting the focal point of the play from where it belonged — with Gregor's parents and sister.

For it is through them that Kafka and, I am sure, Berkoff intended us to see the real meaning of the story which is man's intolerance of suffering and disease. When they realize what has happened, Gregor's father mother and sister are at first shocked and horrified, then they become deeply concerned and even kind. These sentiments give way to anger and fear which in turn become shame, disgust, negligence and cruel rejection. Gregor becomes an obscenity.

But it's a difficult story to transfer to the stage and Richard Grant and Michael O'Brien deserve praise for even attempting it. They make use of some interesting sound and lights effects and one sequence, in which Gregor is feverishly exhorted by his family to hurry on and earn more money, is quite shattering.

Hilary Jones gives a touching performance as Greta, Gregor's sister, and Ian Roberts and Fiona Ramsay are adequate as Mr and Mrs Samsa.

BRIAN BARROW

Fiona Ramsay and Ian Roberts in "Metamorphosis" which has opened at The People's Space theatre

A review of *Metamorphosis*, which was directed by one of my university friends, Richard E. Grant.

novella by Franz Kafka, brilliantly worked into a piece of theatre by the English actor Steven Berkoff.

The cast was very good. The family were played by Henry Goodman (as Gregor Samsa, the son) Fiona Ramsay (the mother), Hilary Jones (the sister) and me (Gregor's father). Michael O'Brien and Chas Unwin and another actor called Whaley played the lodgers. The production was done in a highly stylised way, using mime.

This son of a citrus farmer from the Eastern Cape soon realised he had perhaps bitten off more than he could chew. I struggled desperately until, little by little, I started to get a grip on the play. However, despite my best efforts, my performance was still not satisfactory: I didn't believe what I was doing and neither did Richard. I was supposed to be playing a suburban father whose spirit had been hammered into submission by his pointless toil in the factories of the industrial world, but this life was completely foreign to me. I had no references to help me become the kind of man who would take out his own shortcomings on his son.

At the final notes reading after the dress rehearsal, Richard came right out and said that something wasn't working about my performance. He asked me to try and do something about it. The only problem was, the next evening was opening night. I was staring failure squarely in the face.

The thing is, nobody can actually teach you how to act. Forget about some director coming up with a magic solution to your crisis. It is all up to you as the actor.

I was trudging forlornly up Long Street on my way to my flat in Tamboerskloof, feeling inadequate and useless. What the hell was I going to do? Then I looked up and saw an elderly coloured man coming towards me. He had a bad limp. I stepped off the pavement to get out of his way. When I continued up Long Street, for some inexplicable reason I began to mimic his limp. My grandfather Daniel Roberts had had polio as a young boy and had limped heavily all his life, which meant that I was quite familiar with a limp. I started 'selling' my limp to people passing by and I actually got sympathy from some of them. In that moment I knew how to fix my portrayal of the father in *Metamorphosis* – the old bugger needed to limp.

The next evening, I arrived at the Space Theatre walking normally. On opening nights, things are always very tense and *Metamorphosis* was an extremely complex production. In the dressing room, the atmosphere was highly charged, as the actors prepared to attempt to realise in one performance all the painstaking work of weeks of rehearsal. You could say that when the curtain rises on an opening night, it might as well reveal a boxing ring, and the actors and the audience are the fighters: audience members can get up and walk out, but for the actors, there's no place to run. So the dressing room was accordingly tense.

It was in this atmosphere that I sat painting my face grey-white and black, wondering whether my new idea would work. It came to me that if I was to go down as an actor, then it would be better to go down in flames. When I went to the clothing rail to fetch my wardrobe, it was with my cultivated limp.

'What on earth are you doing, Ian?' asked Richard, his eyebrows arching.

'Practising … this is how I am going to play Gregor Samsa's father,' I said calmly. Most directors and fellow actors would have had strong resistance to such a last-minute change and would have advised against it, but not Richard or Fiona or Hilary or Henry. They just nodded matter-of-factly from in front of their mirrors, their make-up sticks poised in their raised hands.

The play began with the actors, dressed in black and white and grey, with faces painted the same, taking our places in the dark. I limped to my place. Somehow, it just felt right. Then a single spot came up, revealing Henry Goodman lying on his back centre stage, with his fingers and toes raised up into the air, twitching like the legs and claws of a beetle.

Richard sat at the back of the audience beside an old upright piano, plucking its strings to create a rough and discordantly moody soundtrack. The scene was very definitely set.

As the opening lines were spoken (I think by me), 'One morning, as Gregor Samsa awoke in his bed from uneasy dreams …' we actors were mortified to see a cockroach of monstrous proportions scuttle into the spotlight, and stop there, its antennae flicking. There was a gasp from the shocked audience. At that moment, I knew without a doubt that we were in a potent piece of theatre. My voice gained confidence and, with one eye on the giant cockroach, I continued loudly, 'and found himself transformed in his bed into a gigantic insect …'

A deathly silence now descended on the audience as the giant cockroach moved out of the light and Henry Goodman took over, with his miming genius, creating his own roach. As the opening continued to its final curtain, I limped about the stage, gaining confidence with every crooked step. At the end, the stunned audience roared their approval.

Metamorphosis played to packed audiences and we took it to the Market Theatre in Joburg where it was sold out for its entire run. We came back on the Trans-Karoo train with our pockets stuffed with cash. It had been an extremely difficult but truly rewarding experience.

A few weeks later, I was due to play the leading role in *Die Reënmaker* at the Nico Malan Theatre. I knew it was going to be a challenge, because my command of Afrikaans wasn't yet good enough to take on such a role.

Meanwhile Richard had set up another production at the Space. He had managed to get the rights to Robert David MacDonald's play *Chinchilla*, which was about the Russian impresario Sergei Diaghilev, who brought the Ballets Russes to Western Europe. Richard wanted me to act in a mid-sized role, that of Gabriel Astruc, Diaghilev's French financial advisor. *Chinchilla*'s run would end before rehearsals for *Die Reënmaker* were supposed to start, so I agreed.

It so happened that, at the same time, some of us had agreed to audition for a new television series, even though, as stage actors, we saw television acting as something of a cop-out. For us, playing in a television series or movie wasn't really acting in its purest form, especially since it offered the safety of the second or third take. The only reason we decided to audition was because television paid very well, and also my agent, Sybil Sands, had insisted that I go despite my reservations.

It was with feelings of being an *impimpi* (sell-out) that I drove to the SABC building in Sea Point. I was surprised to be met by Murray Steyn, who had studied with me in the drama department at Rhodes. I had found him a great inspiration as an actor and was surprised that he was apparently a crew member and not auditioning himself. He explained that he had recently gotten married and needed a solid income. I was still chewing on this news when I entered the locale and was met with a rather strange set-up.

The director, Alan Nathanson, an imposing man with a large dark beard, was sitting with a retinue of about ten people, a big glass window immediately behind them. Behind that window was the Atlantic Ocean, and the intense glare of the late afternoon sun on the ocean surface meant that you could only see the people in silhouette. I could hardly make out who was who. How rude, I thought as Murray introduced me.

I sat down in the single chair placed before them. Then Herr Director spoke. 'Hello, I am the director. Please read the part of the doctor.' With that he sent the script sliding over the polished parquet floor, with it coming to an abrupt stop at my feet. I picked it up thinking, 'Who the hell does this man think he's talking to?'

Then the mad Irishman, always waiting for a chance to come out and shake his red hair loose, spoke. 'Nah, I don't like that role,' I said. The voice I found myself speaking with had absolutely nothing to do with me. I slid the script back over the parquet floor, and it came to rest by the director's shoes.

There was a reactive coughing and shuffling among the people in the room. Clearly, nobody had ever dared treat him in this manner. Thankfully, Murray was outside the door waiting to usher in the next actor, so he didn't have to feel embarrassed because he happened to know me.

'Oh? So, you don't like the role of the doctor?' said Herr Director with a modicum of malice as he picked up the script.

'No, I don't.'

'Pray tell, why not?'

'I think it's badly written.'

This caused even louder sounds of embarrassment among the silhouettes. Apparently, the writer, Geraldine Aron, was sitting right next to the director (so I found out later).

'I see …' More stunned silence. 'Well, is there perhaps any part you *would* like to read?' he asked, sending the script skimming back over the floor to me.

I opened it in the pregnant silence. I skimmed the pages and found a character called Faizal or something.

'Yes, I'd like to read the character of Faizal, please.'

'Faizal?' There was a muffled giggle because Faizal was a coloured character. I was given the go-ahead and then proceeded to do my best coloured accent, but it was obvious that I was never going to play any role in that TV series. When I was done with the reading, I flicked the script back over the floor and left, my pride intact.

In the end, Sean Taylor got the role of the doctor and played it very well.

No matter how convinced I was, as a young actor, that acting in television and in movies was a cop-out, I soon recognised that my attitude was financial folly. I once framed a cheque for a week's salary from the Space Theatre and mounted it on my wall: it was made out for R8.27! This was for an entire week's work and was signed by dear Cynthia Dennis, the bookkeeper of the theatre.

It wasn't long before I swallowed my pride and went to earn some proper money.

Since I had no immediate plans to be part of the television production, I could focus all my attention on Richard's production of *Chinchilla*, which is set in Venice. In those days, it was extremely difficult to get the rights to plays, because many writers refused to allow their plays to be performed in

South Africa owing to apartheid and the cultural boycott.

However, by some miracle, Richard got the rights to *Chinchilla*. He cast the leading roles with high-class actors from Joburg and everything was set for a great production. About three days before rehearsals were to begin, I answered an early-morning phone call at my flat. It was Richard and he was in a state of complete hysteria.

'Baalie!' (Why Richard took to calling me by this nickname, I have no idea. Perhaps it had to do with the fact that I was older, as in I was an old *ballie*, or gentleman.)

'Good morning, Richard.'

'Baalie, something terrible has happened … We must meet immediately!'

I'd come to expect big emotion over little things from Richard, so I wasn't too concerned as I rode my bicycle through the crisp Cape Town morning air down Long Street. Richard screeched to a halt in his red Datsun 120Y outside our favourite coffee shop and began talking the moment he saw me. It was indeed a dire situation he found himself in. Overnight, all the major actors from Johannesburg had withdrawn from his production. Richard's suspicion was that someone had bad-mouthed him in Joburg as an arrogant upstart, and when the main actor withdrew, the rest of the cast followed suit.

'Oh, my God, Baalie, I am *doomed*!' he cried out.

Again, I found the mad Irishman speaking through my mouth without my consent.

'You know what, Richard?'

'What?' he said, quick to catch on to any strain of hope.

'We're gonna do this play.'

'But, but, with *who*? Rehearsals start the day after tomorrow and I have *no* cast!'

'Well, that's not completely true, Richard. You've still got me.' The cogs of incredulity were grinding behind Richard's eyes.

'We'll recast all those assholes from Joburg. We'll cast people off the streets of Cape Town if we have to. It doesn't matter, but Richard, we are going to do this play!'

Richard's face suddenly lit up. He was actually a tsotsi concealed in drama student's camouflage. Because he was so committed to his quest, he could do anything he put his mind to.

'Baalie!' he said and gave me a huge bear hug.

And that was that. Richard cast the play in two days. Gavin van den Berg, an extraordinary talent, just happened to be in town. He took on the monstrously difficult role of the ballet dancer Nijinsky. Duarte Sylwain and Caroline Newby took Diaghilev and his female confidante, respectively, and I played Gabriel Astruc, the Frenchman. Three weeks later, the play opened to critical acclaim.

However, even though the reviews were good, we struggled to get big audiences. Richard had set out to create the glory of Venice in the Space Theatre in apartheid South Africa, which was no small feat. He then decided to organise three vintage cars, and we got into wardrobe on a Saturday morning and cruised the streets of the city, encouraging people to come and see the show. They did. That was the glory of Cape Town in the 1980s.

The Space Theatre was a real working-man's theatre: some of the most meaningful productions were staged there. It had only a single dressing room for actors. You would sit before your mirror amid the chaos of half-naked actors and actresses moving about, wardrobes being tossed onto a rail, actors looking for this or that, trying to have a conversation with someone on the other side of the room, and so on. It was a warm, friendly kind of chaos, the kind of atmosphere some actors miss so badly they go into mourning when a production finally ends. For a while, the Space's dressing room became your home away from home, a safe place where we all had each other's back.

One evening, as I was busy removing my make-up, I noticed a pair of tan-coloured moccasins enter the small piece of floor beneath my outstretched arm. Now, in South Africa in the early 1980s only Afrikaans-speaking men wore that kind of tan moccasin. I looked around and up above my left shoulder into the smiling face of a bearded man wearing gold-rimmed spectacles.

'Hullo,' he said quietly, with a slight Afrikaans accent. 'I am Manie van Rensburg and I just want to say that I really enjoyed your German characterisation tonight.'

I thanked him and decided not to point out that the character I was playing was in fact French.

'Your play transported me to Venice. From Long Street in Cape Town to

Venice for a fifty-rand ticket. That was something very special – thank you.'

He should actually have been complimenting director Richard and the rest of the cast, but I thanked him again for coming to see the show and went back to wiping off my make-up, expecting him to move on. But Manie cleared his voice; there was more he wanted to say.

'I will soon be making a television series, where there is a small role for a German character that I would like you to play. It's a one-day shoot about two weeks from now.'

He handed me a card. 'Here is my number. Please phone if you want to do it.'

And with that he left. A strange quiet descended on the otherwise noisy dressing room. People were looking at me curiously. I went back to removing my make-up.

'Do you know who that was, Baalie?' asked Richard.

'Ja, he said he was Manie van Rensburg.'

'Not just Manie van Rensburg. That was *THE* Manie van Rensburg, the great movie director.'

'Oh,' I said, because up until that moment, I had only a vague idea of who he was.

'What did he say to you?'

'He said thank you for transporting him to Venice from Long Street, and by that I am sure that he was actually thanking all of you.'

'Ja, and?' Richard insisted.

'He offered me to play the part of a German for one day in a TV series in two weeks.'

The room burst into congratulatory cheers. Everyone was so pleased that I had managed to land a role in a Manie van Rensburg TV series. Even though the members of the Troupe Theatre Company were exclusively English, and only worked in English, everybody knew who Manie was and all of them would have dearly liked to do a movie with him.

Later, when I was about to phone Manie to tell him I wanted the role, the mad red-haired Irishman stepped forward once again, spreading wanton thoughts in my mind. That is why, when I phoned, I told him that not only would I like to play the part but that I also wanted to work on his movie set. Manie, being a civil and gracious person, thankfully didn't put the phone down in my ear.

'What would you want to do on set?'

'I can do anything,' I responded. 'I come from a farm. I can do carpentry, electricity, I can take engines out of cars and fix them. I can weld, brass or steel. I can do glass fibre. Anything.'

'Let me speak to my producer, Johan van Jaarsveld, and we'll phone you on Wednesday.'

That night I couldn't sleep very well. This was unusual for me, because the one thing I don't have a problem with is sleeping. I got the sense that I was being tapped on the shoulder by the hand of destiny and that I had to be open to any directives from the universe, or even from the Irishman inside me.

I also realised that I had placed myself in a difficult situation: I was scheduled to begin rehearsals for the leading role in *Die Reënmaker* at the Nico Malan in a week. If I got the movie job, I wouldn't be able to do it. I would have to let Pieter Fourie, the head of Capab Drama, know – and soon – but I also didn't have the movie job yet. For that, I had to wait three days and then they might just say no. I decided to go see Pieter anyway and tell him of my plans. He could have reacted with outrage, but to his credit he didn't.

'Ian, as dit in jou hart is, gaan doen dit dan. Ek sal nie in jou pad staan nie' (Ian, if you feel in your heart of hearts that you should do it, then go ahead. I won't stand in your way), he said.

I was surprised at the level of understanding he showed, and in my view his response was a typically Afrikaner way of kindly freeing me from my contract. What struck me especially was his words 'as dit in jou hart is'. Up until that point, I was used to a more rigid toughness from my English upbringing and years at St Andrew's College. In my experience, Afrikaners generally tend to be more emotive in expression and therefore in their understanding. I indeed felt it in my heart of hearts.

On that crucial third day, I waited beside the phone in my flat. The young man was nervous, not so much for the fact that he might soon be jobless, and have to give up his flat, but because he might be turned down in his quest to become a worker on a movie set. After cups and cups of Frisco instant coffee, I was so jittery that when the phone rang, I nearly ran out of the room in apprehension of being turned down.

'Hullo, is that Eeyaan?' the voice on the other end asked.

'Yes! Yes, it's me.'

'This is Johan van Jaarsveld. Manie and I have decided that you can work on the movie set as assistant to the production manager, Richard Green. We can pay you R120 a week. Will that be enough?'

'Yes, that's enough, thank you, thank you very much!'

'Good, please be at 40 Strand Street in Pearly Beach by Saturday evening for a pre-production get-together.'

When I put down the phone I tingled with energy, it felt as if I had been reborn. There was no doubt in my mind that I was setting out on a great adventure.

7

The magic of moviemaking

MANIE VAN RENSBURG WAS SHOOTING a six-episode drama called *Dokter Con Viljee se Overberg* at a place called Baardskeerdersbos, a tiny, almost forgotten hamlet in the Overberg, where it seemed as if time had stood still. Production manager Richard Green, me and Mosie, a coloured man from Gansbaai whose surname I have sadly forgotten, did the set dressing, carrying furniture from one house to another. We painted walls, painted tennis courts on lawns, rented horses that could drink wine and smoke cigarettes, and sourced extras – the production had a very tight budget.

Our intensive daily activities reminded me of working with my father and uncle on the farm, so being assistant to the production manager came easily to me. Money was tight and the work was hard, but I loved it. It wasn't long before I started thinking that this was what I was born for.

Working in the theatre had been good, but I was now discovering that, compared to a television or film production, it was more like working an office job. When you work in the theatre, you go to the same building every morning for rehearsals and back again every evening for the performances. On a production that is being shot on location, you constantly move from place to place, often in small backwaters that you've never been to. This hunter-gatherer lifestyle was heaven on earth for a farmer's son.

I had taken my Canon 514 XLR Super 8 sound camera with me and began shooting a documentary of what, to me, was a wonderful experience. Early one morning, as I was filming the rehearsals for a busy street scene, where hired vintage cars drove past on the dirt road while actors spoke to each other in the doorways of their old-fashioned houses, sound man Anton van der Linde came up to me.

'What the heck are you doing?' he asked.

'I'm just making a movie of us while we're making the movie.'

'You're crazy, man. Manie will be the *moer* in. Stop it.'

I reckoned that if the director didn't like what I was doing, then he could tell me so himself, so I carried on, moving my tripod and camera over the road and setting up for a wide shot. Shortly after that, Manie walked over to me and, in our conversation, it turned out that he loved that I was filming the goings-on. As long as I did my job, moving all the furniture on the set, sweeping the carpets and making up the beds, he was happy. The result is that I have a priceless documentary of about 25 minutes of the shoot of *Dokter Con Viljee se Overberg*. Quiet and approachable: that was the kind of person Manie was, and that was why people always seemed quiet and respectful and well-behaved on his sets.

One evening, after a day's shooting, we were gathered in the rented holiday house in Pearly Beach, a coastal town near Baardskeerdersbos, where the crew got together for dinner. Manie and the talented director, producer and scriptwriter Johan van Jaarsveld were playing a game of pool while discussing the production. As I walked past, Manie asked, 'Hoe's jou Afrikaans, Ian?'

He wanted to know whether I could speak any Afrikaans. I told him I had been fluent in the language in the army, but that I had become a bit rusty since then.

'We have a bit of a problem,' Manie said in his quiet way. 'One of the main actors, André Rossouw, has been admitted to hospital and he was due to play a role on set tomorrow.'

'We have tried to find another actor to take his place, but we've had no luck so far,' said Johan.

'We were thinking, if your Afrikaans is good enough, perhaps you can play André's role tomorrow?' Manie again.

I didn't have to think twice before answering. 'I'll do it!'

I put on a confident front, but in actual fact, I was short of Afrikaans speaking experience, since all the theatre productions I had been working on had been in English and all my friends in Cape Town were English-speaking.

'You play Cousin Johnny tomorrow, and if the character works for me, then you can play all André's roles,' Manie said.

Dokter Con Viljee se Overberg was made using actors in an ensemble way: in each episode the same actors would play different characters. Manie said

On the set of *Dokter Con Viljee se Overberg* with director Manie van Rensburg (far left) and producer Johan van Jaarsveld.

he would review the rushes once they arrived on set from Irene Studios, near Pretoria. ('Rushes', or 'rush-prints', are the raw and unedited footage from a day's shoot.) That would take about three days.

'Dink jy jy sal met 'n bry kan praat?' (Do you think you could speak with a burr?), Manie then wanted to know.

This way of speaking Afrikaans, by pronouncing the 'r' in a throaty, drawn-out way, was foreign to me, but I was young, arrogant and hungry. When I left Rhodes University drama department, I had made a pact with myself never to turn down the chance to play a good role because of language. If I felt a role was right for me, I would find a way to learn the language. Now my pact was being seriously challenged. Manie eyed me as he drew on his Camel Filter, maybe thinking he had made a mistake by offering this farm boy from the Eastern Cape the chance to play all the roles of a great actor like André Rossouw.

After dinner, when most of the crew had gone home, I sidled over to Birrie le Roux, the young lady who was doing wardrobe. I had noticed that she sometimes spoke with a slight burr and I asked her to help me get it right. She agreed and we went out to my Kombi Camper and sat there in the crisp, salt-laden, autumn night air as she taught me how to do the dialogue of Cousin Johnny until she felt I could pull it off.

The next morning, dressed as Cousin Johnny, I piloted a donkey cart down a dirt road and brought it to a halt at the exact spot where I had been told to.

'Môre, tant Sarie, hoe gaan dit vandag?' I said with the burr on the two r's. Standing opposite me was one of the great ladies of Afrikaans theatre, Babs Laker.

'Môre, Cousin Johnny, dit gaan goed, dankie!'

And so I found myself acting in a television scene for the first time.

Three days later, the rushes came back and I waited outside in the dark with trepidation. Would Manie find my acting good enough to take over all of André's parts? Manie never allowed actors to watch rushes. Later, when I got to know him, he told me why.

'Actors can never be objective when viewing a frame they were in, because they are always too focused on themselves.'

If there was something a specific actor needed to see, he would be invited to a one-on-one session with Manie during which he would roll film on the editing desk and point out what the actor should take note of. That was the only chance they would get to view rushes.

When the crew came out of the viewing, they seemed to be happy with what they'd seen. To my great relief, Manie was satisfied with my performance and said I could take over all of André's roles. By default, I had become a television actor. There were butterflies in my stomach and it felt like they were flying around happily, carrying little sachets of rich yellow pollen mixed with honey.

Of course, the fact that I now had an acting role didn't mean that my other job went away. Richard, Mosie and I were on the go 18 hours a day, 24/7. Every morning we would arrive first on set, when the early-morning mists still whung over the land, wherever the location was in or around Baardskeerdersbos. I would collect wood and build a fire, because when Manie arrived at 7 am, it was imperative that he get a hot cup of coffee in his cold hands to go with his Camel Filter cigarette. The budget was so tight, we didn't even have an electric urn, so I would boil a large pot of water over the fire. This was second nature to me from my hunter-gathering days.

I have always loved being busy, and being assistant to the production manager reminded me of farming oranges in the Kat Valley. Still, the acting was the highlight. Within five weeks I had gone from telling Richard Grant that we would do the play *Chinchilla*, even if it meant casting actors off the street, to playing one of the leading roles in a TV series that was being directed by one of the leading talents in South Africa. Helter-skelter never scared me.

Once the shoot was done, I went back to Cape Town and became involved again with the Troupe Theatre Company. Every evening after rehearsals, I would go for a run along the Pipe Track, which runs along the western side of Table Mountain, up above Camps Bay. At some point, I would always disturb a flock of guinea fowl and they would take to the air, voicing their displeasure with raucous cries.

What was often on my mind as I jogged high up on the mountain every evening was the bush war in then Rhodesia. I knew people who were fighting in that war and I had been very close to it when I travelled through Rhodesia in 1972 with my then girlfriend's family. I imagined a family of guinea fowl trying to live peacefully in the Rhodesian bush, only to have their world repeatedly shattered by warfare. Did the politicians and generals who directed the war from their offices ever think of the souls of guinea fowl? Did mankind ever think of the kudu, the lion or the elephant when they made war?

I decided that, in my next script, the guinea fowl would state their case. Obviously, my involvement with the production of *Metamorphosis* had also influenced me. I started writing intensively on a second-hand Olivetti portable typewriter that I had found somewhere. After I'd written 21 pages, I told Richard about my script and he was immediately interested to read it. I felt a bit embarrassed by the measly little pile of papers, but if anyone in the wide world was ever going to push the idea further, it would be the wildly imaginative Richard Grant, so I gave it to him. The next morning my phone rang. 'Baalie, this is fantastic. I love it! We're going to do it!' Richard said.

In the production, Henry Goodman, Fiona Ramsay, Fred Abrahamse, Hilary Jones and Bryony Mortimer became guinea fowl on stage. Led by Henry, who was an exceptional mime artist, they were ingenious in the way they mimicked the manner in which the guinea fowl moved their heads, and the rapid scuttling, by which they would, at precisely

Grant en Goodman tref weer die kol

GUINEA FOWL, Images of Africa, deur Ian Roberts, opgevoer deur die Troupe Theatre Company onder regie van Richard Grant, met Henry Goodman (Dada), Fiona Ramsay (Memi), Hilary Jones (Dutu), Bryony Mortimer (Moni), Fred Abrahamse (Preki), Lammie Shoba, Neil McCarthy, Noel Makinana en Ian Roberts; dekorstelle en maskers deur Fred Abrahamse en kostuums deur Birrie le Roux. In die Volksruimte.

DIE Volksruimte het in die afgelope jaar of wat 'n hele paar opvoerings van baie hoë gehalte gelewer, veral dié waarin Henry Goodman en Richard Grant 'n rol gespeel het. Hierdie twee toneelmense – akteurs of regisseurs kan 'n mens hulle nie sonder verdere verduideliking noem nie – skep altyd iets besonders, iets opwindends en boweal iets afgeronds.

PROFESSIONEEL

Guinea Fowl is nog eens 'n professionele stuk werk waarin woord, beeld en beweging, tesame met die visuele voorstelling tot eenheid gevoer is. Die afronding getuig van groot presiesheid in die voorbereiding en van samewerking tussen al die betrokkenes.

Die feit dat die skrywer, Ian Roberts, ook 'n rol in die stuk vertolk en dus byderhand was dwarsdeur die voorbereiding, het sekerlik daartoe bygedra dat die finale produk so puik is.

KRAGTOER

Henry Goodman het met sy mede-tarentale 'n kragtoer uitgevoer. Die groep voëls, waarnemers van en kommentators oor die beeelde van Afrika wat voor hulle (en die gehoor) afgespeel word, het met woord en dikwels net voëlgeluid die aanskouer op die punt van die stoel gehou, end-uit. Die manier waarop die tarentale beweeg en skreeu, was presies reg, en soos 'n mens in 'n goeie professionele opvoering sou verwag, van begin tot end op peil.

Die ander spelers het elk 'n verskeidenheid of rolle vertolk en deur die bank uitgeblink. Lammie Shoba se boesman, Goodwill én terroris is elkeen ráák gesien en Fred Abrahamse het naas sy rol as tarentaal, ook die terroris, bewaarder, soldaat en klerk met groot oortuiging gespeel.

HOOGTEPUNT

Noel Makinana het Joko Scott in 'n drietal rolle vervang – Scott is ongesteld – en pragtig by die patroon van die stuk ingepas, met sy vertolking van die toordokter allig sy beste.

Ian Roberts het soos 'n gesoute akteur opgetree en sy uitbarsting in Xhosa was asembenemend.

Maar dié hoogtepunt is gelewer deur Neil McCarthy,

Deur
VICTOR HOLLOWAY

wat onlangs die Fleur du Cap-prys vir die belowendste student van 1980 verwerf het. Hy het 'n vyftal rolle gespeel, maar niks beter as sy vertolking van die soldaat aan die grens nie.

Dié kêrel, vol bravado, maar met groot vrees wat geleidelik na vore kom en hom uiteindelik tot die rand van incenstorting voer, is 'n stuk toneelspel van die hoogste gehalte.

KEUSE

'n Mens kan beswaar hê teen Roberts se keuse van "beelde", spyt wees oor die afwesigheid van ander. Maar wat hy en sy spelers wel aangepak het, word deurgevoer met groot intensiteit en oortuiging. Dit betref die aanskouer deurentyd en boei hom 'n paar uur lank in die teater – en langer daarbuite.

Grant se regie is uitstekend, en Goodman se "choreografie" van die tarentale merkwaardig.

Elkeen wie se belangstelling in die toneel verder strek as kanaries en kaal meisies, moet na *Guinea Fowl* gaan kyk – dis 'n toneelervaring.

AMONG the cast of Ian Roberts's new play, The Guinea-Fowl, which opens at The People's Space on March 13, are (from top) Fiona Ramsay, Henry Goodman and Hilary Jones.

The play, presented by Troupe Theatre Company and directed by Richard Grant, is about 'change in Africa' and has a cast of black and white actors. There will be previews on Wednesday and Thursday next week.

Another South African playwright whose work will be seen at the theatre in the coming months is David Lan, who has scored major successes at London's Royal Court Theatre. His Painting A Wall, Sergeant Ola and Red Earth have been 'scooped' by The People's Space, and will have their first South African performances at the theatre, under director Mike

An Afrikaans newspaper review of my play *Guinea Fowl*, which I wrote as a young actor.

95

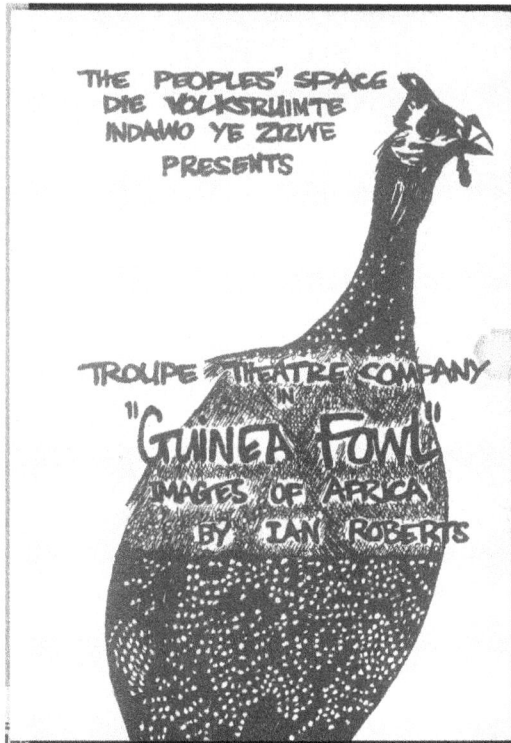

The programme for *Guinea Fowl*, which was directed by Richard E. Grant and had Fiona Ramsay in one of the leading roles.

the same instant and as if by some unheard command, all move together in a certain direction. Joko Scott, Lammie Shoba, Neil McCarthy and I played the humans (soldiers and guerrilla fighters) who invade their world.

Rehearsals were tough, with the script being developed as we went along. On numerous occasions insults were shouted across the floor, but somehow, and thanks to Richard, who manned the ship like a doughty helmsman in a bad storm, things never fell apart.

One afternoon after rehearsals, when we came down onto Long Street on our way home, Lammie Shoba was attacked by a jilted lover, who lunged at him with a long, shiny knife. But Lammie was quick and jumped behind a car and kept circling so that she couldn't get near him. He laughed as the woman threw foul insults at him. At the time, I found this incident somehow symbolic of our torrid rehearsals.

One thing I should say, though, is that in my career it has always been true that in every production – whether for theatre or film – where things had been all friendly and plain sailing, the result would be a well-balanced and level but essentially uninteresting production that failed to attract and inspire audiences. Of course, this does not guarantee that all productions that are difficult to create are going to succeed.

Guinea fowl opened to warm critique and the play did quite well. A personal highlight was when I was approached by the immaculately dressed and gracious Michael Atkinson at the opening-night party. 'Hello, Ian dearest,' he said in the dulcet yet resonant tones of the theatrical leading man. 'I must say that I have been pleasantly entranced by your guinea fowls. Thank you, and well done! Congratulations are in order.' At the time, Michael, who was born in Britain and was a former member of the Royal Shakespeare Company, was at the height of his illustrious career in South Africa as an actor and director.

After *Dokter Con Viljee se Overberg*, I went on to make seven movies and TV series in a row with Manie van Rensburg, and, in so doing, I got to know him very well. It is a long-time dream of mine to impart some of what I learnt from him to students at film schools and acting institutions. One of the things I'll tell them is that movie acting is just like growing oranges. You work hard in the summer, setting the crop while everybody is lying dreaming on the beaches, and in the winter you reap. And what you reap is

The actress Grethe Fox and Manie van Rensburg at their home in Cape Town.
Credit: Gallo Images

directly affected by how well you have set the crop in the summer.

Those were the days when actors very often did not do auditions to get a part in a TV series or a movie, even for a leading role. What would happen was that a director would see you perform on stage and, on the strength of that, decide whether you could play a specific part in their movie. I found this a highly sophisticated approach: why sully the mystery and the magic that an actor might bring to a role with a ropey series of auditions?

Manie regarded the performance potential of actors as a kind of Holy Grail of moviemaking. Often, he was goaded by the crew and the production team to play a small cameo role in the movie he was directing, like Alfred Hitchcock, Luis Buñuel and many other directors. Manie, however, would always flatly refuse. To him, the world of actors and actresses was sacred; the world in front of the camera was holy ground that he would never invade.

In Manie's view, the actor's interpretation of a scene was up to them. It was fully their responsibility. He expected actors to have done their own work at home of visualising the scene(s) for the next day and to arrive prepared. It was because of this that he would seldom, if ever, try to tell or show an actor how to act a scene. The furthest Manie would go would be to tell an actor what about their performance wasn't working for him and then do another take to give them the opportunity to correct it. This meant that if an actor or actress somehow couldn't get it right, Manie would eventually have to fire them.

In 1986, when shooting the opening of the SABC TV series *Heroes*, the three leads – Neil McCarthy, leading lady Carol Ann Kelleher and I – were doing a scene in which she came out of her house to meet Neil and my characters. It was a complex scene with many nuances. It was also very important because it set up the development of their relationship for the next five episodes of the series. As the Americans would say, it was a money scene: it had to work for the series to work.

Manie had set up one of his long, complex tracking shots with the camera moving in among us actors to capture a two-shot, and then tracking again into a single shot on a specific actor for a particular line before tracking away again to hold us all in a walking three-shot. It would be another of his signature long, moving scenes shot in a way that had to be done in one take. We actors knew our asses were on the line to try to hit every mark and perform it flawlessly.

We did the first take and everything seemed to run perfectly, but, strangely, Manie called for another take. We did it again, but Manie, for reasons unknown to us, was still unhappy. He adjusted some of Carol Ann's moves and called for a third take. I glanced over towards sound man Anton van der Linde, with whom I had done five Manie movies by then, and he nodded surreptitiously back at me – yes, something was very wrong.

After the third take, Manie said, 'Okay, cut it there. Right folks, that's a wrap for today.'

For a moment everyone stood around perplexed. It was only about lunch time and already we were done for the day? We watched as Manie walked calmly to the Kombi that would drive him home.

I was excited to get half a day off and decided to go catch a wave at

Muizenberg. That evening, I came back to my sister Jane's place in Pine-lands, where I was lodging. Shortly after, the phone rang and she picked it up: 'It's for you, boet.'

'Eeeeyaaan?' came the calm, measured voice.

'Ja, Manie?'

'Ons moet praat, kan jy hier na my toe kom?' (We have to talk, could you come over?)

As I put down the receiver, I had a sinking feeling. I was convinced he was going to fire me. I started mulling over what was wrong with my performance while I drove on De Waal Drive to his place in Gardens. I didn't know what to think as I climbed the steep old creaky wooden stairs of the semi-detached house where he lived with his wife, the actress Grethe Fox, all the way to the study at the top. There, Manie stood waiting with a beer glass full of J&B whisky, the ice tinkling eloquently in the frizzing soda.

'The whisky's just to soften the blow,' I thought as I took the glass. He looked at me with a fatalistic expression in his eyes.

'Cheers,' said Manie, *now* with a conspiratorial twinkle. 'Sy moet gaan' (She's got to go). He said it softly, yet with definite finality. It wasn't my ass that was getting fired but the shapely behind of the beautiful Carol Ann Kelleher.

I thought he was becoming more and more like a swashbuckling pirate captain of the high seas, where his movie was his ship and he knew when he didn't want to sail up a certain river. I took a long draught of the pale J&B, feeling the soda bubbles tickling my throat and the relief wash over me.

Manie sighed and continued.

'I made a big mistake, Ian. I went to see the girl in a play at the Market [Theatre] in Johannesburg and I thought she was perfect for the role of Isadora, but she isn't.' 'Sorry, man, Manie,' I said, not sure what I should do.

'You don't perhaps know of an actress who would be right for this role?'

I was astounded. The master was placing his trust in me. It just so happened that I knew someone who would be perfect for the role, and, moreover, I knew that even though she lived in Johannesburg, she happened to be in Cape Town right at that point.

'Yes, I can come up with a name …'

'O ja?' Manie raised his eyebrows and he took another sip.

'Her name is Terry Norton and she's a genius actress. As luck would have it, she is currently in Cape Town and not busy.'

Manie thought for a moment – the pirate, weighing up the words of an informant, deciding whether he should trust them. Suddenly he smiled and looked at his watch.

'Terry Norton, you say …' and then handed me the telephone that was attached to the wall. 'Please call Mr Green and ask him if he could come over immediately.'

Even though I felt very sorry for Carol Ann, I had to admit that I found these behind-the-scenes machinations rather exciting. It helped that I wasn't on the receiving end of it! Soon production manager Richard Green arrived and, even though it was now approaching midnight, he was also handed a beer glass of J&B and soda.

Manie then explained the situation to him and asked Richard to phone Terry and offer her the role of Isadora.

'But Manie, it's way past midnight,' he protested.

'I know, Richard, but, as you know, this is very important.'

To our relief, Terry answered her phone, and when she heard who was directing, she agreed there and then to play the role. Richard went home to his wife, and Manie and I crushed the aluminium top of another fresh one-litre bottle of J&B and tossed it out the window. As we talked into the ghost hours, the way the hands on the clock on the wall pointed no longer meant anything.

Manie told me how terrible it made him feel to fire an actress in a leading role. Of course, he knew all hell would break loose in the morning when Carol Ann heard the news.

'I don't know why actors get so cross when I fire them. As I always say: I'm very sorry and it was not them who had made the mistake, it was me. I was the one who messed up when I cast her, she's just not right for it. I don't know exactly what it is, because she was very good on stage, but when you put a frame around her there is something about her that just doesn't say "Isadora" to me. If I were an actor and the director told me he'd made a mistake and that I was wrong for a role, I would be only too happy to leave his movie set.'

Thus we talked until the sun rose up over the mountains above distant Sir Lowry's Pass, and when the Kombi arrived in the street below, we drained our glasses and made our way down the stairs to street level. We climbed in and were driven to the location to shoot a call sheet hastily adjusted not to include the leading lady. The following day, the freshly wardrobed Terry Norton was on set. Luckily, Terry delivered a good performance and Manie's decision was duly justified.

A few years later, in 1990, I was reminded of a related lesson on the set of the feature film *The Fourth Reich*, about the South African boxer and Nazi supporter Robey Leibbrandt, who received military training in Germany at the start of the Second World War and was sent to South Africa to establish links with pro-German organisations and commit acts of sabotage.

I arrived in Oudtshoorn a week after shooting had begun only to find nothing happening on set. Apparently, Manie had decided that he didn't like the leading man, Paul Herzberg, a South African-born actor then living in England. Using Herzberg as lead actor was part of the deal when Manie decided to take on the film as director, but now he was saying Herzberg was not right for the role of Robey Leibbrandt.

Manie was adamant, 'I do not want to make the movie with him as the lead, so one of us will have to go.'

When I got to Manie, he complained that Herzberg had no idea how to play a Boer. Herzberg could not know what it meant to have been born out in the dusty veld in a world of hardship, and to have grown up with grandparents who, after the denigrations of the Anglo-Boer War (1899–1902), had been forced to stand in the corner of the classroom wearing a 'dunce' hat because they couldn't speak English. Manie wanted to replace Herzberg with Ryno Hattingh, who he felt would know where Leibbrandt came from, owing to his Afrikaner background, and would intuitively know how to play the role.

Eventually, the producers decided the leading man had to go so Manie could be retained as director. Richard Green told me how he had to drive the very pissed-off Herzberg to the airport in Cape Town and pick up Ryno, his replacement, who happened to have flown in from Johannesburg at the same time.

Today, many directors are afraid of following their instinct or gut feeling when it comes to picking an actor. Because of modern technology, they have also become removed from their gut. For example, since the Covid-19 pandemic it has become the norm to do auditions via WhatsApp. A director will cast a role without ever coming into an actor's physical presence. Furthermore, they are increasingly wary of taking artistic chances because, should their deviation from the norm lead to failure, they risk being executed on social media, with their demise possibly going viral. Social media hangs over people like a cloud of correction and casts a blanket of commonality over everyone.

That said, I have since realised that directors are frequently not certain about what they are doing. So auditions give them a chance to see what is possible. However, if the X-factor of what an actor can bring to their performance in a movie gets used up in extensive auditions, then the actor might not be able to recreate that magic again when the scene is shot somewhere down the line.

Many years later, I auditioned for *Coup!*, a BBC movie about the abortive coup in Equatorial Guinea in 2004 by the British ex-SAS (Special Air Service) member Simon Mann and the South African mercenary Nick du Toit. I was auditioning for the role of Du Toit. The director was Simon Cellan Jones and he had with him a lady producer whose name I have unfortunately forgotten. The auditions came and went, but I heard nothing further. Oh well, another one I didn't get, I thought, quite disappointed with the turn of events, since South African actors generally walk a financial tightrope and BBC movies pay well.

Then, about two weeks later, the producer phoned, requesting another meeting with me. As we chatted over a cup of coffee, she said, 'Ian, I've watched your auditions again and, quite frankly, I feel you're hiding something.'

Of course I had been hiding something! I told her I had been holding back on the X-factor that would manifest only when I felt it could add to the power of the movie, *not* the audition. Bless the women of this world, who often have the gift to come upon my subterfuge and bring it out into the open. I auditioned for her again and she persuaded the director to pick me for the role. I ended up playing the part.

So much for auditions ... famous directors like Manie van Rensburg, Dirk de Villiers, Jan Scholtz and John Rogers didn't need them. How privileged I have been to work with and learn from them. Directors like these, who manage to retain the rough edges of their distinct personalities, are becoming increasingly scarce. In fact, like the cars whose engines you can still work on with spanners and screwdrivers, they are on the verge of extinction.

8

What Manie van Rensburg taught me

PRODUCING MOVIES IS GENERALLY NOT easy, and it also shouldn't be. What moviemakers are trying to conjure from life is the *kamma-kamma*: they are engaging in a game of fantasy in which they have to make you believe in the story they are trying to tell. There are so many variables, so many things over which a moviemaker has no control, that it's touch and go whether all that work will eventually come together and be something that will entertain viewers and possibly even make money.

Apart from everything he taught me about acting in movies, I also learnt a valuable lesson from Manie van Rensburg about the art of movie directing. Directors are always in the thick of things, and on a movie set the buck stops with them. One night, after Manie and I had looked deep into a few bottles of J&B, he told me a thing he'd learnt the hard way. By then he had taken to calling me 'Ou Grote' (old big one) – a reference to my physical size.

'If you ever become a director, Ou Grote, there will come a day on a shoot where you simply won't know what to do. You will feel stupid and inadequate and not even the crew can help you. Not that they should have to – you are the director and getting paid the big bucks. When this happens, Eeyaan, *this* is what you should do … Call the director of photography and tell him to get the crew – who will be lounging around, waiting for orders – to go and put up the tripod.'

'And where should they do so?' I asked.

'Just say "over there" and point at any position that looks right. Next, you tell the grips to put the camera on top of the tripod. While they're busy doing that, it will become clear to you how you should block and shoot the scene. It has always worked for me.'

With Desiree Freshwater and her brother, whom I got to know while on an SABC shoot in Port St Johns. Credit: Desiree Freshwater

I had an opportunity to test Manie's advice in 1983 when I acted in an SABC production in Port St Johns. After about two weeks on the shoot, I got to Second Beach at about 10 one morning, because I was not in the first scene, to find the crew lazing about in the semi-shade.

'Why are you guys not shooting?' I asked.

They pointed towards the beach, where the director, Ralph Mogridge, stood with his arms folded across his chest, gazing out over the ocean, his back turned on the movie he was trying to direct.

'The boss is completely fucked,' the clapper loader said.

'Ja, he's lost it,' claimed the continuity lady. 'He said it's all too much for him.'

Manie's words came back to me as I walked across the sun-warmed sand towards our director.

'Morning, Ralph.'

He glanced at me as I stood alongside him, supposedly also looking out over the ocean. I could see he had tears in his eyes and looked defeated. Ralph was a gentle, soft-spoken man.

'Ian, I'm finished! I just don't know what to do.'

'Well, I know what you should do, Ralph ...'

He looked at me with a 'this-better-be-very-very-fucking-good' expression in his red-rimmed eyes.

'Oh yes, and what is that?'

'You should call [director of photography] Peter Kuchenmeister and tell him to tell his crew to get the tripod out of the gaffer truck and put it up over there,' I said as I pointed to where a lonely piece of seaweed lay on the beach about 20 feet away from us. Ralph's expression had now changed to one of incredulity.

'You mean at that piece of seaweed over there?'

'Yes. And then you should instruct Peter to tell the crew to get the camera out and to set it up on top of that tripod.'

By now, Ralph was becoming intrigued. 'And then?'

'Then it will become clear to you how to shoot the scene.'

I walked away to get a cup of coffee, while Ralph stood for a while wiping his eyes. Then, suddenly he turned around and shouted for Patrick Ndlovu, the first assistant director.

'Patrick, tell Peter to come and see me, please.'

After Ralph told Peter what to do, the crew were suddenly up and about and doing things. Soon Ralph became the boss again. The next moment he called the actress to him.

'Maralyn, I think you should walk along towards the camera from those rocks over there and then you, Mbaza (a local Xhosa man who was playing the role of a beachcomber), you wait here with me, and when I cue you, you walk towards Maralyn carrying the mussel shells.'

Within a few minutes that special magic that is unique to a movie set had returned. The magical words that had gotten us back on track hadn't been mine, though, but Manie van Rensburg's.

In those days, there was another magic to be experienced on set – at least by the director and production crew. For example, on the SABC shoot in Port St Johns, after, say, three days of shooting, the exposed film had to be boxed, driven to Umtata and then flown to Johannesburg, from where it would be taken to Irene Studios. There, the film was developed and rushes made, which were sent back by air. If you were working in a remote location like Port St Johns, the rushes would take about four days to reach you.

This time lapse gave rise to an increasing and unspoken sense of expectancy, a sort of excitement at getting the chance to watch the shots of scenes by now almost forgotten. This sense of expectancy has unfortunately vanished from moviemaking since the arrival of video take-off software. Directors like Manie used to stand alongside the camera to watch the scene play out in front of their eyes and were thus part of the immediate audience for the actors. Nowadays, directors have vanished from beside the camera. They usually sit in tents with as many video screens as they have cameras rolling. In my view, technology has stolen the subliminal dynamism and magic of live performance that used to infuse movie sets. As for its potential for creating magic, I find this so-called technological progress tragically retrogressive. These days, I mostly stand far away and watch as actors and actresses, yearning for instant gratification, crowd around the video replay to see how they acted in a recently shot scene. Acting has become centred on thinking and analysis; the gut has been forgotten.

It is absolutely crucial for an actor to take criticism. You have to learn early on to be able to take criticism and, even more importantly, to react objectively to it. Either become adept at that or get the hell out of the industry, because an actor can never objectively observe himself in relation to the play or the movie. No matter how good you are, in the search for excellence, you *must* listen to the director. My mark of how good an actor or actress is lies in their ability to adapt to the situations presented to them. For instance, if one arrives on set with a completely different idea of the character one is attempting to portray to what the director is expecting, then how quickly can the compromise be reached?

At one point in 1986, when I was working on the TV series *Heroes*, also directed by Manie, I was wondering, because of a lack of feedback, whether what I was doing was working. I knew that, as directors went, Manie was unusually in awe of actors and therefore unwilling to comment on, or indeed direct, their performances. He'd once said to me, 'I will do everything to create the world for the actors to move through, then it's up to them.'

Then one morning he said to me: 'Daar's iets wat ek jou op die rushes wil wys' (There is something I want to show you on the rushes).

We went into the editing suite, which had been set up in a rented house in the little town of Philadelphia, where we were shooting. The editor laced the rough cut of a scene and left the room. Manie and I watched my performance as a motor car mechanic in a garage owned by a Jewish man, played by Percy Sieff. When the scene ended, Manie drew long and hard on his Camel Filter.

'Ek voel jy speel die man asof hy 'n bietjie dom is, ietwat stadig. Wat dink jy?' (My sense is that you are portraying the man as if he is a little dumb, somewhat slow. What do you think?)

I realised what was bothering him. I told him I had based my character on a man called Kenny Quinn, a mechanic at the Mitchell Ford garage in Fort Beaufort, the town closest to my father's farm. Manie was allowed into my secret as to how I had created a characterisation. He was as deeply fascinated by my tricks as only another trickster could be.

I had developed the technique of finding someone I knew in real life and tagging my characterisation onto their ways of being. This is not subtle mimicry but more like placing my knowledge of that person like a ghost in my mind and using that as a spark for my performance. Manie said he liked what I was doing but wanted to point out that my character shouldn't come across to the audience as dumb. The story didn't allow for it. I thanked him for his guidance and made the adjustments to my character. The movie came first.

As a general rule, most South African television and movie productions have low budgets. One of the many results of this is that actors aren't pampered like Hollywood stars. For one, it's not like each of us has a private caravan on set to withdraw to. Over the years of having to do 'caravan-less' shoots, I have developed a number of tricks to preserve the magic I have in mind for a specific performance. I have found ways to create a 'caravan space' around me.

For example, I purposefully stay off set to prevent the fragile 'thing' that I sometimes feel inside me from being trampled by platitudinous conversations over a cup of coffee while waiting for the lighting to be finished. Great directors like Manie van Rensburg have developed what I can only describe as a sort of sixth sense when it comes to this. They just seem to know when you, as an actor, should not be disturbed, so they won't call you for some often unnecessary run-through rehearsal that could dissipate that elusive magic that might be brooding within you.

In 1981, I was chosen to play Hermaans Cronjé in *Verspeelde Lente*, a television adaptation of a novel by Jan van Melle. It tells the story of Pop le Roux, a beautiful but poor young woman, played by Elize Cawood, who marries a rich, older landowner instead of the man she loves – *bywoner*

Playing around on an abandoned double-decker bus in the Tankwa Karoo. Before we started shooting *Verspeelde Lente*, I went to visit a local family for a few days to improve my Afrikaans.

(sharecropper) Hermaans. When shooting *Verspeelde Lente* in the Tankwa Karoo in the early 1980s, there was a brilliant scene, written by Johan van Jaarsveld, in which the mother of my character talks to him about the failure that was his father and how they came to be in a destitute state. All the while, Hermaans is sitting at the dining table eating pumpkin and porridge.

The genius of the scene is that, throughout, Hermaans says nothing: he just listens. I knew that the power of the scene lay in his mute reaction, not in the mother's monologue. On the day we had to shoot that scene, I was infused with an array of emotions, which I knew were right for the coming scene. As we drove out to the desert location in the early morning, before sunrise, I did not join in the normal banter in the Kombi.

After getting our make-up done and doing wardrobe, I walked 70 metres into the desert and went to sit on a large rock, away from everyone else. Manie must have observed this and decided not to call a rehearsal, which was unusual. We were rolling very expensive 16 mm film and things had to be just right on the first take, which means that normally I would've been called for a rehearsal.

On that day, the rock out in the desert was my caravan. It was vital to me that I be given the space to keep the smatterings of my planned performance together. The small nuances that distinguish a carthorse from a racehorse performance are like ghosts in an actor's being, and, as I have learnt, they can vanish so very easily, never to return.

Eventually, production manager Richard Green walked towards me and said quietly, 'Okay, we're ready for you.'

I climbed down from the rock and walked down the hill to the old house that was the location. As I entered, I saw that the table was set with a plate of porridge and pumpkin. Against the rough mud-brick wall facing the table was the cameraman; next to him, with his back to the wall, stood Manie – again, part of the audience. Sound man Anton van der Linde stood with his boom on the other side of Isabella Bosman, who was playing the role of Hermaans's mother. Instead of the usual 'Good morning', 'How are you?', 'Just let me just check the focus' or 'Get the boom out of shot!', the set was completely quiet.

I walked forward and sat down in the chair.

'Aksie' (action), Manie said quietly and Isabella began her monologue. Over the next few minutes, all the emotions I had been keeping inside me were displayed on my face as my movie mother told me the sad story of my father's struggles in life.

When Isabella completed her monologue, no one called 'cut' to end the scene. I knew that directors sometimes deliberately let a scene roll on at the end to try and get further emotion to register on the actor's face. I looked up at Isabella, but she shrugged. Still the camera rolled that expensive film. Eventually, Richard said, 'Well, uhm, I think we should call it a "cut".'

When I looked up, I saw Manie leaning against the wall, tears streaming down his face. As he took off his spectacles, he gave a sort of low moan and wiped his eyes. He was so overcome by emotion that he had been unable to

My character, Hermaans Cronjé, his mother (Isabella Bosman) and the minister at the funeral of Hermaans's father.

Hermaans's mode of transport in the Tankwa was his bicycle.

call 'cut'. Coming from an essentially English background and having only recently become familiar with Afrikaner poverty of the early 20th century, and the phenomenon of Afrikaner *bywoners*, I was intrigued by the intense brew of emotions that lay at the heart of Manie's reaction.

With the passage of time, and as I got to know Manie better on a personal level, I began to understand where this depth of feeling came from. As a small boy, he was deserted by his mother for reasons that are unknown to me. Over the years, I have known quite a few men to whom this has happened, and it is probably the most monstrous thing that can happen to a small boy. I had a caring mother from the time I was born to the time she left this mortal coil, so it was only from other men that I came to understand the extent of the void that an absent mother leaves in a boy's, and later a man's, emotional world. This is why some men can't stop drinking whisky and others can't stop smoking dope … because they can never quite fill the hole left by their mother's absence.

Perhaps as a result of this, Manie also had great sensitivity and empathy for his fellow man. It was this awareness that made him a great leader and an astute captain of the pirate ship *Movie*. For example, whenever meals were served on set, he would always wait until every last actor and crew member had been served their meal before he would take his. Clever caterers who had gotten to know him would hide his meal so that, when he did eventually come to the table, they would be able to give the boss the very best of what they had cooked up. Such was their respect for him.

Quite a few times on Manie's sets, everything would be put on hold. 'Go and drink coffee, the director is busy rearranging the script,' we would be told. I still have an image in my mind of Manie and Jeanne Bonello, the continuity lady he liked to work with, sitting on folding chairs in the middle of a large, tarred parking area outside the entrance to the *dorpsaal* (town hall) in Philadelphia, our base for *Heroes*. Laptops had not arrived yet, so the new scenes were being typed on a portable Olivetti on a folding table, with a Roneo duplicating machine standing by to print them. The sun rose higher until I felt they should find some shade, but no, they sat there until the new scenes were written. These were handed to us as the scene was set up, and then we'd shoot. Manie would never shoot a scene unless he felt it was correctly scripted. On this he would never compromise.

Similarly, if an actor had any problem with the way a scene was put

Manie van Rensburg reading a script with his Olivetti in the background.
Credit: Gallo Images

together, or had any issue with the script, Manie was always approachable and willing to listen. On numerous occasions I complained to him when I felt the script forced my character out of line in a scene. He would listen intently and consider my opinion – as he did with other actors. When he agreed with me, he would change the scene or the set-up of the scene. This created an enduring sense of trust between Manie and the actors he worked with.

One morning, I arrived on the set of *Heroes* at a disused military camp outside Darling. It was a wet and drizzly winter's day and I felt particularly gloomy. Normally, I would arrive on set with a reasonably good idea as to how I wanted to play a scene, but this morning I felt thick-headed. As I walked towards Manie, he smiled and then strangely asked, 'Do you know how you are going to play this scene this morning?'

'You know, Manie, for a change, I have no bloody idea.'

'Well, that's fine, because I know exactly how you can play it.'

I was astounded: how did he know that on this particular day I was stuck, after I'd known perfectly well how to play my character for the past five weeks we had been shooting every single day, except Sundays? Manie had worked out a brilliant move for my character, who was part of a group of Ossewa-Brandwag right-wingers who had been arrested and imprisoned in a camp.

I played the scene as he directed; it was brilliant choreography and it worked excellently.

Having been a cameraman on the first movie he'd worked on, Manie often liked to take over the camera when shooting some of the incredibly complex scenes he liked to choreograph. These long takes could not easily be 'cut into' because the camera was constantly moving and cutting would interrupt the flow of the shot.

What complicated matters more in a particular scene on *Verspeelde Lente* was that the scene had to be actioned just as the setting sun touched the tops of the distant Cederberg mountains and cut just as it vanished below the horizon. That left a total of about six minutes to film the scene, without any break.

It was a rare love scene between Elize Cawood (as Pop le Roux) and me (as Hermaans Cronjé) – the SABC didn't allow love scenes that went further than a kiss – and we had to play it in one take. Manie liked to put actor's asses on the line with challenges such as these! However, with Afrikaans not being my home language, I was struggling to get it right.

Manie sat on the moving dolly behind the camera. As the red sun touched the top of Tafelberg over the Cederberg, he called 'aksie' and we were launched into the scene. Manie had the habit of making deep breathing sounds when he struggled to keep the camera absolutely still as he moved along the tracks, with the nimble-footed focus puller walking alongside, keeping everything in focus.

Elize and I got through all the tricky moves, playing out the foreplay to our love scene, which would end with us lying on the ground, embracing, in the corner of an old stone kraal. But seconds away from finishing the scene, I bombed. I forgot my dialogue. From that moment onwards, I thought, I would forever be the asshole actor who blew the magnificent sunset scene.

However, the next moment Manie's face rose up from behind the camera, not scowling but bearing a conciliatory smile as he gave precise directions in a calm voice: 'Okay, boys, put the tripod here ... Set up the camera. Close up on Mr Roberts. Hurry up, the sun is setting!'

There was no 'Damn, look what you've done! You've gone and wrecked my scene.' The crew moved quickly and efficiently to capture the inset shot. Within seconds, the pick-up close-up on me was in the can and the camera had been moved back onto the dolly. I noticed with relief that the sun was only halfway down.

The infamous love scene with Pop le Roux (Elize Cawood) in *Verspeelde Lente*.

'Aksie' was called and Manie was again breathing deeply, like a yogi in an ashram, as he filmed Elize and me carrying on with the scene as if nothing had happened, until eventually we lay on the desert sand of the Tankwa, kissing passionately. As if to symbolise the destiny of my ill-fated character Hermaans, the sun had slipped irrevocably behind the Cederberg.

The way Manie shot the scene predetermined the eventual outcome of the passionate kisses and sexual urgency between Pop and Hermaans as written in the script. Their relationship was slipping away just like the setting sun and would descend into darkness.

As Elize and I got out of our wardrobes and the crew packed away the equipment, with light supplied by a generator, we all knew we had just been involved in something exceptionally special. It was indeed a kind of magic.

There was magic and there was often loads of laughter too. At the time we were shooting *Verspeelde Lente*, the road between Calvinia and Ceres was (as it probably still is) the longest uninterrupted dirt road between two towns in South Africa. We had heard that air force pilots sometimes used the road to check the instruments of their Impala training jets.

Now, the Tankwa Karoo is an extremely quiet place, there being so few living things out there to make a noise. In 1981, when we were there, you would only see another car every five or so hours. One day, our small film crew was busy shooting a scene where Hermaans is riding along on his bicycle, when the rich farmer – played by Brian O'Shaughnessy – comes riding past in his expensive car, leaving Hermaans in a cloud of dust.

Suddenly – as in high-explosive suddenly – the contented peace of our beautiful desert film set was shattered by an Impala jet blasting over us at full speed, only four metres off the ground. The sound man ripped his headphones off and we all stood agog, watching the silver blob making for the Sutherland mountains. In the stunned silence Manie piped up, 'Franz Marx …'

Instantly, an image formed in our mind's eye of the actor-producer Franz Marx sitting at the controls of the Impala, jealously gazing down on this mysterious new project being directed by his competitor Manie van Rensburg, who had picked a virtually unknown actor and actress for the leading roles. We imagined how this would have been too much for Franz and, being a resourceful man, how he had managed to commandeer a jet from the air force to come and take a look at what we were doing.

Slowly, the crew started to laugh and soon it built up into a roar. Some of us were lying on the hot stones holding our bellies. It took some time to get the set back into operating mode again!

9

The movie comes first

ONCE I STARTED MY ACTING career, I only visited Baddaford Citrus Estates occasionally, even if the lessons and memories of my childhood informed who I would become as a man and an actor. I would receive regular updates from my parents about happenings on the farm. One day in 1986, while I was shooting the television series *Kwela Man* in Cape Town, I received shocking news from the Eastern Cape: my uncle Dan had been attacked and nearly killed on the farm.

Two men had arrived at the kiosk on the main road where juice and fruit were sold. They asked to see the farm owner, because they wanted to negotiate a price on a lorry-load of out-of-season cold-storage oranges, which was a good cash business for us. My father, who would normally negotiate these deals, was tied up with something, so my uncle went to see the men.

On the way, he drove past my parents' house, where he was stopped by Thembekile Qeqe, the man who worked in my mother's garden for many years. Thembekile told my uncle he didn't trust these men and pleaded with him to take a weapon along. 'These are very bad people, I have heard them talking,' said Thembekile. Something in his tone made my uncle go home to pick up a small 7.62 mm CZ pistol, which he put in the top pocket of his shirt.

When he got to the kiosk, the men approached my uncle. They spoke Xhosa, which he didn't understand, at which point he asked them to get into his car so that he could drive them to the nursery to find somebody who could translate. As he pulled away, he heard the deathly sound of a 9 mm pistol being cocked behind him. He turned to look and the gun exploded. The bullet barely grazed his cheek, but it seared his face with powder burns and the shocking report burst his eardrum.

The gunman tried again to shoot, but his weapon jammed, so he began beating my uncle on the head with the butt. Instead of knocking my uncle unconscious, the blows woke him from his stupor and the shock of the gunshot. He leant forward, pulling the CZ out of his top pocket. After miraculously managing to cock it, he thrust the muzzle under the man's jaw and pulled the trigger, killing his attacker instantly.

My uncle owed his life to Thembekile. Some farm labourers caught the other assailant and, after beating him, handed him and the body of his comrade over to the police when they arrived. When I heard the news, I felt as if the very source of my being had been attacked and I became incensed with rage. I asked to be released from the production as I was dead set on travelling to the farm to try and establish who had been behind the attack. It wasn't good enough for me that my uncle had survived, one assailant was dead and the other was in custody.

At the time, attacks on white farmers were almost unheard of and, on top of that, my uncle was known for his consideration for black people. I felt there had to have been another reason for the attack than mere criminal intent, and I wanted to find out what it was. However, when I spoke about the incident to two of our African cast members, Peter Sephuma and Nomsa Nene, they showed great empathy. In our discussions, I realised that South Africans of all races are exposed to severe violence and that there might not necessarily be a more nefarious reason behind the attack.

I decided to continue shooting on *Kwela Man* because the movie came first.

I phoned my uncle, whose voice was faint when he answered, and he wept over the phone. What had really gotten to him was the fact that his attacker would have killed him for absolutely no reason. And that, because of this attack, he had been forced to kill a man. I later learnt from my cousin Jonathan that the attack on his father was not politically motivated, as I had thought it might be, but that the attackers were criminals with robbery on their minds. They had, in fact, been on the run from the law.

The 1980s was an incredibly turbulent time in the country, with an increase in struggle activities and rioting, especially in the townships. The National Party government responded by proclaiming two national states of emergency. In some instances, the political violence also had an impact on the film industry. For example, on the first day of shooting *Kwela Man*, our small convoy was stoned by youths who emerged from behind bluegum trees along Borcherds Quarry Road near Cape Town Airport. I was driving a friend's VW Kombi, with Peter Sephuma in the passenger seat, when the windscreens of the four vehicles in front of us shattered, sending shards of glass up into the air. I was still contemplating whether I should try to make a quick U-turn when Peter leant over, stuck his head out the driver's window and started screaming insults at the youths in Xhosa. I immediately joined in.

The youths were so shocked at hearing their mother's vaginas and the scrotums of their fathers and grandfathers, and all the detestable ancestors before them, simultaneously insulted by both a black and a white man that they stopped throwing their half-bricks at us. To this day I have an image in my mind of a wild youth poised with his arm extended backwards, ready to hurl a brick, yet struck motionless as we passed. We had to get a replacement for the cameraman, whose arm had been broken.

Part of the shooting for *Kwela Man* was done in a coloured suburb called Philippi, and one morning we were paid a visit by about a hundred young ANC supporters from the nearby Crossroads settlement. The producer, Danie Nortje, and actors Joko Scott, Peter Sephuma, Nomsa Nene and I went to face the group, who told us we had to leave or they would burn our vehicles with petrol bombs and throw us out by force. We told them they had no cause to mess with us and that there was no way we would leave. They were welcome to come and try to throw us out. They never did and we carried on shooting.

Whenever you were in conversation with Manie, you became aware of the focused attention of a rare and formidable intellect who was actually listening to what you were saying. I chose my words carefully whenever I spoke with him. However, as frequently happens on movie sets, some people (most often actors) would make casual conversation with him that was not particularly relevant or important. Whenever this happened, I would notice Manie implementing his escape technique: he would simply turn his back on the person and walk away. This left many an actor suddenly deserted.

'Hang on, where has he gone? I was still talking to him,' they would exclaim in shock, while I would conceal a smile, having seen this happen before.

You would think the relative silence and sense of respect you experienced on Manie's sets would have made them somewhat austere and even uncommunicative places, but the opposite was true. Manie had a maxim he mentioned to me a few times: 'Whenever you are directing, and you come upon enthusiasm on a movie set, Eeyaan, you must never trample on it. Enthusiasm is always very good for a movie.'

In 1995, I was directing a major 13-episode drama called *Honeytown*, in Johannesburg. One day, sound engineer Anton van der Linde and I were chatting about Manie during a coffee break. We had heard disturbing stories through the movie grapevine that he had been seen drunk at such and such a place. Apparently, he had fallen and hurt his back badly. This left the two of us, who had done so many movies with Manie, very disturbed.

We decided to go round to his place after work, because we wanted to voice our concerns to him face to face. Manie's house was situated high up on a ridge in Melville, with a breathtaking view extending far out over the northern suburbs of Johannesburg. We began with a few beers, while Manie showed us how the Alexander technique had helped him get past his back injury, so that he could walk comfortably again. It was a beautiful and strangely comedic setting for an impromptu ballet performance as he showed us a few postures, with the ever-darkening lines of the distant Magaliesberg as a backdrop.

After sunset, we went inside and began drinking whisky. Eventually, Anton and I got to the purpose of our visit: we told him we were concerned about him and that there were stories going round that he had been drinking a lot. On hearing this, Manie suddenly became very focused and sharp, wanting to know exactly *who* had said that he was drunk. Anton and I didn't have these details, so we got caught out on that, and the purpose of our visit seemed to fade away as we carried on talking about the TV series we were making, and which Manie was happy to hear I was directing.

When we got up to leave, we walked out into the street, where Manie said goodbye to me and wished me luck as a director. Raising his hand before his face and forming a camera frame with his index and pinkie fingers, he said, 'Onthou dié skoot, Eee-yaaan' (Remember *this* shot, Ian). Then he started to move the 'frame' in front of his face as if it was a camera on a dolly, tracking a bit unsteadily on his feet between Anton and me before panning round onto his girlfriend and back to me. He was creating a complex tracking shot like the one he had created when shooting the sunset scene with Elize and me on the set of *Verspeelde Lente*.

'Ek sal hom nooit vergeet nie. Dankie, Manie' (I won't ever forget the shot. Thanks, Manie), I said. I have no idea where my next words to him came from.

'Jy is 'n baie groot gees, Manie' (You're a very big spirit, Manie).

He smiled his swashbuckling pirate-captain smile at me.

'Jy ook' (You, too).

These were the last words I ever exchanged with this extraordinary man. Two weeks later, Manie shot himself with the same shiny, chrome-plated .357 Magnum we had sometimes used as a prop on his movie sets. On the morning that I heard the shocking news of his passing, I hurried over to his house.

I was relieved to find Manie's body had already been taken away. His girlfriend rushed towards me and hugged me. She smelt like terror; it is a smell that I had come to recognise, because by then I had sadly had to hug a few people who had been exposed to extreme trauma.

I walked into the room where it had happened. It smelt richly dank and there were some young Afrikaans cops about. They were angry that one of their kind had killed himself. Angry almost to the point of disgust.

'Kyk, daar klou nog stukkies van die man se brein op die plafon' (Look, there are still parts of the man's brain on the ceiling), one of them said as he kicked a cardboard box out of his way. I looked up unthinkingly and was immediately sorry I had.

'Hoekom is jy so kwaad, jong?' (Why are you so angry, young man?) I asked one of the policemen who seemed particularly upset.

'Kom kyk hierso, meneer. Kom kyk net hier' (Sir, just come and take a look).

He led me to the side of the bedroom, where the cupboards were filled with empty booze bottles, J&B whisky prominent among them, and boxes of pills – for pain and other things. The young cop pushed some of the items on the floor around with his shiny black shoe.

'Dit is wat hulle hier in hierdie huis gedoen het, meneer. Hulle het al hierdie dêm goed gebruik.' (This is what they did in this house, sir. They consumed all these damn things.)

I had had enough – I needed to get out of there. I left for the set of the

TV series I was busy shooting in Hillbrow. It was a cold, foggy winter's morning. On set, everybody was in a state of shock at the news. I stared out at the bleak world in which we would now have to attempt to shoot magic shots without Manie van Rensburg. I looked up and saw the sun breaking through dense heavy clouds, setting them momentarily afire with pure, golden light.

I tore a piece of paper off my notebook and wrote the following poem:

On Manie's death
The smoke down here,
and the clouds up there
are blowing, much the same.
But the smoke down here's
direction is changing, swinging, shifting –
And up there the gradual cloud
still moving in the direction of the weathervane.
While we, the left-behind, are
just the uncertain timid vacillations
of our buffeted mankind.
The smog down here is grey
Heavy with smudge.
Up there, cumulonimbus castles –
vast and crystal white,
reflecting another *helderder,*
untainted light.

One day in 2023, Richard Green and I were on a call and reminiscing about our days together on movie sets. Our friendship had started in 1980 on the set of *Dokter Con Viljee se Overberg* and had run over about forty years. Eventually we got to the last movie Manie directed, *Taxi to Soweto* – a project I wasn't involved with. Richard proceeded to tell me an interesting story about the shoot.

As I have mentioned, as a director, Manie could never be persuaded to play a small cameo role in any of his movies. The day after the crew's wrap party for *Taxi to Soweto*, the production office was abuzz with hung-over crew members packing up all the rented gear that had to be returned. The

Manie, director of *Taxi to Soweto*, with a taxi driver. Credit: Gallo Images

camera had just been packaged when the phone rang. It was Manie and he had a strange request: he wanted to reshoot the final scene of the movie.

It was a complex scene to reshoot: not only did it involve the leading characters but they also needed a crane to get some height for the camera. Much of the equipment had to be unwrapped again and the crane was rehired. The following day, the crew was out on location early to catch the good light. Everybody knew what to do because the scene had already been shot two days earlier.

Nobody knew why they were out there shooting the scene again. But there was to be an important difference between the two shots: as the camera came down to head height and stopped moving to allow the taxi to drive out of frame, the crew all stood there watching. The cameraman had secretly been given instructions to pan to the crew and to end the shot on them. This meant that the titles would roll on the film crew. Standing purposefully in the centre of the frame and looking straight into the camera was Manie van Rensburg. This movie would be the end of his directing career and he had planned the shot so that he would be in his farewell frame.

Like I said: magic.

Over the years, Manie and I developed a saying: 'The movie comes first.' Chances are it originated over a glass of whisky and soda. What we meant by this was that whatever might've been happening in the life of an actor or crew member, it had to be put on the back burner for the sake of the movie. Whenever we were on set and shooting, filming always took preference. This was a non-negotiable thing. 'The movie comes first' is also a helpful maxim to rely on when destructive emotions start to fly around on a set. It is like a hitching post to tie your horse to while you wait for the dust to settle.

Another insight I have gained over the years is: when confusion reigns on set, just focus on being true to your character. Sometimes there are so many egos colliding on set, and attractions and distractions, that an actor is forced to become blatantly self-centred to try and maintain their focus on the role they are playing. If you don't maintain the integrity of your performance, nobody else will, and the progression of your character could falter. This could, and often does, lead to an erosion of the integrity of the movie as a whole.

In 2015, I was busy shooting *The Wild*, a soapie for M-Net, on location out on a game farm near Heidelberg, in Gauteng. Every day, the noise made by the crew on set became louder and louder; at one point, the actors who were trying to rehearse a scene could hardly hear each other speaking their lines. For me, this showed a great lack of discipline and trampled on the principle of 'the movie comes first'. For a long time, I have felt it is as if crews have lost their reverence for being on a set, as if their sense of wonder has disappeared.

We were in a barren winter mealie field where two game-viewing vehicles had stopped side by side. The scene had to play out between the occupants of the vehicles. Realising that the first assistant director, and even the director himself, were incapable of getting the crew to be silent, and after asking numerous times for silence, I climbed onto the back seat and shouted at full volume, 'Listen to me! You're all a bunch of assholes!'

My voice cut through the hubbub and a rare quiet settled over the mealie field. 'None of you crew will appear in this movie, only the actors, and you're making so much noise, we can't hear each other to rehearse the scene. I am leaving the set now and when you have learnt some manners, you can come and call me!'

The red-haired Irishman had shown himself again.

I climbed down from the vehicle and walked off across the barren soil, kicking the blackened, dusty mealie stalks as I went. I chose not to attend the ensuing lunch break and was sitting in my dressing room when there was a knock on the door. A cameraman called Marc Brower, who I had worked with on *Verspeelde Lente* in the early 1980s (back then he had been a clapper loader or focus puller), entered with an angry expression on his face.

'Ian, who the fuck do you think you are?'

'What do you mean, Marc?'

'You have absolutely no right to shout at a crew like that!'

I looked up and sighed. 'You're right, Marc.'

'Ja, it is completely unacceptable! You need to go out there and apologise.'

I told him that while I was sorry for being rude, there was no way I was going to do that.

'Tell me, Marc, how did you forget the magic?' I asked him.

His eyes narrowed. 'What magic?'

'You were on the set of *Verspeelde Lente*, Marc. At which point did you forget the quiet reverence we had for our craft? Don't you remember the sincere respect we had for the mere fact that we were able to be out on set making a movie?'

Marc didn't answer. He was clearly still angry with me, but I could see he was starting to think back to that time.

'You've forgotten the magic of Manie's movie sets. It has been blasted out of you by the strange conditions we have to work under these days. All I'm doing is trying to get back some of the magic, Marc. Yes, I was rude, but you know what? I'll throw another bloody tantrum after lunch if the crew haven't learnt to control their swollen hormones and loud mouths. And I won't apologise either … The movie comes first. That's another thing you've forgotten.'

I was called out on set after lunch and we actors rehearsed the scene, with the crew now miraculously silent, as they should have been in the first place, and then shot the scene, perhaps in one take. I was not needed on set for a number of hours, so instead of driving back I went for a walk in the opposite direction. Soon I found myself near the N3 highway and saw a stormwater drain passing under the tarmac. I thought it would be great to crawl through it under the wide four-lane road. I could actually feel the vibrations of the big trucks on my back through the concrete.

Eventually, I exited on the other side and found myself in another mealie field. I started making my way across it towards some buildings. Suddenly, I saw movement in the field in front of me and noticed a big dark snake making its way over the sand between the mealie stalks. I stopped. The snake stopped. I stood absolutely motionless. It turned its head towards me, its dark tongue flicking.

The snake quickly moved a few metres away and then suddenly vanished. I walked slowly forwards to find its hole in the ground. The moment was over. I have come to regard seeing a snake in your path as a bringer of good things in the future. Maybe this was a sign of 'keep going with your quest for actor-friendly movie sets'.

I walked on, exhilarated by the gift of the powerful energy of nature. There had been no sound except the distant rolling of vehicles on the highway.

I know that people thought I was being rude and arrogant out there in the mealie field, but my longing for those magical movie sets remains. It is an intense longing in my actor's heart. This yearning was fulfilled in September of 2023 when, after not doing a single movie for five years, I was cast opposite Sandra Prinsloo in a film called *A Kind of Madness*. The director/screenwriter, Christiaan Olwagen, maintained the same kind of atmosphere on his movie set as Manie did. I was in actor's heaven.

10

A rebel with a cause

EARLY IN 1988 I WAS back in the theatre, playing one of the lead roles in David Mamet's *American Buffalo* at the Baxter Theatre. Even though I really enjoyed TV and film work, doing a theatre production was like going back into the engine room of acting. Stage work is like stepping into the boxing ring: There's no place to hide out there and it hones the actor for film work. During our rehearsals and performances of *American Buffalo*, I learnt more valuable lessons about my craft.

Director Peter Goldsmid was one of those unusual arty beings who I sometimes feel are completely out of place in South Africa. Peter had pulled off the remarkable coup of getting the rights to produce the play in South Africa, despite the cultural boycott against the apartheid state. The play was set in a second-hand shop (or junk store) in Chicago, so we spent a good while learning how to speak with a Chicago accent.

Finally, it was the last two days of rehearsals. *American Buffalo* is a tough play to perform: the main character, Teach – played by Sean Taylor – is a man with great intentions that he has never realised. He is a kind of *windgat* (boastful) loser. At the end of the play, Teach realises that, despite all his noise and remonstrations at the world, he actually is quite an asshole and a desperate one at that.

Sean was struggling to get to this point of a breakdown, a challenge for most actors, including me. During rehearsals, we realised that Sean's performance of Teach just wasn't taking off and, more importantly, Sean knew he wasn't getting the ending right.

Then, at one of the last rehearsals, things suddenly fell into place: Sean began to weep for his character's realisation; he wept for all humanity and our fallibility. At the end, there was silence in the rehearsal room, broken only by Sean's sniffing.

Nicky Rebelo, the other actor in this three-hander, looked at me, impressed with Sean's performance. But Peter Goldsmid wasn't moved.

'Ja, that was quite good, guys,' he said dispassionately, as he raised his arms and clasped his hands behind his head. I was astounded. What the hell's wrong with him? Did he not see and feel how electrifying Sean's performance was?

'The play is getting there,' he carried on matter-of-factly. 'But all that drizzling at the end was a little over the top, Sean.'

Now the shit is gonna hit the fan, I thought.

'What … did … you … just … say?' Sean asked as he moved towards Peter, his voice now razor-blade sharp. His sniffles had vanished and his eyes glared.

'I said I thought all that weeping at the end was a bit indulgent.'

Sean grabbed a heavy glass jug half-filled with water that stood on a small table and lunged at the director.

'You useless fucking piece of shit!' shouted Sean as he raised the jug above his head.

But just before he could smash it down on Peter's head, I managed to grab his arm and pulled the jug out of his grip. Nicky and I manhandled Sean into a corner of the rehearsal room and the director quickly left. Peter never came back.

Now we three actors were on our own. We approached John Slemon, the manager of the Baxter, to ask if we could take over and direct each other. Being of Irish descent and a good friend of Sean's, he agreed. Despite this near-fatal hiccup, *American Buffalo* was a very successful production.

Over the years I developed my own process of bringing on a breakdown. Many years later, on the set of the film *Malunde* (meaning 'street kid'), my character – an ex-army, rough, Recce-type guy – had to have a breakdown on cue. About four days before we were to shoot this scene, the director, Stefanie Sycholt, came up to me and asked if I was prepared for it. For an actor, this question is difficult to answer. The truth is that you never really know whether you'll be able to deliver and do the character justice. If your character is the leading role, then the pressure is even greater, because if you fail, the movie fails.

After the first take of that crucial scene, I knew my arse was on the line. The German director of photography, who didn't really like me, hung his head behind the camera, staring at the tracks. The director was also not impressed and came up to me.

'Your performance is nowhere near where it should be, Ian,' she said.

'Listen,' I said desperately, 'you get everything right for the next take, okay? Just roll the camera when I come back on set.'

I had one last card to play. I walked off up the hill to where the little wardrobe caravan stood deserted in the pitch-blackness. I groped around and, finding my jacket on a hanger, took out the packet of Texan Plain cigarettes and matches I had bought. At that point I had given up smoking, but this was an emergency. I lit a Texan and inhaled the powerful rum-steeped smoke deep into my lungs. After I'd finished that cigarette, I was already feeling quite spaced-out, but I lit another. Texan Plains were very strong cigarettes with no filter.

Halfway through the second one, I knew I was high enough on nicotine to try to act the scene. An expectant silence hung in the air as I entered the set. The director said, 'Action!' and, as if by magic, the performance I so desperately needed came out of the cold night air to me. Even the German cameraman seemed to be impressed.

The most important lesson I ever learnt about acting happened during a performance of *American Buffalo*. It was ten long years since I had left Rhodes and begun acting professionally. Throughout all that time, but mostly on stage, I had been secretly petrified of bombing out in front of an audience, forgetting my lines or simply losing the plot. I had learnt to cover up small mistakes and carry on, but that fear always lurked, giving me sweaty palms and sometimes a constricted voice. In TV and movie acting, the pressure was less: the audience on set was smaller and there was the comforting option of a second or third take. I knew I had to lose not only my fear of an audience but also my inbred desire to please.

One night on *American Buffalo*, in front of a packed theatre, Nicky, who was playing an adolescent boy called Bobby, failed to return on his cue with the bagels and yoghurt Donny (my character) and Teach had sent him out to buy. When it became clear that Nicky was a no-show, Sean and I surreptitiously made eye contact. All the dialogue for the next section of the play was about bagels and yoghurt!

We carried on with some fabricated dialogue to buy time, but when a full five minutes had gone by, Sean suddenly blurted out: 'Where the hell's the kid? I'm gonna go fetch him!' He promptly walked offstage, leaving me gawking at the empty door, having to face my worst nightmare alone. The audience stared back at me, deeply engrossed in the play. They say that if you want to teach a person to swim quickly, throw them in at the deep end. Well, I felt as if I was a mouse facing a tsunami. I glanced timidly at the audience. Maybe I should just come clean and tell them the show is over.

Stage acting teaches an actor how incredibly fast your brain can operate when you are under serious threat. With my mind still racing through my options, I looked at the audience. For the first time in ten years of stage work, I really saw who they were: I could see their facial expressions, what they were wearing, and so on. For a change, *I* was studying *them*.

I ran my hand over my shaved head, feeling the stubble and mulling over the fact that I should have shaved it before the show. But then I thought, they don't know … they can't see how long my stubble is … and I was surprised to feel the knot in my gut slowly unravelling. I was losing my fear! I picked up the old-fashioned phone and dialled a number, taking as long as I could:

'Hello, Abe, how's ya doing?' I said and listened to 'Abe' for as long as a telephone conversation would allow, but still no Bobby and still no Teach.

'Oh yeah? Dammit, Abe! That's no good … did the woman say why she's leaving ya?'

As I listened to 'Abe', I realised I was beginning to enjoy this spur-of-the-moment scriptwriting!

'Abe, I hate to say this, but that is so typical! When we're playin' poker tomorrow night you can tell me all about it.'

My racing mind decided to get back to trying to save Mamet's plot.

'So, tell me, Abe, ya didn't happen to see Bobby, the kid, down on the street, did ya?'

Pause … pause … pause …

'Oh? Ya saw Teach? What the hell is he doing on the street? Was he carrying any bagels?'

And so I held the audience captive for what felt like a very long time, until eventually Sean re-entered, bleak-faced and breathing noisily through tight lips.

'I just saw the kid,' he said. 'He's coming wit' da yoghurt and da bagels. Asshole got lost, but he's coming!'

And soon Bobby entered the stage, also pale-faced and out of breath with yoghurt and doughnuts from an all-night café down the main road from the Baxter. He had had to run there, because a stage cleaner had eaten the props.

Later, when I was removing my make-up in the dressing room, I looked at myself in the mirror and knew I had changed forever. Butterflies before a show? Yeah, for sure. But scared of an audience? Never again.

One night towards the end of the run of *American Buffalo*, we were in the Baxter bar after a Friday-evening show when the filmmaker Dirk de Villiers walked up to me. When Dirk entered a room, everyone noticed. He was a tall man with long, greyish hair and a beard, strange knock-kneed legs, a booming voice and a kind of gambolling persona that was reflected in his robust movements.

After I introduced him to Nicky and Sean, my fellow cast members, Dirk took me aside. He needed to talk to me in private and it was a matter of some urgency, he said.

'I have been trying to cast the leading role in this TV series about Boer prisoners of war on St Helena island called *Arende*. Those grootkoppe [bigwigs] at the SABC want me to cast a regte Boerseun [a true Afrikaner by birth and upbringing] to play the role. I have just been up to Pretoria and Johannesburg to do exactly that, maar hulle is almal fokken moffies, man [but they are all too fucking effeminate]! Even if they're not, they come across like it when you put a frame around them! And I've got to start shooting next week!'

Incidentally, the actress Trix Pienaar – who lived in a train at Pringle Bay, close to where the series was to be filmed – had already told me about this series. It was written by the talented writer Paul C Venter. She thought I would be perfect for the leading role. I wasn't a mainstream Afrikaans actor, but I was intrigued. I had just come from doing extensive and intense work with Manie van Rensburg, who was quiet and circumspect when it came to expressing himself. Dirk was exactly the opposite. He was a very different kind of director, a sort of kindly, lumbering freight train, running on an endlessly curving track.

'Ian, what I'm saying to you is, I want you to play the role of Sloet Steenkamp in *Arende*.'

They say that when the student is ready, the master shall arrive. I had worked hard at my craft, often under tough circumstances and for very little money. I felt as if destiny was knocking on my door. Normally I would have said I needed a day or two to read the scripts, but I already knew from Trix that it was an excellent script – and the idea of playing a rebel had always been very enticing to me.

'Thanks Dirk, I'm very keen, but there's just one problem.'

'What's that?'

I took off my hat to show him my shaved pate – a requirement for my role in *American Buffalo*. Dirk raised his eyebrows and straightened to his full height to study the top of my head. This was a potentially insurmountable problem if we were going to start shooting the following week. Would I have to wear a wig? Dirk pulled out an old-fashioned blue chequered handkerchief.

By now a few theatrical cognoscenti and common barflies had gathered to watch Dirk's performance. Dirk started knotting the corners of the hankie. Soon, all four corners were knotted to form a kind of a cap. He leant forward and placed it on my head. The hankie covered my bald pate perfectly and my remaining hair completed the illusion of a full head of hair.

'There! Sloet Steenkamp!'

A stroke of genius! People clapped.

In retrospect, that piece of quick-thinking magic from Dirk in the Baxter bar set the tone on set for the entire production of the first ten episodes of *Arende*.

The next day, I had a meeting with Dirk at the offices of C-Films in Cape Town. In those days, I used to set my own price for acting in a production.

'So how much are you going to charge me to play this role?' asked Dirk.

'Given the size of your budget,' I replied, 'what do you think my role is worth to this production?'

Dirk thought a bit and said: 'I'm guessing about twenty grand.'

'Fine, if it's good for you, then it's good for me,' I replied, and we shook hands on the deal. That is the way I did my deals on all of the eight TV series and movies I did with Manie van Rensburg and Johan van Jaarsveld, and now also with Dirk de Villiers. Soon after, I started reading the pile of Paul C Venter scripts, which amounted to ten 56-minute episodes of the

On the set of *Arende* with Gavin van den Berg (Captain James Kerwin) and the famous hankie on my head. Credit: Barry Lucas

Dirk de Villiers, the director of *Arende*. Credit: Barry Lucas

first season of what was to become the immensely popular Afrikaans series *Arende*. I was inspired.

By this time, I had developed a technique for preparing for big roles on a TV series. The longest location shoots in those days were 13 episodes, or a full 12 and a half hours of edited film. This meant there would be many scenes I had to prepare for as an actor. So, my trick was to merely get a broad picture of the story and not to waste focus by getting hung up on the details. This gave me an idea of how much to deliver in the performance of a specific scene, because in those days TV series were very seldom shot in chronological order.

When I finally finished reading, I knew that the heart of the story was the obsession of the main character, Sloet Steenkamp, with escaping from St Helena and regaining his freedom from the British. As I've mentioned, I come from a British background. My great-great-grandfather, Daniel Roberts, left the British Isles in 1820 to settle in the Bathurst area of the Eastern Cape. My great-grandfather Llewellyn fell out of favour with the local Boers when he supplied refreshments and oranges to passing British forces in 1900. My mother, Lynn (who had Irish roots) and my father, Llewellyn, could not speak Afrikaans. I had a lot of learning to do about the Boers, not to mention the Anglo-Boer War.

Luckily for me, Dirk gave me a copy of the diary of a Boer fighter who had been a schoolteacher before the war and had been captured at Paardeberg. The diary, which was copied at the War Museum of the Boer Republics in Bloemfontein, was written in a mixture of Dutch, French and English. The language in Venter's scripts wasn't nearly as mixed as that of the diary, but it was still fair in the way it captured the Afrikaans of the time, which was not yet formally recognised.

I had always had a sort of secret admiration for the Boer generals Christiaan de Wet and Louis Botha. I came across a photo of Botha holding a *bosberaad* (bush meeting) with some of his officers on a hilltop in the Eastern Transvaal, and they were all sitting on the ground. That spoke to me. My admiration grew as I discovered more and more about what the Boers had done during the war. Every young actor will be lucky to find a heroic figure who can inspire him; for me, one such figure was the Boer general Jacobus Herculaas 'Koos' de la Rey. In 1988, I had just started to learn about the Boers and their history. I devoured Johannes Meintjes's biography of De la Rey, *Lion of the West*.

In preparing for my role as Sloet Steenkamp, I drew further inspiration from a curious incident that had happened to me while I was acting in *American Buffalo*. Every evening, I would drive from Pinelands, where I was squatting at my sister Jane's, to the Baxter Theatre in Rosebank. Right towards the end of the run, it so happened that an acquaintance from Rhodes University, an enigmatic and beautiful female art student, came to see the play. Afterwards, in the theatre bar, the drinks were flowing and so were the emotions.

Eventually, on our way home, my girlfriend at the time exploded with fury because she thought I was being unfaithful. After I had managed to drive the Kombi home under a hail of insults, slaps and punches, my girlfriend cornered me in a room at my sister's house, but luckily I managed to slip out. I started running through the dark streets of Pinelands with the cool night wind soothing my face. I should have gone back, but some instinct kept me running all the way to the Pinelands Golf Course. The gaunt trees and dark shadows under the bushes lining the fairways seemed to welcome me. I eventually stopped running and stood in the dark calm beneath a large bush, looking out at the world of lights, at the flashing cars on the nearby N2 highway, and at the human drama out there. I felt as if I was looking out at the world from a position of concealment. It was invigorating.

This incident helped me later to find the key to unlocking the character of Sloet Steenkamp. Maybe I was being cowardly, but it was as if, by not going back to try and sort things out with my then girlfriend, I was being shown what it was like to be a loner in the shadows, looking out at the world. This is how actors should respond to the dance of life – get out on the floor, take the gap and execute fast swirling steps on the edge of your inabilities and inadequacies. If you're lucky, inspiration will come. How else can you learn?

Thus it was that I drove from Cape Town to Pringle Bay in April 1988. I was given a place to stay by Pieter Grobbelaar, the production manager. It was a north-facing house situated on the promontory that juts out westwards into False Bay from the foot of the Hangklip Mountain. It had a large upstairs room and a larger downstairs area where the bedrooms

Arende set scaffolding at the old harbour in Hermanus. Credit: Barry Lucas

and bathroom were. The upstairs room had a giant window that looked out over the beautiful bay and a small balcony to the side. Actress Jocelyn Broderick and I shared the house, but I decided I wanted to stay upstairs even though there weren't any bedrooms. I felt so close to nature in that part of the house. So I fetched a big king-sized mattress, dragged it up the stairs and put it on the floor.

I had also just bought the cassette of Fleetwood Mac's latest album, *Tango in the Night*, and brought my big, portable double-deck Hitachi cassette player with me. I must thank the engineers at the Hitachi company for building that sweet machine, because I still dream of the perfection of that sound.

Movies are generally get-up-before-dawn affairs because it's expensive to keep a film crew going, which means that producers try to get as much done in the 12-hour shift that a crew is supposed to work. Furthermore, the quality of the light is always the most beautiful and interesting just after dawn and just before sunset. While filming *Arende* I would drive my Kombi to the set in the first light before dawn.

The first season of *Arende* is set on St Helena island in a concentration camp aptly called Deadwood Camp. The set had been built on a small plateau between Pringle Bay and the mountains, which were generally treeless with grey rocks interspersed with fynbos, much the same as on St Helena. The art director, Ade Prinsloo, was a very lively, energetic man and he had conjured up a camp out of old corrugated-iron sheets, pine offcuts and bits of canvas. On the other side of the road that divided the camp, he

The hospital at the recreated Deadwood Camp in Pringle Bay. Credit: Barry Lucas

had created the 'administration' buildings, using more formal set-building techniques.

Tragically, Ade passed away during the filming of the first season, but what he and his crew achieved was a miracle when you consider the limitations of SABC budgets. Every day, we would leave our cars outside the movie set so they were out of camera shot. Only certain cars were allowed in, such as Dirk's gold Opel, whose boot carried important protection against the cold, drizzly winter mornings – a couple of bottles of ginger brandy, buchu brandy and port, among others.

At the end of the day, when we returned to our accommodation, a number of us would find that our cars always took a turn down the dirt road to the Hangklip Hotel, which had a lovely bar. It was a large, oblong place that was dimly lit and had dark corners where anything could hide and who knows what could happen. Sometimes at night, the fog and mist would drift off the Atlantic into the bar, and the beam of the nearby lighthouse would sweep round, lighting up the gaunt mountain at brief intervals, creating a sort of pirates-of-the-high-seas atmosphere.

The hotel's trump card was the owner, a German man I knew only as Otto. He served beer in ice-cold quart bottles and a range of excellent imported German schnapps, and his kitchen always had a fresh supply of perlemoen (abalone). Every night, at some point in the party, I would have perlemoen fried in garlic butter before going home. I would be up again at the crack of dawn to further engage with the character of Sloet Steenkamp, a man obsessed with escaping from St Helena.

11

On the set of *Arende*

IT WAS THE BEGINNING OF the Cape winter, which meant that some days were cold and wet, but that didn't bother us at all. Because we were working on a tight budget, we grabbed all the daylight we could. It also drizzled and rained quite often, which meant that the tents and shacks we were shooting in were wet and dingy. But, no matter that, the vibe on set was one of obsession.

Dirk was a man obsessed with his project; the cameraman, Jakes de Villiers, was equally crazy-passionate and exceptionally talented; and Ade's set-building was brilliant. The various cast members seemed infused by the same spirit of obsession.

Viewers saw this in the frames of Limpie Basson playing Petrus Johnson, who was the father of the much-derided pacifist Paul, played by Gert van Niekerk. The main agitator for the *bittereinders* (the Boers who did want to surrender and fought to the end) was the passionate Buks Retief, played by Johan Esterhuizen (mentioned previously in the Maynardville rain debacle). André Roothman played the more conciliatory and scholarly PJ Buys. Collectively, they made up the occupants of the tent that Sloet Steenkamp shared in the Boer concentration camp, a world that Paul C Venter's script set out with great attention to detail.

Day after day, different talents were brought together to create a single, flowing statement of images. This magic was enriched by Louis van Rensburg's rousing music and by a director who was not hamstrung by a particular vision of style or genre that he needed to impose. It all combined to form pure art.

On my first day on set, I wore my knotted handkerchief cap. We filmed a scene at the latrines the British had set up for the inmates of Deadwood Camp: a trench dug straight into the ground, with a long horizontal wooden beam on which one would lean one's arse while doing one's

Director Dirk de Villiers with my *Arende* co-star Gavin van den Berg.
Credit: Barry Lucas

Sloet Steenkamp with his wife, Annette, played by Susanne Beyers.
Credit: Barry Lucas

Limpie Basson (second from left), who played the role of Petrus Johnson, and other actors on the set of *Arende*. Credit: Barry Lucas

Sloet Steenkamp, Boer rebel and prisoner of war. Credit: Barry Lucas

business. These once-free men of the wide-open veld were forced by the British to defecate in a trench alongside each other. It occurred to me that everyone knew everyone else's business in this camp: there was no privacy for the Boers.

It was then and there that the beginnings of a distaste for the British and what they had done to the people of this country began to grow in me. Maybe the Boers had become accustomed to this kind of invasion of their privacy, but to me it was a horrific denigration. This feeling helped me to understand Sloet's increasing obsession with regaining his freedom, even if against all odds. It was one thing to get out of Deadwood Camp, but entirely another to get off the island.

Sharing a tent with Sloet were a number of conflicting characters. All were pro-war except Paul. Sloet was not that interested in the internecine politics of his tent because he was focused only on escape. However, when the other tent inhabitants victimised Paul, Sloet stood up for him.

To portray this aspect of Sloet's character, I drew on an experience from my army days in 1971, 17 years earlier. The troepie in the bed next to mine was a softie called Nachenius. In our bungalow of thirty men was a bully who went by the surname Harmse. He was thick-set, with a face to match his powerfully built body, which seemed to ooze testosterone from every pore.

Once, after a heavy day's drilling on the parade ground in the blistering sun, we returned to our bungalow exhausted, dirty and pissed off. Harmse had taken his shirt off to reveal his big sweaty muscles before ambling over to start provoking dear Nachenius, who lay on his bed, petrified. This went on for a while, but eventually I had had enough, and again the mad red-haired Irishman in me decided to show himself.

'Harmse, why don't you just fuck off?' I said, tiredly.

Harmse spun around, quickly as a cat in a fight: this was the cue he had been hoping for.

'Roberts, jy wil my seker opfok, nè?' (Roberts, you probably want to fuck me up, hey?), he said as he stepped round Nachenius's bed towards me.

'Nee, Harmse, jy's verkeerd. Ek wil eintlik fokkol met jou te doen hê. Los net vir Nachenius uit.' (You're wrong, Harmse. I actually want fuck-all to do with you. Just leave Nachenius alone.)

I knew I had only one shot at him, and that if I failed to deck him with my right-hand punch, heaven knows what would be left of me. Luckily, a friend of mine, who was a karate seventh dan, came in and took on Harmse in my place. Still, recalling this incident helped me immensely in my performance of Sloet: it gave me a far better idea of what it meant to have to stand up for someone who was being bullied. In most cases, it was a dangerous thing to do.

In the first season of the show, Sloet's obsession with escape leads him to dig a tunnel under the barbed wire. It is while Sloet is staring out through the barbed wire, scheming where his exit hole to freedom should be, that a young British officer, Captain James Kerwin, played by Gavin van den Berg, who has a habit of going for a run in the mountains outside the camp, comes running back along the fence towards the gates. What does Sloet do? He begins racing the captain along the *inside* of the fence, with Kerwin on the *outside*. This was the genius of Venter as a screenwriter.

I had first met Gavin in 1981 at the Space Theatre in Cape Town, but I didn't know him and his background very well, so I phoned him before we shot the scene. Gavin was born in Lourenço Marques (today Maputo) in Mozambique a few years after me. While my four grandparents were English, Scottish, Welsh and Irish, Gavin's parents were completely bilingual. He went to English and then dual-medium schools and eventually studied speech and drama at Wits University, majoring in English and Afrikaans. As an actor, Gavin had a very special quality.

I found it quite ironic that he – who had an Afrikaans background – was playing Captain Kerwin, a toff English officer who was a product of Sandhurst, while I was playing a Boer, even though my parents could not even speak Afrikaans and I had had an English upbringing.

In our first scene together, Captain Kerwin is dressed in a spotless and freshly ironed long-sleeve vest and long johns, with canvas pumps on his feet. He takes up the challenge presented by the scraggily dressed, unkempt and barefoot Sloet. This was powerful visual symbolism. Gavin, for whatever reason he saw fit, used an affected and stylised way of running upright and poised, hands pumping open at his flanks, while I have always sprinted like a wild boar. These differences further enhanced the contrast of the civilised, sophisticated European pitted against the wild man of Africa.

Later, Sloet escapes from the camp and runs for the coast. Dirk and Jakes constructed amazing shots of Sloet running at full speed over the bushy, rock-strewn landscape towards the rugged coastline of St Helena. For me, this was not acting. It came from deep within me: I have always tried to escape the strictures imposed on me and yearned to be a free soul. It started with the corduroy dungarees I so hated as a small child because my fingers were too clumsy to take them off. Then came my love of camping, disappearing into the mountains after lectures at Rhodes University and running the Pipe Track on Table Mountain every evening after rehearsals … Even today, I try to escape into the bush, the mountains or the sea (on a surfboard) to a place where there aren't any people around.

The more I learnt about the history of the Boers, the more of a gut feeling I, the son of English settlers, got for what drove the rebellious Sloet Steenkamp to behave the way he did. His wild attitude really came to the fore in the escape scene (in the second season), where Sloet hurls himself into the chilly ocean off the steamship that is taking the prisoners of war back home. He decides to jump off the ship because he knows that, once they arrive in Cape Town, he will have to swear an oath of allegiance to the British Crown. That was something he would never do; he would rather drown.

On the day we shot the scene, the temperature in False Bay was 12 degrees. I had on Sloet's threadbare clothes, while cameraman Jakes and his assistant were down in the freezing water, but at least they had wetsuits. I had to jump off the ship and plunge into the Atlantic because we couldn't afford a stuntman. We were still using Arriflex 16 mm film cameras: camera 2 was on the ship to capture my jump to freedom from above, while camera 1 was underwater. This was quite an extravagance on the part of Dirk's production company – *two* cameras rolling on one shot. Generally, South African directors had to get the shot with only one camera.

The genuine old steamship was rolling on the False Bay swell as Dirk began his run-in before calling 'Action!'

'Right, Eeyaan! Is jy reg?' (Right, Ian! Are you ready?)

I clung to my last vestige of safety, the railing of the ship's bridge.

'Ja, Dirk. Ek is so reg soos wat ek kan wees onder die donnerse omstandighede' (Yes, Dirk, as ready as I can be under the damn circumstances).

'Oukei, rol klank!' (Okay, roll sound!)

The sound man pressed record on the Nagra tape recorder and then swung his long boom out over the side of the ship as quickly as he could.

'Spoed!' (Speed!), he shouted.

'Rol kamera!' (Roll camera!) The camera focus puller pressed the knob on the Arriflex. 'Ons rol!' (We're rolling!)

The guy with the clapperboard held it in front of the lens. 'Episode drie. Vier-en-twintig. Take een! (Episode three. Twenty-four. Take one!)

'Merk hom!' (Mark it!) shouted the second camera operator.

There was a resounding clap, and I could see the camera panning around and focusing on me.

'Set!' shouted the operator. The frame was set, the focus sharp and the next moment Dirk first shouted, 'Good luck, hey!' and then 'Aksie!'

I launched myself into space, plunging down towards the dark, shifting waters. I crashed though the surface into the frigid world below, just missing the underwater cameraman. Soon I clambered up the ship's old rope and wood ladders to get dry wardrobe and have my hair blow-dried before I returned to 'first position'. It took two takes to get the shot. I couldn't remember when last I had been so cold.

Because of budgetary constraints, we filmed *Arende* out of chronological sequence, which meant that I had to maintain a good idea of the development of Sloet's character as the story progressed, and I had to shift my portrayal depending on the scene. By the time we had filmed almost all the scenes for the first season, my shaved head from *American Buffalo* was covered with a stiff crop of dark-brown hair, and I was eventually allowed to discard the handkerchief from the House of De Villiers.

After we finished filming in Pringle Bay, Dirk and I headed for Matjiesfontein, where the opening scenes of the first season would be shot. It was early and we had to catch the morning light for this important scene. On the side of a dirt road, east from the Lord Milner Hotel, a wooden chair had been set up against a rock face. Sloet has been captured by the British and charged with high treason because he is still a citizen of the (British) Cape Colony. He has been condemned

With director Dirk de Villiers and co-actor Gert van Niekerk. Credit: Barry Lucas

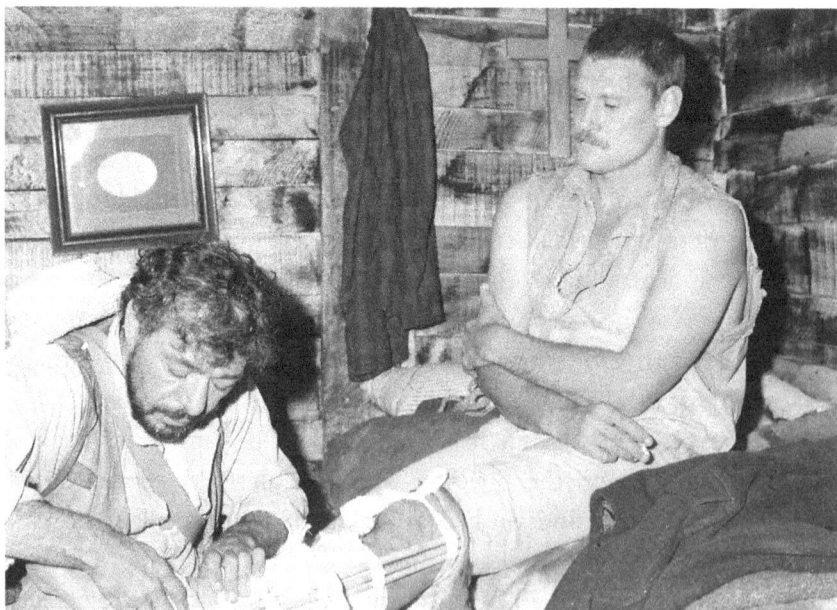

Actor David Pieters, who played the fisherman Sam Gobbler,
practices bandaging my leg off set. Credit: Barry Lucas

Gavin van den Berg with the actress Jocelyn Broderick (Jo-Ann Wilks).
Credit: Barry Lucas

Members of the cast and extras on the set of *Arende*. Credit: Barry Lucas

to death by firing squad. Since I had been playing Sloet for the previous seven weeks, I had a good idea what he would have felt on that day.

In the scene, Sloet is sitting on the chair, blindfolded. In one hand he holds a handkerchief that he has been told to drop once he is ready to be shot. I felt uneasy and frightened behind that blindfold, because I knew many Boers had been executed in exactly the same way. I could hear the sounds of soldiers, Sloet's executioners, being marched into a straight line twenty paces from me. As the tension grows in the scene, a buggy approaches, carrying a man in a black suit (played by Albert Maritz) with the message that Sloet's sentence has been commuted to exile on St Helena.

What does Sloet do when he hears the news? Instead of being happy that his life has been spared, he remonstrates violently. While soldiers undo his hands, he shouts that exile is a sentence far worse than death. As his blindfold is removed, he rips his shirt open and begs the soldiers to shoot him. The audience is left in no doubt about the depth of his hatred for the British.

While we were still filming in Pringle Bay, I had been working hard to develop Sloet Steenkamp as a character. On one weekend off I decided to climb the gaunt cliff face that rose above the Hangklip Hotel. I began via a thickly wooded kloof, eventually getting high enough to reach the back of the mountain, whose high rugged cliffs face the sea. I was entering a world virtually untrodden by humans. Pure nature. Ancient, gnarled trees grew among these rocks, which had protected them from fires over the ages. I felt privileged to move among them. I felt as if I was walking in the presence of the fugitive wild spirit of Sloet Steenkamp.

Within fifty metres of the peak, I noted how the ancient rocks had been eroded into long troughs by rainwater over hundreds of thousands of years. I couldn't ignore the sense of being a mere smidgeon in the boundlessness of eternity. I felt that Sloet had also experienced this. Realising your insignificance in the face of eternity leads to a loss of fear. I understood then why Sloet was not scared of any consequences he might face in his quest for freedom, and why he did not care much for the opinions of others.

Eventually, I reached the top and gazed out over the edge of Hangklip down on our little world of *Arende* in the same way that an eagle would see it. I felt powerful and energised as I gazed out over the ocean, the only sounds those of seagulls and other birds soaring playfully in the air. As the sun began its descent, I made my way down the mountain. I had achieved much in my quest to understand Sloet's character better. Instinctively, I felt the common ground between him and me. It was a gift from the gods who live on top of Hangklip.

The filming for the second season mostly took place at a farm outside Barrydale called Die Waterberg. The British were out to get Sloet Steen-kamp, who had managed to get hold of a horse after his escape. There is a scene in which he has to pick up a drunken Khoikhoi man, who is wearing an ostentatious ostrich feather in his hat, by grabbing his arm and swinging him up onto the rump of the horse, to sit just behind the saddle.

Before I continue, I need to make four brief points. First, it has been said that once one has fallen off a horse 11 times, it can be assumed that you are finally a horse rider. Now, I had already gone well beyond that number long before the second season of *Arende*, but still I was wary of horses. Second, one should try to avoid riding horses in the Karoo, since there are generally too few places between the billions of rocks for one to fall without breaking one's bones. Third, stuntmen should be called in to do horse stunts, because for an actor to merely ride a horse convincingly is, in and of itself, already a stunt (except for Gavin van den Berg, who got into a saddle for the first time and looked as though he was born there). Fourth, I have learnt that it is much easier to get clever on a horse when it is riding *uphill*. Falling off is much worse when going *downhill*. Directors who try to save money by making actors ride horses should know this.

Dirk de Villiers didn't seem to have any knowledge of points two to four. He made me – an actor, not a stuntman – ride a horse in the Karoo on a *downhill* part of a dirt track. I was supposed to come cantering along on my horse and pick up a coloured man with an ostrich feather in his hat about halfway from the camera position. And so the scene was set, with me on top of a twitching horse called Bloukrantz.

When Dirk shouted 'Aksie!' I cajoled Bloukrantz into a canter, trying as best I could to look like a person who had been riding horses in the Karoo since he was eight years old. Indeed, everything went well until I arrived

Sloet and Reverend Theo Bloemfontein, played by Albert Maritz.
Credit: Barry Lucas

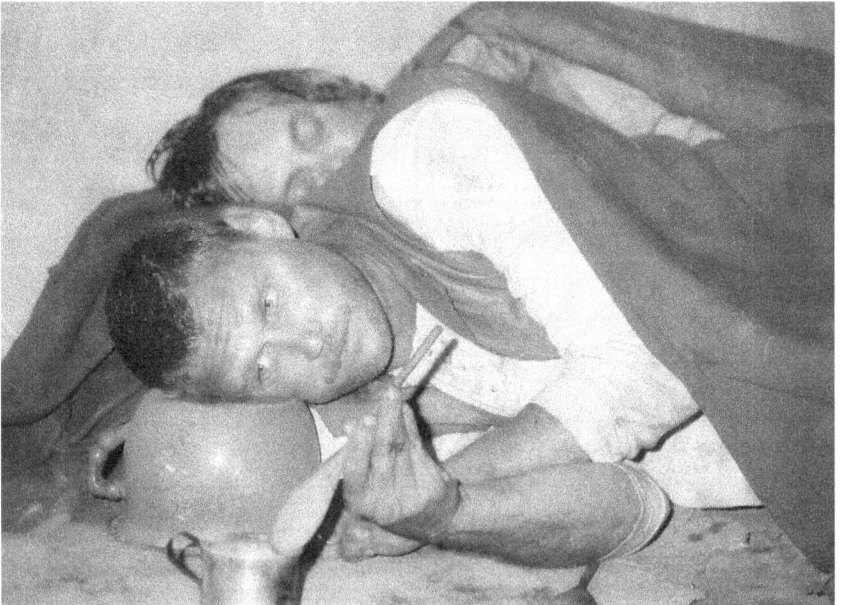

Sloet in a prisoner of war camp with a fellow inmate, played by Neels Coetzee.
Credit: Barry Lucas

at the point where I had to pick up ostrich-feather man. I managed to lean down and grab him with my right arm and unceremoniously yank him upwards so that he landed on Bloukrantz's broad rump.

'What a luck! This shot might actually even work out!' I thought.

All that Bloukrantz, ostrich-feather man and I had to do now was canter past the camera and out of shot. But there was a problem: my co-actor was an extra who had never acted before and, worse, had never ridden a horse! Now this poor man was expected to stay on top of Bloukrantz's heaving rump.

'Ooooo, jirre, meneer, help my! Ek gaan myself vrekval!' (Oh lord, mister, help me. I'm going to fall to my death!) he shouted.

'Hou vas, boetie. Ons moet net die donnerse shot klaar kry!' (Hold on, brother. We just have to finish this shot!) I said, talking out of the right-hand side of my mouth so that the camera, which was to our left, would not pick up that I was talking. We had only about twenty metres to go, and I urged on Bloukrantz. It flashed through my mind that my grandfather Cecil McWilliams, who fought in the British cavalry, had been such a good horseman that he won the Grand National, the race where they jump over hedges and things.

Ostrich-feather man was getting increasingly agitated behind me. 'Oh lord, mister, help me!' he said again.

'No man, we're nearly there!' I shouted as loudly as was possible for a man using only one side of his mouth. 'Grab my jacket and hold on!'

The desperate extra grabbed my jacket and held fast. Only ten metres to go.

Just when I started to think we were going to make it, the leather girth (strap) under Bloukrantz's stomach snapped. The pressure of my having to overcompensate on the stirrups to accommodate my passenger's desperate hanging on my back was just too much. The saddle lurched sideways and there was nothing I could do but launch myself off the horse sideways to my left.

As if in slow motion, I saw to my horror that I was going to fall on a rock-hard earthen wall. The angle of the wall prevented me from doing my old falling-off-a-horse trick, which entailed rolling over as I hit the ground. To make matters worse, ostrich-feather man fell on top of me, so my left leg hit the wall with the combined weight of both of us.

The force smashing into my upper left leg had felt very great and I knew I had been seriously injured. I pushed ostrich-feather man (who was fine, having used me as a landing pad) off me and felt my leg. I was amazed that it was not broken as I staggered upwards, with dust and dirt and dried grass falling off my clothes.

'Sorry, sir,' said ostrich-feather man, dusting himself off. I said nothing because I was distracted by the goings-on of the camera crew. I could have sworn I heard laughing. Even though it might have appeared very funny to people twenty metres away, 'funny' was the last word that came to my mind as I struggled to stand upright.

Then I heard Dirk shouting: 'Haai, is julle oukei?' (Hey, are you okay?)

I was in too much pain and shock to talk, so I just turned around and started limping away. I was hurt and angry that I had been forced into doing a stunt I wasn't trained for. I heard Dirk shouting behind me again and realised he must be following me, so I quickened my pace as much as I could.

'Meneer Roberts!'

I just kept walking. The way I felt, I could have walked right over the mountains to the Atlantic Ocean, about sixty kilometres away, and gone for a swim.

'Sorrie, man!' I could hear Dirk was breathing heavily. 'Stop nou, jong, asseblief!' (Stop, man, please!)

I stopped and turned to face him. He came to a halt about ten metres away.

'Fok jou movie in sy hele militêre moer in, Dirk!' (To hell with your movie, Dirk!), I bellowed.

I turned away and carried on walking, now definitely heading for the horizon. Still Dirk huffed and puffed behind me. After half a kilometre, most directors would have turned around, called off the shoot for that scene and sent the first assistant director to go and fetch the runaway actor. Not Dirk. He knew we had something in common: we both believed in the dictum that the movie comes first.

'Stop nou, jong, ek word nou moeg' (Please, stop, man, I'm getting really tired) he said, rather out of breath.

I stopped and turned and so we faced each other in something reminiscent of a Western gunfight.

'Sorry, man, are you okay?'

'No, Dirk, I'm not okay at all.'

'I'm really sorry, the stuntmen are so expensive.'

'Ag, man, I suppose I'll live.'

Dirk shifted his weight from one foot to the other. He knew what he was about to ask was beyond audacious, it was ridiculous. 'So, will you be able to do another take, then?'

I couldn't believe the man. My leg was already swelling in two places. He was completely out of line in trying to do the shot without using stuntmen. Yet, here he was, asking me to climb back onto Bloukrantz's hastily repaired saddle and do it all over again …

Dirk was completely mad! But so was I. Both of us were crazy. In fact, the entire crew was slightly ditzy: welcome to the set of *Arende II* – a dangerous place – and welcome to the South African way of making movies.

'Sure, Dirk, let's go shoot the scene to smithereens.'

'Now you're talking, my friend,' he said, smiling victoriously, and we walked back down the mountain to the set.

12

When an Afrikaans *meisie* calls you her *kêrel*

AS IF *ARENDE* WASN'T ALREADY such a turning point in my career, it also brought a turning point in my personal life when Michelle Botes arrived on set. In one scene in the first season, Sloet, in a desperate attempt to avoid Captain Kerwin and his posse, who are out hunting for him on horseback, climbs down a precipitous rock face to the sea, slips and falls, and badly injures himself. (As usual, I had to perform that stunt myself on the cliffs near Hermanus.) Sloet is, for all intents and purposes, finished: with a badly injured leg, he is hardly able to move but is saved by a St Helena local, a fisherman with a small boat, a lot of courage, a big heart and an even bigger hatred for the British. His name is Sam Gobbler, excellently played by the Cape actor David Pieters.

Sam comes upon the physically broken Sloet, lying half in, half out of a tidal pool, with the raging surf threatening to engulf and destroy him once and for all. Sam drags Sloet back to his wooden cabin, romantically situated among the cliffs right at the edge of the sea. Now, Sam has a beautiful young daughter whom he calls Princess, enchantingly played by Michelle Botes. Princess is immensely attracted to the dashing Captain Kerwin and he to her, even though he cannot express it very well owing to his English obsessions with class and the stiff upper lip, and all that complicated and cluttered jazz.

So, when Princess's father brings a large, wild and injured Boer back to their cabin, she is very unhappy ('They will put us in jail for hiding a prisoner'). But her father is adamant: he is going to nurse Sloet back to health and then smuggle him onto a ship via his connections in Jamestown harbour. Sloet regains his strength while Princess tolerates her father's foolishness, until late one night Sloet bumbles into the

Director Dirk de Villiers with actress Michelle Botes, who played the role of Princess Gobbler. Credit: Barry Lucas 'bathroom' where Princess is bathing in a large tin bath. She is naked. Now, although Sloet is completely committed to escaping back to South Africa, where his beloved wife waits for his return, he can't stop himself from gazing at Princess's beauty. However, the movie scene 'Sloet Steenkamp gazing at Princess' was also 'Actor Ian Roberts gazing at actress Michelle Botes' ...

I had met Michelle once before, as the girlfriend of my friend Anton van der Linde, sound man and co-worker on many Manie van Rensburg movies. Sometime before, I was visiting Anton at his *possie* in Woodstock in Cape Town when through the door came this beautiful apparition: his girlfriend, Michelle. I had never seen such a beauty in all my gallivanting days. She had a shock of vibrant curly dark hair, a strong and yet somehow delicate jawline and square shoulders, and was dressed in beautiful flowing, hippie-like clothes – like a gypsy wearing bits of silver and gold, which glinted in the shafts of sunlight in Anton's house. She pulled out a packet of French Gitanes cigarettes and lit one. I watched her, mesmerised, as she held the cigarette between her thumb and forefinger, and exhaled the glorious, aromatic blend of burley, Turkish and a bit of Virginia tobacco. I inhaled as much of the smoke as I could. She spoke Afrikaans in a deep, husky voice. And on top of all this, I was told she was an actress.

On *Arende*, the production manager, Pieter, in all his wisdom had put Michelle into the same seaside shack as me and Jocelyn Broderick. So now she was sharing a house with me. Then came a weekend off for the movie and everybody was excited to be heading back to Cape Town, but suburbia was the last place I wanted to go. I decided to hang out in Pringle Bay, maybe walk in the mountains or catch a surf at Koeëlbaai, and at night do my food and drink with Otto at the Hangklip Hotel. But that Friday night Otto said he also needed a break and was shutting the hotel for the weekend. I was very sad about this, but luckily Hansie the barman took me all the way to his favourite drinking spots in Kleinmond.

Hansie, his friends and I partied right through Saturday to Sunday evening, when I made my way back to the shack. And there I was blessed with the vision of Michelle coming back from her visit to Cape Town. Two days had made her even more beautiful than before. She flitted in like a will-o'-the-wisp, carrying a large wicker basket loaded with coffee, cookies and things for the house that she unpacked in the kitchen. For the single man, there is a strange power in the image of a woman carrying a basket full of sustenance to share in a cosy cottage while a storm rages outside. We were both young and unencumbered since Michelle had since broken up with Anton.

On one of the days when they weren't shooting scenes with Sloet, I walked into the surrounding fynbos and was astounded to find many different kinds of small flowers. I began to pick some because I knew Michelle would be on set that afternoon. The friendship between Michelle and me had started to grow into something special. I knew she loved these little flowers that grew wild all around the set and that few people seemed to notice. Since I am a secretive Cancerian, I didn't want anybody to know that I was crazy about the girl, so I picked up an empty hessian sack that lay discarded at the edge of the camp and hid the flowers in it. When I got time off again, I went out and gathered more flowers. After the evening wrap, I nonchalantly gave the sack to Michelle.

Back at the shack, Jocelyn, Michelle and I had begun sleeping in one bed, the big mattress I had put on the floor of the large room with the giant windows upstairs. After a party at the Hangklip Hotel, we would lie on the bed in the darkness, watching the shifting sea in the moonlight and fall asleep lulled by its crashing and murmurs on the rocks below, accompanied by the sounds of Fleetwood Mac.

Our lives were shifting like the tides, and it was good. It was this vibrancy, this madness for living – this magic – that infused itself into the scenes we were shooting every day on set. However, given my dictum of 'the movie comes first', Michelle and I decided to hold off on making our relationship formal until the first season of *Arende* was in the can.

As shooting for the first season drew to a close, Michelle and I were needed less and less on set. By that point, our relationship had become quite serious. I can't recall exactly when or how we decided to get married, though. There was certainly no ring with a diamond in a little velvet box; I did not go down on one knee, and Michelle cannot remember saying, 'I do.' It was as if by some magical consent of the universe we both knew we were going to get married. We never even bothered to get engaged. She phoned her mother, Suzie, in Windhoek with the following words: 'Ek het my kêrel gevind, Ma. Ons gaan trou. (I have found my 'kêrel', Mom. We're going to get married.)

I happened to overhear this conversation. Now when an Afrikaans girl says 'my kêrel', then you should know she has chosen her man. I decided I had better inform my parents, too.

'I've met the girl of my dreams, Ma. We're going to get married at that little church up in the Hogsback mountains,' I said when I shared the news with my mother one day towards the end of June 1988. This was three weeks after we had finished shooting the first series of *Arende*.

'Good heavens, my boy, that's wonderful. Who is this girl?'

'Her name is Michelle Botes, she's an actress,' I said.

'Gawd mawd, my boy … she sounds Afrikaans.'

'Yes, she is, Ma.'

Even though my mother was of Irish descent, she was something of a royalist and avidly watched any coverage of the British royal family on television. One of her McWilliams forebears had also gone on campaign against the Boers in the Anglo-Boer War, so I suppose she might've felt that Afrikaners were slightly foreign, at least to our family.

I told my mother a little more about Michelle and why I had fallen in love with her. Even though she hadn't met Michelle yet, she didn't question my decision. In previous years, my mother would often ask me why I was taking so long to get married, to which I would reply: 'Well, look at Prince Charles … he's not married.' That satisfied her for a while, but then Charles went and got married in 1981 at 36, and now I was also at that age. I suspect she was very relieved when I told her about Michelle. She always said, 'My boy, I don't care what kind of woman you end up with, as long as she's kind.' And Michelle was kind.

'So, when do you want to get married?'

'Soon! On the ninth of July.'

My father and I had a different sort of conversation. He was always concerned about the practical side of things, like money. Even though I told him I had been earning well on the TV series we'd been making, he insisted on putting up a large sum for the wedding.

Meanwhile, my formidable agent, the legendary and now late Moon-yeenn Lee – I had switched to her agency, MLA, with the blessing of my former agent, Sybil Sands – had landed me a role in another movie that was being shot in Joburg. It was a story about the repercussions of the Immorality Act, which forbade sexual relationships between people of different races. The leading roles were played by Jana Cilliers and Bill Flynn; I played a policeman. The scenes I had to do were to be shot in Braamfontein, and at night, but I was scheduled to be on the set of *Arende* the next morning to shoot the first scenes of the series. I had to be in Matjiesfontein in the Karoo, about a thousand kilometres away. Once the Joburg shoot was done, I hit the road south in my VW Kombi panel van and drove through the freezing night. After shooting those last scenes, my hotel room in Laingsburg waited for me, but I had a girl in Cape Town whom I was going to marry. So on to Cape Town I went.

I went to stay with my sister Jane who, no matter what her situation was, would always welcome me into her house. Michelle and I would soon be leaving for the farm, where my parents were feverishly putting together the wedding ceremony. My parents were two of the most understanding people I have ever known. Even if they didn't quite comprehend why their children did things in certain ways, they would always find a way to understand them eventually.

I was, however, not yet fully convinced of the marriage thing. I told Michelle I had to go into the wilderness on my own to seek out answers to some life questions, and specifically whether I should get married or not. Most women would have broken it off at the mere suggestion of doubt, but Michelle was not that sort of woman, so she waved me goodbye with a beautiful smile.

I bought a small self-igniting stove with a couple of gas canisters, a rucksack, a sleeping bag, a little pot, some food, tea, coffee, sugar and powdered milk, and set out for the wilderness, just like in my hunter-gathering days. I drove out to the farm Elandsvlei in the Tankwa, the semi-desert that stretches between the Cederberg mountain range and Sutherland, and went to the same people I had lived with when we shot *Verspeelde Lente*. The next day I set off into the foothills of the Cederberg, heading west.

Ever since visiting Elandsvlei for the first time in 1982, I had been mystified by the tabletop peak of Tafelberg – the highest point in the range – which is gaunt and snowcapped in the winter. I hiked towards this magical mountain because I believed the spirits that occupied its peak would be able to answer some of the questions that mortals couldn't. On the first day I made quite good progress, but I soon realised the mountain was much further away than it appeared.

That night, a bitterly cold wind blew and I was on top of a treeless plateau. As things became more miserable, I desperately needed shelter – a big rock, a dense bush, anything. I couldn't see well in the dusk and I had forgotten to bring a torch. The only way out was back down off the mountain, where I knew there was a kloof with bushes and firewood … but that would have meant defeat.

I was just about to turn back when I heard the sound of a sheep bleating. Sheep = wool = warmth, I thought, as I made my way towards the sound. I came upon a stone kraal filled with sheep. Attached to one side was a kind of tent – just a piece of canvas stretched out to form a shelter from the wind. Inside were two adolescent sheep herders. Speaking in Afrikaans, I asked them if I could share their tent – I had coffee, tea, sugar and powdered milk to bargain with. They agreed, and so it happened that the three of us shared the small space, our combined warmth comforting against the freezing wind.

I had often slept with Pese and Kununu Piet, Djonni Kieghlaar and Pieter Trompetter in a small tent in the Eastern Cape bush, but I didn't know these guys at all, so I was wary of falling asleep. What was to stop them from hitting me over the head, taking all my stuff and vanishing into the night with their sheep? My imagination kept me awake for long, until one of the herders began snoring. Comforted, I eventually fell asleep too.

The next morning, as the three of us made coffee, I realised my wild imagination had sullied the innocent spirits of my compatriots. I told them I wanted to climb Tafelberg, but they told me it was impossible: three days weren't enough time, it was too far, and there were too many other mountains in the way. So I changed direction and headed south towards a small river among the cliffs. In the late afternoon I found it and began the steep, rock-strewn descent to the stream. There, at least, I had water. Beside the stream lay a giant boulder, and underneath it was a place where I could crawl in to sleep. I was lucky because night was coming quickly and I had no tent or safe place to sleep.

Sloet supports Paul Johnson, played by Gert van Niekerk, in his last moments after he was shot. Photo: Barry Lucas

As I settled in, I boiled some water for tea on my Italian gas stove (which, unbelievably, I still have and use to this day). The shepherds had told me to be wary: there were hungry leopards in these mountains. I crawled further into the recess under the boulder and lay there, looking out at the landscape lit up by a bright moon and listening to the faint tinkling of the water running over the rocks.

I woke in the middle of the night. I could hear something was moving about my fireplace, but the moon had set and it was too dark to see. When I woke the next morning, I saw that a leopard had left its spoor in the sand around my boulder; all it had found was a couple of tea bags and an empty sardine can. As I sat by the stream sipping my coffee, it occurred to me that maybe the visit from the leopard was a sign that I should go ahead and get married.

At that moment, I suddenly heard a rush of wind. I looked up and saw a giant eagle flying above me. It landed on a cliff on the far side of the stream right opposite me and sat in the early-morning sunlight in all its glory, staring at me. I focused my binoculars on it: it was a beautiful, powerfully built black eagle and I was convinced it was ogling me with its fierce eyes.

In the final scene of the first season of *Arende*, Paul C Venter draws all the threads of the story together to bring the season to a close. A sports day is held between the British soldiers and the Boers, and a mock confrontation turns sour as the Boer pacifist Paul Johnson climbs high up onto a water tower, carrying a revolver as a symbol of the violence that he detests. The British troops mistake Paul's actions for aggression and a shot rings out. The bullet hits Paul and he falls, crashing to the ground.

As he lies dying, he looks up at Sloet and speaks his final, gut-wrenching words: 'Ek sien 'n arend, Sloet! Hy vlieg hoog in die lug. En hy's vry, Sloet. Hy's vry! (I see an eagle, Sloet! He's flying up in the sky. And he's free, Sloet. He's free!)

I was in awe. Here before me, in the Tankwa desert, was Paul's eagle. Sloet, it seemed to say, go fetch that princess in Cape Town and marry her! Suddenly, as if punctuating my thoughts, the great bird launched itself off the cliff and flew upwards, circling above me, higher and higher. I followed it with my binoculars until it vanished from sight. I reached for my notebook, took my ballpoint pen, and wrote the following: 'The eagle has risen, taken up its thermal and left.'

Two weeks later Michelle and I were married. The ceremony was held in the small church on top of the Hogsback mountains and the reception at the King's Lodge Hotel, attended by many special friends and various Eastern Cape farmers. At the end of the evening, Michelle and I walked through an avenue of raised arms while a six-piece jazz band from East London played.

We ventured out into a white world that gleamed with purity and perfection in the headlights. It had snowed on the Hogsback and, as we drove, our tracks stretched out behind us, dark in the whiteness. We were driving out into the darkness, as if into outer space on a one-way journey to infinity.

13

Camel Man

IN BETWEEN THE SHOOTING OF the first and second series of *Arende*, Moonyeenn put me forward as a candidate in the worldwide search for the new Camel Man (the representative of the Camel cigarette brand). It was rumoured that the current Camel Man had developed lung cancer (maybe from smoking too many Camels?). In due course, I was selected as the entry for Africa.

This exciting opportunity came shortly after the birth of my first child, Cara, which was a humbling, 'reset of your place in the universe' kind of life event. After eight hours of labour in the magnificent water birth unit of the Johannesburg General Hospital (today Charlotte Maxeke Johannesburg Academic Hospital), the sister in charge came to me with a worried expression on her face. 'The baby is under stress, we need to give an epidural.'

I went to Michelle and told her what the sister had suggested. 'I don't need an epidural, I need a Camel Filter!' was her firm response.

I carried her down to the little smoking room, with a nurse trippling alongside us with the drip on wheels. (At the time, we weren't aware of the harmful effects of smoking during pregnancy.) With her ancient, dark eyes, Michelle stared at me as she smoked the Camel to its butt and put it out. 'Give me another …' I watched as she smoked the second Camel, but about halfway through, she stubbed it out. 'I'm ready,' she said and we hurried her back to the water birth unit.

Some minutes later, Cara entered the world. As the only man there, I stood with my knees shaking and, as the midwife lifted our baby out of the water, it was as if the earth shuddered. Nothing can prepare you for that moment. I recalled Manie van Rensburg's reaction when I told him I was going to get married. He nodded knowingly and said, 'Trou is fokkol, Ou Grote. Maar as sy kind kry, gaan jou lewe nooit ooit weer dieselfde wees nie.' (Getting married is nothing. But when she gets a child, your life will never be the same again.)

Getting the Camel Man job would have been a godsend for us as a young couple with a new-born baby. I was flown to Los Angeles so that the American casting agents could take a closer look at me. It was the first time I had flown first class. In those days you could still smoke on planes, so, as people settled in and fell asleep in their luxury seats with their eye masks and ear plugs in place, I went to the lounge upstairs to smoke. I shifted around the many windows, gazing down enthralled at lightning bursting in the giant cumulonimbus night clouds over Kilimanjaro. I have always been a night person and I don't think I slept at all that magical night.

The next morning, at Heathrow Airport, I boarded a TWA flight and flew over the stormy North Atlantic towards the land of the free. I watched amazed as, far below, giant swells rolled across the deep sea, their crests breaking in massive columns of tumbling white foam. We crossed the North American coast and flew over the snow-white mainland, which seemed vast and endless.

I was on my way to fabled Hollywood, but as my excitement grew, I also became more and more apprehensive: I was going to compete with actors and models from all over the world. I felt the butterflies of insecurity fluttering in my gut, but eventually another, calming thought started to grow in my mind: no matter how big a foreign star might be, the camera frame that surrounds him will be exactly the same as surrounds me. I also remembered what I had learnt about camera lenses and the size of frames from my photography studies in the 1970s; I planned to use my knowledge to my advantage.

No one arrived to pick me up at Los Angeles International, but that didn't upset me as much as the fact that I could not retrieve my French Opinel pocketknife, which I had been forced to hand in at airport security. It had vanished somewhere between Jan Smuts Airport and LA. While I was scheming what to do next and how to reach Moonyeenn, a man I had met on the plane walked up to me. 'Is everything okay there, son?' he asked. This was James Retty, a specialist agent in Hollywood, who would go ahead of big stars like Clint Eastwood and Meryl Streep to quality-check the hotels or apartments where they would be staying.

'No, James,' I answered, 'not good. I was supposed to be picked up.'

'Do you know where you're staying?'

'I showed him a piece of paper with my hotel details.

'Santa Monica – that's no problem. I live close by. I'll drive you there.'

I was astounded to find the type of friendliness and helpfulness one could expect in the Eastern Cape at the airport in Los Angeles. As James drove me in his yellow Cadillac down a broad highway towards Santa Monica, I thanked him profusely. He even made sure I was checked into the hotel before he left. The hotel was rather weird: the thin walls were made of wood, so I could hear the people in the rooms next door. This was very un-South African.

Even though I had got mildly drunk while eating lobster in first class on the flight, it failed to save me from getting severely jetlagged. At about 3 am, I gave up trying to sleep, got dressed and walked out through the foyer and into the brisk night air. I was strolling down a wide street lined with respectable-looking houses, well-lit by streetlamps, when I noticed a big police car following me. I just kept walking. Eventually they pulled up alongside me.

'Good evening, sir. Where do you come from?'

'I'm from Africa.'

'Africa?'

'Yes – South Africa, actually.'

'Okay, well, even if you're from Africa, sir … there's no way a man like you should be walking any further down this street. You best turn round and get the hell outta here.'

I'd spent enough time in Johannesburg that I didn't have to be told twice about no-go areas. I walked back to the main road and found an all-night pizza takeaway. Having had my fill of lobsters, I didn't need a pizza as much as the warmth of the place. So I hung out there, watching the people, some of them coming from parties, mostly a little drunk or stoned or both, and looking for a snack.

I was still enjoying this real-life movie when an altercation took place. I heard a man shouting rudely at the young Hispanic guys behind the pizza counter and immediately recognised the accent. The bad-mannered man was South African and was speaking English spiced with Xhosa. Had I flown nearly 16 000 kilometres only to be faced with the drunken boorishness of a compatriot? 'Mamela mnqundu wakho,' I wanted to say. 'Thula! Uyangxola njengesidenge!' (Listen to me, asshole! Shut up! You are making the noise of an idiot!) I was astounded, because the chances of such a thing happening to me on my first night in America were about 50 trillion to one.

I was finally growing tired and decided to leave rather than get involved. Once back in my hotel room, I slept well, despite the noises coming through the walls. The next day, I was picked up by a neatly dressed young movie driver in a large Yank tank and driven through the legendary LA fog to the Los Angeles County Arboretum and Botanic Garden. Three giant *Aloe ferox* loomed large at the entrance gates, their spiked leaves gaunt against the fog.

'Howzit guys, it's so good to see you in this strange frikken place, my African brothers,' I said, thinking out loud.

'What's that you're saying, my man?' asked the driver, looking at me in the rear-view mirror.

'Naa … just running some lines.' Of course, there were no lines in an audition for the Camel Man, because he never said anything, but I didn't want the driver to know I was talking to the plants.

I was delivered to make-up, which was in one of those shiny, stream-lined caravans you see all over the States. On set, a heated discussion was taking place between the agent of a young American actor and the director. The agent was telling the director that his client, who was standing beside him and who looked quite strong to me, was certainly not going 'to climb that fucking tree – it wasn't in the brief anyway!'

'I'll climb it,' said the mad red-haired Irishman, speaking through my mouth.

Everyone turned and looked at me.

'Where's your agent?' the director asked.

'She's back in Johannesburg, South Africa.'

He seemed very pleased that I had no agent with me. He rolled the cameras and I began climbing. When I was halfway up, he asked me to cross on a rope from the tree to another one nearby. Once I was halfway across, he asked me if I could jump down to the ground. For a Hunter-Gatherer, who had once climbed to the top of giant pecan-nut trees to pick bags of pecans for money, these were Mickey-Mouse-easy things to do. After I had played a range of scenarios at different locations, I arrived at a large lake in the arboretum.

In the next shot, I had to take a drag of a Camel cigarette and blow out the smoke while gazing contentedly over the lake. A cameraman handed me a smoke, but it was the weakest Camel on the market, a thing I would only smoke in a severe emergency.

'Sorry man, but haven't you got a proper cigarette?' I asked.

'What? Don't tell me you're actually a goddamn smoker?'

'Yes, I am, and I'd prefer a Camel Plain right now. It's been a long day.'

The man searched through the box of Camel products he'd received and, voila, he handed me an unopened pack of glorious Camel Plain.

'You're the first man through here who smokes.'

I took a deep drag and blew the smoke out over the lake. I didn't have to act the satisfaction.

Back in the aluminium caravan, while my make-up was being removed, the sassy young make-up artist started chatting with me. 'You're the guy, man. You're the guy,' she said excitedly. 'The rest of these queens couldn't sell a camel to a fucking dealer in Baghdad.'

Five days later, I had to go and present myself to a few agents in LA. In the large foyer of a building near the Warner Brothers studios, an agent in a suit, who introduced himself as Mr Fenton, came to shake my hand.

'Girls,' he called out, 'come and take a look at who we've got here. He's from Africa.'

Numerous well-groomed ladies arrived and checked me out smilingly. I felt quite exposed, but Mr Fenton seemed to like their reactions to this apparent exotic curiosity from the sun-drenched plains of Africa. Then he and I got talking.

'What's your box office?' he asked.

I had never heard this question before but assumed he meant what the last movie that I had played in had earned at the box office.

'The last movie I did took four million rands,' I replied.

He seemed to like that, because the rand and the dollar had nearly the same value at the time. He told me that if I moved to America, he was quite sure his company would be able to get me work.

When I got back to Joburg, Moonyeenn told me the Camel people liked me very much and that they wanted to negotiate a fee for me to go and shoot a series of ads in the jungles of Borneo. She had already sent in the first quote for my services: $750 000. This was a weep-with-joy promise of future security. If I made it big as an actor in La-La Land, I would probably never have to work again.

Still, I was hounded by my conscience. During my early years acting in the theatre, I generally earned a small income and my fellow actors and I felt strongly about prioritising our craft above money. I remembered how one of my fellow Capab actors, Marthinus Basson (who went on to become a famous stage director), once turned down the chance to make big money in a TV advertisement for a wine brand.

'How the hell would I feel if I did the ad and then had to walk past a bunch of drunk hobos?' I remember him saying.

I had never forgotten Marthinus's taking the moral high ground. I kept thinking of the billions of non-smokers around the world whom I could potentially encourage to start smoking, and the smokers who might be emboldened to smoke even more. Having had my own love affair with tobacco, I knew the power of tobacco marketing.

If I had still been a loner, I would perhaps have gone to the States and set myself up in LA, but I also knew that I would still have to make that moral decision sooner or later. I had to make it before Moonyeenn's negotiations continued or I would break her trust. The tension within me became quite oppressive as I wrestled with the notion of selling out for money.

Eventually, however, the politics of the day forced a decision on me: because of the government's apartheid policy, I was refused a visa to travel to, or work in, Borneo. The Americans withdrew their offer and I never had to sell a single cigarette to anyone. Thank heavens for that!

The second season of *Arende* was shot in Barrydale in the Klein Karoo in 1990. I stayed at the Barrydale Hotel – the only hotel in town. I was needed earlier on the shoot, so Michelle came down from Joburg a bit later. I was curious to see how Paul C Venter would move the story from St Helena back to South Africa, so I started to read the script straight away. I didn't read far, though, because the beginning shocked the shit out of me: the producers had killed off Princess in the very first episode! Call me biased, because I was married to the actress who played Princess, but I felt that they had made a cardinal error. It certainly went against all my storytelling instincts.

They say actors should not be taken seriously when talking about scripts, but by that time I had already written three theatre plays, apart from having learnt the ancient art of storytelling around the campfire with the Hunter-Gatherers. I tossed the script onto the floor and made my way down the main street to Dirk de Villiers's house, where a get-together of cast and producers was in full swing.

Before I sipped the beer that was put in my hand, I went up to Paul himself, who was also at the party. He was standing next to the commissioning editor and other bigwigs from the SABC. I said what was on my mind, but the voice that came out of my mouth had the edge of that mad red-haired Irishman.

'I don't like the first episode at all!' I said, so that everyone could hear. The party went quiet.

'Oh, no?' said Paul calmly. Why not?'

'You're making a big mistake. You can't kill Princess!'

Then Dirk de Villiers spoke up. 'The writer of the text wrote it as he saw it, mister!'

'But you shouldn't mess with the *ménage à trois*!'

My case was this: the romantic leads were Captain Kerwin and Sloet Steenkamp, with Princess wedged in between them. Her natural beauty and wildness were perfect for letting the storyline unfold, but now they were killing her off.

I don't recall exactly how the situation was defused, but before the sun rose the next day, Paul came to my hotel room to speak to me privately. He told me he had struggled all night over what I'd said, and he'd come to the conclusion that I was right, but that it was sadly too late to do anything about it.

Afterwards, I learnt the true reason why the character of Princess had to be cut: Michelle was due to star in another television series, and the powers that be at the SABC felt that if she continued to appear in *Arende*, she would become overexposed. It didn't make any sense to me – would anyone ever describe a Hollywood star as 'overexposed'? – but that is the official reason why Paul was forced to kill off her character.

In 1992, we shot the last episodes of the final season of *Arende* in Douglas in the Northern Cape. Off days gave me the chance to explore this small farming community and the areas around it, situated near the confluence of the Vaal and Orange rivers. I knew it was on a farm in this district, and more particularly somewhere on the banks of the Vaal, that my great-grandfather Llewellyn had been badly burnt while installing a water pump. The accident had been so bad that he died ten days later in hospital in Kimberley.

As I mentioned in Chapter 1, I had some distant relatives, the Jacksons, who farmed on the northern bank of the Vaal River. I went to see them and they directed me to the neighbouring farm. While visiting the desolate site of my great-grandfather's accident, it occurred to me that, as an actor, I should try to experience this feeling of desolation. I knew I had to tap into the feeling, and that perhaps one day it would be needed for a performance.

The Jacksons had another farm on the southern side of the Vaal, where they had built a sort of Western-style cabin. That evening, I was invited to join them at the cabin for a braai. The Jacksons were great horsemen, and they liked to recall the days of Jesse James or Wyatt Earp in the way they carried their guns and wore gloves, chaps with tassels and boots with spurs. During the braai I was buzzing contentedly inside about what I had done that day: I had paid homage to Llewellyn, my great-grandfather.

Arende was eventually dubbed into many languages and broadcast all over the world. I once happened to go into a sound studio to experience the voice of Sloet Steenkamp being dubbed into Chinese! All 36 episodes of the series have been seen around the world, under the title *Cape Rebel*, and have been rebroadcast in their entirety five or six times in South Africa. While we were elated at the success of the series, sadly, not one of the actors has ever been paid a single cent in royalties. Patrick Swayze once told me that if *Arende* had been made in the US, all the leading actors and actresses would have been so wealthy they would never have had to work again. But I digress.

In December 2019, 31 years after I first set foot in Pringle Bay to shoot *Arende*, I returned to the seaside town. I was on my way to do a concert at the Hangklip Hotel and I was early, so I chose to drive down the side road to see if the little seaside shack where we stayed while filming the first ten episodes still existed. The little house was still there, although the colour had changed from a bold and striking mauve pink to a demure and boring creamy white. I was sad to find that the dirt road that went past the hotel, one of the few remaining out-of-the-way places with a certain mystique, had been tarred. So much had changed.

14

Acting from the gut

I AM OFTEN ASKED BY fresh-faced young people how they should go about becoming actors and actresses. I always tell them the same thing, which is to go out into the real world and get a job. If they look surprised, I say: 'Go out and work. Or do anything – but work with people. Make money. Have fun. Thereafter go and study … and *then* you will be ready to learn how to act.'

I held a smorgasbord of positions before I finally started my studies: army conscript, citrus farmer, apprentice quantity surveyor for a construction company, factory manager, door-to-door salesman and shop manager for a clothing store. Only *then* did I become a BA student at Rhodes University, majoring in speech and drama. I believe all the experiences I had while working equipped me better to make the most of studying at university. If I hadn't gone out into the tough world and often failed, I would not have been able to appreciate this privilege.

All my years of performing on stage and screen have taught me many valuable lessons on acting. One of them is that an actor's Big Performance only comes from having enough life experience.

As I honed my skills as an actor, I came to the conclusion that, for me, there are four kinds of actors: mules, donkeys, horses and racehorses. Mule actors are solid and dependable. They give the same performance every night, but their acting runs the risk of being predictable and boring. Donkeys, too, give the same performance every night, but they are capable of breaking out of the boring rigmarole of their performances, although only on rare occasions. Horses' performances are more muscular and intriguing for audiences; these actors are generally good-looking and highly capable, and critics often describe them as 'excellent in their roles'. Finally, you get the racehorses, who are skittish, jumpy and vulnerable, sometimes giving appalling performances, but who have the capacity of taking their performances 'out there' – to a place that words cannot describe. In those moments they achieve that highly sought-after quality of magic.

I believe that if actors live mollycoddled, protected lives, they will never be able to give 'out there' performances or portray characters who display extreme emotions or do extreme things. The character Teach in *American Buffalo*, for instance, is just such a character: to achieve his character's breakdown at the end of the play and deliver a racehorse performance, Sean Taylor had to expose many old personal hurts. He had grown up in a time when boys didn't cry and when crying indicated weakness or unmanliness. So to break down live in front of an audience meant he had to revisit vulnerabilities hidden deep inside himself and reveal them to the audience. He had to reach for the edges of his personality to achieve this. That is why I say you cannot expect racehorse actors to always be tame, pleasant-natured mules in their everyday lives.

This begs the question: where does an actor find inspiration when creating or portraying a character who displays extreme emotion? Vincent van Gogh would probably have gone out into nature with a canvas and painted whatever vista or lighting grabbed his attention. An actor has only a script with a character description that probably lists a few physical characteristics. The difficulty lies in making that character a flesh-and-blood person.

As I have mentioned, during my career I have mostly based my characterisations on people I knew – those who seem to have a link in my mind to the character in the script. But it won't help to simply mimic that person. There are plenty of genius mimics, but a mimic cannot be the leading man. As an actor, you must develop your own version of that character. And even that might not be enough, because you've also got to be blessed by your lucky stars, for instance by having an excellent group of actors or a great director. I have also found that the stars like to honour hard work.

When I was studying photography in the 1970s, I first had this revelation regarding music. Dollar Brand – the original stage name of the famous pianist and composer Abdullah Ibrahim – was to give a concert at the Feather Market Hall in PE. My friend and fellow student Rob Pollock and I had bought tickets, but then Dollar Brand cancelled the show because people of colour were not allowed to attend. He moved the show to St Stephen's Hall in New Brighton, a black township. Back then it was a dangerous place for two young white men to be. Rob and I almost got kicked out, but we were not deterred.

As soon as Dollar Brand stepped on the stage, he brought a miraculous calm and peace with him. He began by placing burning incense sticks in the cracks of the stage floor. During his brilliant performance, he seemed to get his strength and inspiration from a place beyond that township hall. I saw for the first time that if one is open, one can be infused with creative spirit. Even though at that time I had no idea I would become an actor one day, years later it was precisely that inspiration that helped me to get closer to my characters, especially to Sloet Steenkamp.

In the second season of *Arende*, when Sloet, after a harrowing journey, finally arrives at his farm at dusk, he faces his mortal enemy, Captain James Kerwin, who is waiting to ambush him. Sloet gazes at Kerwin with hatred in his eyes. As an actor, how do you recreate this anger? In acting school I had learnt that for an emotion such as hatred to come across as real, it has to be seated in your gut. At the time, I had no idea how to perform these extreme emotions, but then I realised that nobody else did either. Even if the director, for instance, had at one point in his life looked at someone with hatred, how could he possibly communicate that to me, the actor? The truth is that an actor is on their own.

Back then, I had been desperate in my performance; you could even say I was grasping at straws. I decided to interpret Sloet's emotional state as being grounded in failure. In that moment of pure hatred, all Sloet's dreams of success are shattered. He is utterly defeated, and that is a feeling most of us humans are familiar with and can relate to. In my quandary, the gods of acting reminded me of a tip once given to me by Richard Haines, the great South African stage actor, while we were working together on *Auf Achse*, a German TV series. For a male actor, he told me, displaying anger in a performance is predictable and dull. Instead, he explained, one must maintain some kind of vulnerability because it keeps one's performance enticing to an audience. This is particularly relevant for young actors, who are often driven by a gung-ho masculinity, which makes their performances one-dimensional and therefore stale. Actresses mostly escape this malady since they are generally more emotionally aware.

I believe that an actor learns many of his skills from acting on stage.

This is why I often call stage work the engine room of learning to act. In the theatre, you can never cease to develop your performance. You must constantly try to improve it, night after night.

I give actors who are rehearsing a play the following advice: when the thought of doing another run-through makes you want to puke, you are close to being prepared to perform in front of an audience. Then comes the challenge of not only keeping a character true but also adding different dimensions to your performance. I explain this by using the following analogy: hold your hand out in front of you and imagine that your performance is your forearm, which ends in your relaxed hand. That performance will get you by. But if you want to keep an audience intrigued, you somehow have to undermine their expectations. Now clench your fist and look at the muscles moving under the skin of your forearm: those shape-changing, rippling muscles represent what your performance should strive to be like.

Another technique I have perfected over the years is the ability to cast the coming scene out of my mind. It sounds rather biblical, but I've learnt that an actor should never 'overwork' a section of the script when they prepare for a scene in a movie. If you delve too deeply into your preparation, you are, first, assuming too much about how the scene will be set up by the director, which is a mistake because in movies there are too many variables. In other words, the more prepared and rock-solid you've rehearsed yourself into a performance, the less flexible you will be on set and the more it will throw you when your expectations are not met in the moment.

Second, when you overwork a scene, your character risks being played from the *face* and not from where it really should be played – your *gut*. Of course, there are exceptions, like when you have to prepare a long monologue. These are not common in movies, but when you do encounter one in a script, you have to work long and hard to be completely secure in the monologue. Then the director can throw anything he likes at you and you'll be able to take it.

Without any conscious intent, I have found that sometimes, when trying to bring a character to life, an instinct in me would force me to withdraw from the world of the set. Generally speaking, a movie set is a wonderful place for an actor to be. Everyone is excited to be working on a new project that will help pay the bills, and old friendships are rekindled. Yet at times I felt the need to distance myself.

I'm often described as 'the crazy actor who camps in the bush', but becoming an outsider has been a deliberate decision on my part. I've always wanted to remain something of a stranger on set and to the other actors, since this has enabled me to choose how to interact and joust with the movie set – actors and crew – as an entity that I am part of but, at the same time, apart from.

For example, throughout the six years it took to shoot all 36 episodes of *Arende*, I was inadvertently exploring my relationship as an actor with movie sets and the notion of maintaining a level of apartness. It took many hours in many bars with different kinds of strangers, and hiking up many nearby mountains, to maintain a modicum of remoteness from the world of the screen. I must thank all those garlic farmers, travelling salesmen and ad hoc boozers in the Hangklip Hotel, Froggy's Barrydale Hotel, the Royal Hotel in Douglas and the Pofadder Hotel for their company. Their stories about the realities of their worlds kept me from being completely absorbed by the mini-world created by the actors and the crew on the set of *Arende*, which helped me to maintain the integrity of the character of Sloet Steenkamp.

From a young age, long before I became an actor, I always felt *different*. Over the festive season, for instance, when everybody is supposed to be in a party mood, I always feel a little depressed, a little distant. I remember an incident from my childhood, when my parents took me to go and play at the house of a friend in Fort Beaufort. After a while, I found that I liked neither him nor his other friends and the games they played, so I soon disappeared. When they realised I was gone, they searched high and low and eventually found me sitting inside a cupboard, enjoying the silence and the smell of the exotic wood. They shook their heads because to them I was something of a freak. In retrospect, I agree.

Over the years I've realised that there are times when I don't fit in with the people around me, which has had the effect of making me feel even more inadequate at trying to be a 'good guy'. I've always known that I am an outsider, and I believe every actor has to arrive at that magical island where it's okay to be different and set up shop on the beach.

Google can teach you many different things, but certain acting tricks can only be learnt through experience. While working on the TV series *Heroes* in 1984, Manie van Rensburg was unhappy with the performance of one of the actors. In movie parlance, to 'feed' another actor is to give them the lines you speak in the scene so that they can react in close-up, but you are not on camera. To 'feed' this particular actor, Manie placed me so close to the camera that my ear was touching the lens.

'I need you to help me out here, Ou Grote. Just blow him out of the water,' he said softly in my ear and winked conspiratorially.

Having watched the flat performance of this actor during all the previous takes, I knew exactly what Manie meant. So I overacted as grossly as I could. The other actor was so surprised he was shocked into an acceptable, cuttable performance.

Fifteen years later, acting in a big international movie in Zululand, I had to call on that trick again to aid the performance of the leading lady, a famous American actress and smouldering blonde beauty. She was such a big name that the entire movie budget emanated from her status. She was the queen of the set, and you got the feeling that if she didn't like you, you would be on the next bus back home.

But then one day, when we were shooting a pivotal scene, the so-called money scene, she struggled to get it into the can. The director was a wonderful man, but he did not know how to work with actors. The scene involved me and the young actor Nick Boraine: we played the roles of two men who had to bring the leading lady the terrible news that her husband had been gored to death by a buffalo.

In the scene, Nick and I had to come round the corner of a stoep where we would run into the leading lady. On the first take (to us South Africans, an extremely expensive one, with three cameras rolling 35 mm film), our leading lady just stared back at us blankly after we had told her the news of her husband's demise. Initially, I thought perhaps we South African actors were too weak for her, that our acting wasn't up to standard. She had acted opposite several Hollywood stars and maybe they knew how to do stuff that we had never learnt.

However, after the second take, when she again did nothing more than stare at us blankly, I knew the problem lay with her and not us. The director was standing behind us, shaded from the blistering Zululand sun by a thorn tree. When he called 'cut', I looked around to see an expression of helpless defeat on his face.

Nick and I returned to our first positions around the corner of the building, waiting for the third take. I recalled Manie's advice to me on the set of *Heroes* and said to Nick, 'You know what we've got to do now?'

'No, what? The woman's nowhere, she's dead in the water!'

'That's exactly it, Nick. So we've got to blow her *out* of the water.'

'And how the hell are we going to do that?'

'Simply do the worst, over-the-top bullshit acting you've ever done,' I said.

'Like what?'

I could see that Nick, who was a sensitive young man and by nature averse to grossness, was struggling to get his head around my suggestion.

'Like gross commedia dell'arte, broad and terrible acting.'

'No way, man, I can't do that!' he said, wide-eyed. 'What about my performance?'

'That was already in the can after the first take, boet.'

'ACTI-O-O-O-N!' was called and we set off again for our meeting with the leading lady.

She walked up the stoep and stopped when she saw us. The Panavision camera on the long tracks stopped. Everything stopped. And then Nick shouted very loudly: 'Your husband's fuckin' D-E-E-A-A-D! He was gored by a fucking buffalo bull!'

A look of true shock spread over her face. Her mouth was moving almost imperceptibly but with no sound coming out.

I then spoke my own line as gently as I could. 'It all happened very suddenly and quickly. He did not suffer at all.'

And then the leading lady burst into tears. Everyone was deeply moved. Behind me I heard a breathy, 'Yes, yes, yes!' It was the director jumping up and down.

Some months later, I was sailing to Japan on a Safmarine container ship that, for a price, took passengers on board. At Port Klang in Malaysia, I left the ship to go into the town. On the quayside, a scrawny man was squatting beside a pile of DVDs that were for sale. And there, way before the film's release in Hollywood, was a rough copy of the movie. I bought it and played it when I got back to the ship, fast forwarding to *that* scene. There it was, a little hazy at the edges and with poor sound, but still the real deal. It would blow you clean out of the water.

When it comes to intimate relationships with fellow actors on movie sets, the line I have always taken is: never consummate a relationship while the movie is still being shot. However, I have often worked on films where there is almost *no* distance between the actors, where everybody 'loooves' each other, where the director is so cool and nice, and the leading man is shacked up with the leading lady. On such sets I sometimes feel as if there is something wrong with me, that I don't have enough 'looove' in me, or that I am incapable of having meaningful relationships with all the beautiful people on set.

I've noticed, however, that often those movies turn out to be quite boring when they hit the screen. They seem to have no fire, no knife – no edge. I firmly believe that great storytelling needs some confrontation: it requires friction both in the script and between the people involved in the telling of the story. Philosophers or psychiatrists might tell you the reasons why, but I just know it to be so.

Sexual tension is one of those languages that all audiences instinctively understand without thinking too much about it. Words can describe the feeling, but its essence is beyond words. I have always known that if the female and male lead characters in a movie do not consummate their sexual attraction to each other in the script, it is a big mistake to do so off set. That is when you should remind yourself that the movie comes first.

As the production of *Arende* progressed, so did my relationship with Michelle Botes. We knew there was something very special between us, but for some reason we kept our relationship platonic. Not consummating our love for each other helped us – and our characters – to live in the sea of promise. It is a very energising way of being, and in acting it can be used to attain a heightened sense of being. This indescribable 'something' speaks to the subconscious of an audience and awakens their curiosity. It is also crucial to maintain it, especially if a movie needs that sexual tension to keep the audience locked in all the way to the end.

As I've mentioned, 'the movie comes first' is a helpful maxim to rely on when destructive emotions start flying around on set. And such emotions can also fly around on stage during theatre productions. I vividly recall how emotional actors, actresses, directors, stage hands and playwrights could become when we got to the end of a run. As the dressing room resounded with declarations of love and exclamations of how desperately everybody would miss each other, again, I was often the odd one out. I was only too happy to slip out after a final performance. Coming to the same stage to play the same character night after night would become a sort of bondage from which I would look forward to freeing myself. I'd usually set off into the night on my own, driving in whichever direction my car was pointed – as long as it was out of town. Sometimes the destination would be unknown, but those escapes have led me on some great escapades.

Actors often have a tough time with the public, especially if they portray characters who fire up the imagination. Actors who have played the baddies in soap operas have some of the best stories to tell about how members of the public struggle to distinguish between them as individuals and the characters they have played.

This became apparent to me one day in 1984 while we were on location in the West Coast village of Paternoster shooting a TV series for the SABC called *Die Seeduiker*. On this day, the legendary West Coast fog rolled in off the icy Atlantic Ocean, and eventually it became so thick that we could no longer see the lighthouse. We hung around for a while, but when it became obvious that the fog was not going to lift, the director, Jan Engelen, decided to call it a wrap.

We had a day off! This was quite unusual on an SABC shoot, because the budgets were tight, so most people got into their cars to return to Saldanha, where we were staying. The next moment, stuntman Jannie Wienand stood in front of me with a naughty smile on his face, his blue eyes twinkling brightly.

'Ja, ou Ianie … What are your plans? You know, soon it's gonna be ten o'clock and then the bar is gonna open. Why don't you and me have a dop?'

Just then the doors to the bar at the Paternoster Hotel swung open and in we went. The owner, a swarthy, dark-haired man with an Italian name, was still cleaning up the mess of the night before, but he gave us cold beers anyway. Inside the bar were things he had gathered over years

As captain Ben Stals in the television series *Seeduiker*.

of partying, which included pairs of panties, from different countries, hanging from the rafters.

Jannie and I quickly fell into a pleasureland where time passes without anyone really noticing. Soon other people came to the bar and we were having a fat jol. But, at about 1 am, a group of men entered who exuded a darker, more negative vibe. They were physically big guys, all in their mid-twenties. Even in my happy, inebriated state I noticed they wore a sort of uniform, which made me wary. In the interests of uninterrupted jolling, I decided I would avoid them, but not Jannie: he was in full swing.

'Hallo, manne! Weet julle wie dié ou is? Hy is die famous akteur Ian Roberts.' (Hello, guys! Do you know who this guy is? He is the famous actor Ian Roberts.)

Oh, stuff it, Jannie, I thought, why are you blowing my cover? Can't you see they are full of nonsense?

But it was too late. By then Jannie had called me over to meet the uniformed group of young men. 'These ouks are police reservists. They are just the kind of people you want to be friends with if the shit hits the fan,' Jannie said, sounding very pleased with himself.

After shaking the hands of about four of them, I found myself facing a large man who, unlike the others, decided against getting to his feet to greet me.

He lounged in his chair like a slothful bear as he smiled crookedly at me. Like any well-mannered St Andrew's College boy would do, I leant forward to shake his hand, which was big enough to hold a dinner plate. His fingers were more like big pieces of boerewors, with forests of black hair growing between the knuckles. His hand enfolded mine, but instead of releasing it, he held on and pulled me a little off balance. I quickly shuffled my feet into a balanced boxer's stance so as not to be compromised if he pulled again … which is exactly what the big man did.

He looked me straight in the eye.

'Sê my net een ding, boetie … het jy vir Pop genaai?' (Just tell me one thing, pal … did you fuck Pop?)

Recall that Pop le Roux was the lead female character in *Verspeelde Lente*, which had aired on SABC in 1983 and was avidly followed by Afrikaans audiences. In it, I played the role of Pop's lover, Hermaans Cronjé, while Elize Cawood played the role of Pop (meaning 'doll' in Afrikaans). Elize had been beguiling in the role, with her auburn hair and simple, threadbare clothes that hid a budding sensuality. She fired up the testosterone levels in many a viewer (and crew member on set) as the series played out weekly over 13 episodes. In those days, sex scenes were taboo on television, but the sexual tension between Pop and Hermaans was palpable and one of the scenes strongly hinted at their consummating their love.

I suppose I should have been happy: as actors, Elize and I had succeeded, because the giant in front of me had been taken in by our characterisations. Still, I realised his question was loaded and there was no easy way out. If I answered 'yes', he would *donder* (hit) me with his fat left hand because *he* had fallen in love with Pop and I was messing with *his* woman. If I answered 'no', I would still be in the shit because he would *donder* me for being a 'fokken moffie' (fucking nancy).

Theatre work teaches actors to think at lightning speed when something bombs out on stage and thankfully my experience came to my aid in that moment.

'Kyk meneer,' I said, 'Pop is nie eintlik Pop nie … sy is net 'n karakter gespeel deur die aktrise Elize Cawood. En Hermaans Cronjé is nie eintlik Hermaans nie. Hy is 'n karakter in 'n teks wat ek vertolk het. En Ian Roberts het nooit vir Elize Cawood genaai nie …' (Look, sir, Pop isn't really Pop … she is just a character played by the actress Elize

Cawood. And Hermaans Cronjé isn't really Hermaans. He is a character in a text that I portrayed. And Ian Roberts never fucked Elize Cawood.)

Boereworsvingers looked at me long and hard as if he had been cheated.

'Jy dink jy's foooh-kin slim, nè?' (You think you're fucking smart, hey?) he said as he released my hand, to my great astonishment.

I moved as far away from him as I could. I motioned to Jannie that we should get the hell out of there, but Jannie was having a ball. I was in a pickle since he had the car and Saldanha was a long way to walk. So, I stayed, but I stopped drinking immediately. I wanted to be quick on my feet should something happen. I realised that the 'sex scene' in *Verspeelde Lente* evoked such intense feelings for the police reservist that he now saw me as a threat.

While I was sobering up, everybody in the bar was getting increasingly soused. At a certain point, I looked over to see the indomitable Jannie engaging in a *vingertrek* (finger wrestling) competition with the giant, who now stood on the other side of the bar with the owner, who seemed to be a friend of his. Poor Jannie's scrawny fingers were quite crooked from all the motorbike falls and mistimed stunt punches. The next moment I heard his forefinger make a sickening 'thwick!' sound as it was straightened by the giant's boerewors fingers.

'Oukei, jy't daardie een gewen, ou pel, maar nou challenge ek jou vir armdruk!' (Okay, you won that one, mate, but now I challenge you to arm wrestle!) Jannie shouted with gay abandon.

I couldn't believe his audacity.

'Ag nee, man, lossit' (Ahh no, man, leave it), the giant declined and turned his back on Jannie.

'Kamman!' (Come on!) Jannie said, wanting to make good for getting his finger so brutally straightened. But the giant seemed deaf to Jannie's challenge and walked off.

I was still trying to figure out what to do next when the mad red-haired Irishman inside me chose to speak.

'Lafaard!' (Coward!) my mouth said loudly, contemptuously. Boereworsvingers heard it, but what was worse was that everyone else in the bar also heard it. The room became deathly quiet. Boereworsvingers turned round slowly to face me.

'Wat de fok het jy gesê?' (What the fuck did you say?) shooting a look of total destruction at me.

Shut up, you Irish prick! I said to myself. This is a very dangerous situation! I realised that I was cornered at the far end of the bar. The toilets were behind me, but I remembered that the windows were high and difficult to escape through. I could already see the headline in the newspapers: 'Actor found beaten to a pulp in Paternoster.'

Not that the Irishman was afraid at all. He kept talking. 'Ek het gesê jy's 'n lafaard. Jy't nou net die man se vinger getrek, hoekom is jy nou bang om sy arm te druk?' (I said you're a coward. You just finger-wrestled the man; why are you now scared to arm-wrestle him?)

The giant roared with rage as he erupted in an explosion of movement. Vaulting clean over the bar, he bounded towards me to throw a killer right-hand punch at my head. But I was already sobered up and raging on adrenaline. I was too quick for him and ducked easily under his punch, which, if it had connected, would have smashed me straight into the afterlife. At the same time, I did some fancy footwork to evade him, moving quickly towards the left and in the direction of the promised land: The Exit.

Suddenly, as if by magic, Jannie came between us.

'Ek sê jou wat, ek speel jou 101 en as ek jou wen dan los jy my vriend uit, oukei?' (I tell you what, I'll play you 101 and if I win you then leave my friend alone, okay?)

I was trapped. Jannie the Stuntman was now the ringmaster of his own dangerous circus as he played a game of darts with me as the prize. Neither Boereworsvingers nor Jannie was very steady on his feet, yet miraculously Jannie managed to hit the double that was supposed to buy my freedom. I was relieved that we could finally get the hell out of there, but it was not to be.

'Kom uit my pad uit, dwerg!' (Get out of my way, dwarf!) the giant roared, shoving Jannie so violently out of his way that Jannie had to use all his stunt experience to avoid serious injury.

With murder in his eyes, Boereworsvingers stomped towards me. This is it, now he's going to kill me, I thought sadly. But, incredibly, Jannie rose from the floor and, moving as fast as only a stuntman can, grabbed the cop by the lapels of his jacket.

'Nee, nee, nee, boetie! Wat maak jy nou? Ons het mos 'n deal gehad!' (No, no, no, brother. What are you doing? We had a deal!) and then began bulldozing him backwards towards the wall, which was thankfully near the exit.

It looked like some Charlie Chaplin comedy: Jannie was literally half his size, but Boereworsvingers was helpless to stop his ever-gathering backward momentum. He crashed into some coat hangers that were fixed to the wall and slid down to the floor, groaning in agony.

'Kom, Ianie, hardloop, my maat!' (Come on, Ianie, run, my friend!), shouted Jannie. I needed no further encouragement. A refreshing cold drizzle fell on us as we ran wildly to Jannie's Toyota Corolla. As we ripped the doors open and jumped in, the drunken police reservists and some bar patrons came running after us, shouting warnings of dire retribution. The Toyota's wheels spun in the dirt as we raced down the road. Jannie and I hid in the cellar of the Saldanha Hotel for a couple of days until they stopped searching for us.

We later heard that Boereworsvingers had sustained heavy damage to his spinal column. Apparently, he was stuck in hospital for quite a while.

'Too bad,' said Jannie with a dismissive sniff when he was told the news. 'Hy't kak gesoek en kak het hy gekry.' (He was looking for shit and shit is what he got.)

And Pop le Roux came out of all of this with her honour intact.

15

An honorary Afrikaner

ONE DAY IN THE EARLY 1980s, on the set of *Dokter Con Viljee se Overberg*, I was drinking coffee with two renowned Afrikaans actors, Jannie Gildenhuys and Limpie Basson.

'Jy weet, seun,' Jannie said to me in his calm, sophisticated voice, 'soos hulle sê, jy's Ingels gebore, maar eintlik is jy 'n Boer' (You know, son, you might have been born English, but you're actually a Boer).

'Ja, eend, in jou hart is jy eintlik 'n Boer' (Yes, Ian, at heart you are a Boer) Limpie chimed in, nodding, replacing my name with the Afrikaans word for 'goose'.

My years as a screen actor have therefore made me realise not only how powerful a medium TV is, but also how important it is to choose the roles you play and in which productions.

Screenwriter Julia Cameron writes about what she calls the artist's 'vein of gold'. In the world of the performing arts, actors also have a vein of gold – a type of character they can play exceptionally well and which seems like a natural fit. Looking back on my early years as a professional actor, however, I remember that this is precisely what my fellow actors and I rebelled against. As up-and-coming stage actors, we could not conceive of the idea that we should be typecast or play only one kind of character. One of the (perhaps ironic) benefits of being an actor in South Africa is that you often have no choice but to play whatever role you're offered. Because of financial pressures, just to survive, you must take on roles that don't always 'sit right' with you.

However, in many ways Sloet Steenkamp was my vein of gold, and thankfully it didn't lead to my being typecast thereafter. After my performance in *Arende*, I became extremely popular in the Afrikaans community, and it was mostly thanks to Sloet that I became something of an honorary Afrikaner to many people.

Over the years, I have been approached by many smiling members of the public, their eyes shining with joy at having finally met 'Sloet'. Barry Steenkamp, the bass player in Die Radio Kalahari Orkes, often tells me: 'As jy R10 gevra het vir elke foto wat mense saam met jou wou neem, was jy vandag 'n miljoenêr.' (If you asked R10 for each photo people wanted to take with you, you would be a millionaire by now.)

There is some truth in that, especially since the advent of smartphones with cameras. I'm happy to oblige, though; if I can bring some joy or positivity into people's lives by posing for a photo, then so be it.

The Austrian poet and novelist Rainer Maria Rilke said, 'I hold this to be the highest task for a bond between two people: that each should stand guard over the solitude of the other.' Applied to my life as an actor, I take the other person in the bond to be the public in general. The actor is caught in a dilemma – to be successful, you need an audience and to be financially successful, the bigger the audience, the better. The downside is that this can compromise one's privacy and the opportunity to find solitude.

It does help that in South Africa celebrity means something different from what it means in, say, the US. When I was in Los Angeles in 1988, I was taken to a bar by Sam Jones, who had recently played the lead role in *Flash Gordon*. Everything was fine for the first couple of Coronas, but then a girl recognised Sam and we were basically hounded out of there by wannabe actresses and fans. Locally, I had a taste of major celebrity when I worked on *King Solomon's Mines* and wanted to have dinner with Patrick Swayze at a restaurant at the V&A Waterfront. I had to organise a private room to prevent us from getting swamped before we had the seafood soup.

With me, it has never been like that, mainly because South Africans are not as celebrity-crazy. Afrikaans people, for example, often first apologise for invading my privacy, which I appreciate as being very respectful, and it makes me respectful in turn. Often I am approached by a well-mannered young man or woman, who simply want to tell me how much they appreciate the roles I've played. 'En wat is jou naam?' (And what is your name?) I would inquire. 'Ag, ek is niemand' (Ag, I'm just a nobody), to which I would respond, 'Nobody is a nobody!'

As I mentioned earlier, during my research for the role of Sloet Steenkamp I read up a lot about the Anglo-Boer War and became intrigued by what I saw as the Afrikaners' pioneer spirit and their quest for independence. The entire 36-episode saga of Sloet Steenkamp and all the wonderful characters created for the series were about one thing – the drive to escape. Sloet couldn't stand being contained and neither could the Dutch farmers, or Voortrekkers, who decided to leave the British-controlled Cape Colony for the hinterland between 1835 and 1840. They tried to escape the tentacles of the British colonial octopus by establishing their two republics of the Free State and the Transvaal.

The British took their highly developed class system with them wherever they went and imposed it rigidly. I suppose the most enduring example of their intransigent hard-headedness would be the network of blockhouses they erected across South Africa in an attempt to curb Boer resistance during the Anglo-Boer War.

I can't help but think that the modern equivalent of the great escape by the independence-loving Boers is the waves of emigration of Afrikaners to Canada, Australia, the US, New Zealand, Argentina and even England. What a loss to our country!

Several years ago, my cousin Dan Roberts emigrated to the UK, but after six years he came back home and, together with Rian Malan (also a recent returnee), began writing songs in Afrikaans. I was very surprised by this development and asked him why he now suddenly wrote in Afrikaans. 'As a bilingual South African, if I wrote a song in English about an experience in London, the resultant point of view would be broad and could easily have been written by someone who comes from the broader English-speaking diaspora across the globe,' Dan explained. 'However, when I write in Afrikaans, the point of view immediately becomes very specifically a point of view of a South African, because Afrikaans only exists there in any meaningful way. This voice implies a perspective that is more "embedded in the soil" and is aimed at an audience that is very specifically located and experienced.'

If one looks at the character of Sloet Steenkamp, he is also very 'embedded in the soil', and the same can be said of Boet from the Castrol ads. I think it might be this understated, earthy quality, which I have managed to portray, that has captivated different South Africans – from petrol pump attendees in the early hours of the morning in Aliwal North to drunken locals in a bar in Hopetown to highbrow businessmen from Pretoria. The attraction to this quality transcends race and language.

The one thing I know for sure, is that I am rooted in Africa. In 1992, I spent several weeks in England while we were shooting *The Power of One* for Warner Brothers. We stayed in a high-end hotel in Guildford, a town southwest of London, which even has an old castle in its centre. On off days, I walked many kilometres exploring the countryside and other towns. Despite my supposedly English background, I recall feeling very strongly that I didn't really belong there at all.

Today I live in Lydenburg with my Afrikaans sweetheart and her family and my two young twins, who speak Afrikaans as their first language. My mother once pointed out to me how much she valued the way Afrikaners expressed emotion, instead of concealing it like us, which was the English way. Afrikaans speakers are such a diverse group, and to hold a stereotypical view of them would be a sad misjudgement. There is much that I appreciate about Afrikaners; perhaps that is why I have liked trying to portray them in different series and movies.

The truth is that I've always been something of a chameleon. For a boy who grew up essentially English and was educated at an Anglican Church school, it was a great step forward to act not only in Afrikaans but also in Xhosa and Zulu. It was all made possible by my first tribe: the Hunter-Gatherers of Baddaford Citrus Estates.

According to apartheid laws, black, coloured and Indian actors were not allowed to act in white art theatres. This led to the sad and strange situation where white actors had to perform the roles of black characters. The first experience I had of this was in 1981, when I was selected to play a black character in Capab's production of *Die Swerfjare van Poppie Nongena*, which was based on the award-winning novel by Elsa Joubert (adapted for the stage by Sandra Kotze). The irony is that this book highlighted the plight of black South Africans as a result of the Group Areas Act.

Lida Meiring played the main character, a domestic worker called Poppie, and Willem de la Querra, Marthinus Basson and I played Poppie's black family (Brümilda van Rensburg and Marko van der Colff played the white characters). 'Hoekom moet ons nou hierdie swart mense se rolle vertolk? Laat hulle dit self doen' (Why do we have to perform the roles of these black characters? They should do it themselves), said Marthinus, who generally avoided politics but had a strong moral compass. We refrained from painting our faces black, but we effectively became Afrikaans-speaking black people.

Although I have always been fluent in Xhosa, my involvement with vernacular languages, or 'vernac' as people refer to African languages in the movie business, officially began in the mid-1980s. In 1986, I was cast as a character in the TV series *Kwela Man* and had to act in Xhosa. I played the role of the boxer Blood Steyn who, in the final episode, has a big pro fight with the lead character, played by the late Joko Scott. By then, I had already shared many a stage with Joko, who hailed from Gugulethu in Cape Town.

One day, while we were busy shooting the final episode, Joko became overexcited, hopping about from foot to foot like a professional boxer. Minutes before, his hands had been bandaged like a boxer's. He glared at me: 'Today, mlungu! Haaaa! Today I am going to shaya you properly, ndiza kubeth' unye, jou fokken Boer' (Today, whitey! Haaaa! Today I am going to hit you properly, so that you shit, you damn Boer).

He was obviously looking forward to knocking Blood Steyn into oblivion in the tenth round. This was the first but not the last time that I would be referred to as a 'fokken Boer'. Even though I had no Afrikaner roots, I refrained from correcting Joko. I also didn't tell him that I had done a lot of boxing back in the day. At a certain point, Joko failed to 'ride'– or dodge – my punch. My right hand crunched into his jaw, lifting him upwards. He crashed to the ring floor, already semi-conscious. Soon enough, he went back to addressing me as 'Mfondini bra Ian' (Dear friend Ian).

My next involvement with a Xhosa role came in 1988 when I directed my first TV series for the SABC. It was called *Iliwa Libhek' Umoya* (literally, The Cliff Watches the Wind). This was followed by *Inkom' Edla Yodwa* (literally, The Bull That Eats Alone) in 1989, in which I performed my first leading role in Zulu: I played an officer in the prison service, Lieutenant Koot Laurens, alongside the by then famous Henry Cele, who played Saul Gumede, a prisoner. Shortly before, Henry had shot to stardom for his performance as King Shaka in the immensely popular series *Shaka Zulu*.

Zulu and Xhosa are both Nguni languages, so my fluency in Xhosa gave me the grace to take on the challenge, but my quest to sound convincing in Zulu cost me very many late nights learning words and perfecting my pronunciation. Being able to speak the lines, I realised, was just the beginning, for to act in a language like Zulu, you have to strive to become Zulu in your entire being. For instance, how do you express yourself with hand movements and how do you hold your head when you speak? Even if you get the dialogue right, you won't be convincing if you don't get these things right.

As Lieutenant Koot Laurens, I would do a scene with Henry in pure Zulu inside the prison; then the location would shift to the administration building and my character would do a scene in Afrikaans in the office of the governor, played by Afrikaans actor Kerneels Koertzen, in which we would interact as Afrikaners. Later in the day, I would do a scene with the prison chaplain in English. I had to work hard at maintaining continuity in the character of Lieutenant Koot as he passed through all these different realities. There is no university degree or guidebook on Google for how to do this – either you get it right, or you don't.

Over the years, my portrayals of Xhosa or Zulu characters, or white characters who spoke these two languages, became immensely popular in black communities. Despite my white skin, African viewers seemed to accept my transformation each time. *Inkom' Edla Yodwa* was so popular that when it came close to the final (13th) episode of the series, viewers became so upset at the thought that the story was going to end that they started to place pressure on the SABC to give them more. The national broadcaster eventually gave in and broadcast the entire series again.

My ability to speak Xhosa led to another interesting role, this time in the long-running Afrikaans soapie *Egoli*, produced by Franz Marx. I was offered the unlikely role of Don, a wealthy Afrikaans man who comes into the life of Louwna, the leading lady, played by Brümilda van Rensburg. Don suffers a serious stroke but survives and makes a slow recovery.

Initially, Don cannot speak, but after a while his speech returns. However, he can only communicate in the first language he ever spoke – Xhosa. Like me, Don had grown up on a farm in the Eastern Cape. As part of my research for the role, I investigated how some stroke victims suffer paralysis of the mouth and struggle to speak. There was a big chance that I might make a complete arse out of myself, but the money was good and I took the challenge.

Now, it is no joke trying to play a white man in a wheelchair who can only speak Xhosa through a stroke-skewed mouth. One day, I was doing a scene as Don with Nenna (played by Shaleen Surtie-Richards) and a young blonde actress from East London. Louis van Niekerk was the man on the studio floor who relayed messages from 'the box above' (where the director and editors sat) down to us actors. The first take had gone quite well, I thought, but then Louis told us we had to do another take.

This was not unusual on a soapie, so we did a second take. Again, Louis listened to the voice in his headphones. We had to do yet another take, he explained. I thought the two we had already done had gone according to plan, so three takes was pushing it.

'Hoekom moet ons nou nog een doen?' (Why should we do another one?) asked Shaleen.

Louis cocked his head, apparently listening even closer to his headphones.

'Ian, jy speel 'n bietjie over the top' (Ian, your performance is too over the top) he said.

On the fourth take, I pulled my mouth less crooked and twitched a bit less. After they called 'cut', Louis still cupped his hands over the headphones. Then he cleared his throat.

'Julle moet nóg 'n take doen' (You have to do *another* take).

Shaleen and I looked at each other. What the hell?

'Hoekom dié keer?' (What's the matter this time?) I asked.

'Meneer Roberts, jy speel nog steeds heeltemaal over the top' (Mr Roberts, you're still overacting) Louis said.

I had had enough. 'Wie sê so?' (Who says so?)

'Meneer Marx' (Mr Marx), he replied.

'Sê vir meneer Marx ek wil hom nóú sien' (Tell Mr Marx I want to see him right away), I said and rose up out of the wheelchair. Louis led me out past the cast, who were all shocked to silence – in the almost twenty years of *Egoli*'s existence, no one had ever dared take on 'meneer Marx'.

I walked past the remonstrating secretary into Frans's hallowed office, where he sat behind his expansive desk. As I entered, he promptly started raging at me. I listened to him silently, still struggling to understand what had prompted his attack. I looked over at Louis, who leant against the wall with his head hanging. I could swear he has a smile on his face.

Eventually, Frans ran out of steam and fell back in his chair, breathing heavily and glaring at me. Now it was my time to speak.

'Nou ja, baie dankie, Frans, vir jou exposé oor hoe goed 'n akteur jy is en daarby hoe sleg 'n akteur ek is' (Now then, thank you, Frans, for your exposé on how good an actor you are and how bad an actor I am).

Franz had a smug look on his face. Clearly, he thought he had won the battle. I continued.

'Maar sê my net een ding, Frans: Het jy al ooit in jou groot ervaring as 'n akteur 'n swart man gespeel? En nogal in Xhosa ook?' (But just tell me one thing, Frans: in your vast experience as an actor, have you ever played a black man? And in Xhosa, too?)

He folded his hands behind his head.

'En sê my, het jy ooit in jou groot ervaring al die kans gehad om 'n man te speel wat 'n stroke gehad het?' (And tell me, have you, in your vast experience, ever had the chance to play a man who has had a stroke?)

At this point, Frans was starting to look rather glum.

'Nou vra ek jou, Frans: Hoe op aarde kan jy vir my probeer sê hoe om die rol te speel?' (I'm asking you, Frans: how on earth can you try to tell me how to play it?)

Franz started ranting again about my arrogance, but I silenced him by holding my finger in front of my mouth. 'Shush, shush!' I said and turned around. As we walked back to the set, Louis looked at me and whispered under his breath, 'Jy't die man goed gesê, boetie' (You really showed him, brother).

We did a fifth take and I played the character pretty much the way I had done in the first place. But this time without any comeback.

In the early 2000s, I was cast as Sir Henry Curtis in an American television adaptation of *King Solomon's Mines*, which aired in 2004. I acted alongside Patrick Swayze, as I mentioned before, and Alison Doody. It was shot in different locations in South Africa, starting in the Eastern Cape, then in Prince Albert in the Karoo and in Stellenbosch.

I got on very well with Patrick and we would sometimes talk deep into the night about life, love and everything else. He never drank anything stronger than Coke and told me how he had decided to turn his life around after he was once found in a gutter, soused out of his mind. I told him about my own relationship with alcohol. He had been taken to rehab. I had fallen into a depression for a year but eventually managed to heal myself.

One day in the stony Karoo, near Prince Albert, a stunt had to take place in which Patrick's character, Allan Quatermain, rides a horse down a steep and, needless to say, rocky hillside to a small hut where the blonde Alison is being held captive by the baddies. He was supposed to gallop up to the hut under fire, pull the girl up into the saddle and ride away with her. South Africa's best horse stuntman, Gavin Mey, who had saved my ass many times before on productions involving horse stunts, was hired to do this dangerous scene.

However, the horse simply froze when faced with the steep rocky crags, and Gavin couldn't do the scene. The director, Steve Boyum, who incidentally had been a stuntman on Francis Ford Coppola's magnificent *Apocalypse Now*, started changing the shot to make it safer and more acceptable to Gavin, when Patrick said, 'I'll do that shot for you, Steve.'

Now, on the average American production, this would never happen, since it would be too expensive should the leading man get hurt. Few people know that Patrick, apart from being a great dancer, was also an accomplished horseman. Steve, amazed at Patrick's guts, agreed. Everyone watched, their hearts in their mouths, as Patrick rode the horse through the death-defying shot in one take. For some reason, the horse went along with it this time. 'Patrick, that is the bravest thing I've ever seen a man do,' was all I could say.

Another cast member was the actor Gavin Hood, who also directed movies. He played the role of Bruce McNabb, one of the bad guys. Once, when we shared a moment on set, he told me he was working on a movie script based on a novel by Athol Fugard. I would often come upon him and two other actors working late into the night; it was on the set of *King Solomon's Mines* that the film script for *Tsotsi* was born.

A few months later, I got the role of Captain Smit, the long-suffering cop who eventually takes down the main character Tsotsi, played by Presley Chweneyagae. My fluency in Xhosa and (to a lesser degree) Zulu helped a lot, since Gavin intended to submit the movie for the Oscars in their foreign-language film category. A great percentage of the script therefore had to be in a language other than English, which in this case was Zulu, Afrikaans, Xhosa, bits of Tswana, Pedi, Sotho, and so on.

Once we got started, I soon realised certain things did not translate easily from English into Xhosa. In the scene where Tsotsi is captured, Captain Smit shouts at Tsotsi to stop, levelling his 9 mm pistol. The English text read, 'Put your hands on your head' and I decided to translate it directly into Xhosa – 'Bek' izandla zakho ngaphez' kwentloko!' However, this would be a highly unlikely thing for a South African cop to say in a high-pressure situation. 'Stop, jou bliksem!' (Stop, you bugger) would probably have been more appropriate. Although Captain Smit's Afrikaans was also allowed to slip in, I decided, strangely, that he should speak Xhosa in that moment. Many black South Africans still remember me for that line, and I'm often called 'Mr Bek' izandla zakho ngaphez' kwentloko' at filling stations and supermarkets!

Tsotsi won the award for the Best Foreign Language Film at the 2006 Oscars.

I don't remember much about my acting career in the late 1980s and early 1990s – when we filmed the second and third seasons of *Arende*. There is a distinct reason for this: my family and I were exposed to a horrifying experience that, I believe, caused a lot of stress and, as a consequence, some kind of amnesia with me. Michelle and I had been together for a few years and Cara, our blonde-haired baby girl, was two years old when three men broke into our rented house on a farm north of Honeydew in the dark of the night. The main antagonist was a slightly built Zulu-speaking man.

I remember waking up with the cold steel muzzle of a pump-action 12-bore shotgun thrust between my eyes. The man was backlit by the light in the passage and screamed blue murder at me.

'Jou fokken Boer! I will kill you! Where is your guns? Jou fokken Boer! Where is your money?!'

In situations such as these, it doesn't help to point out that you are actually English-speaking, *not* Afrikaans, and that you have absolutely *no* guns and, being a South African actor with a wife and a young child, *no* money to speak of. To our attackers, I was simply another white man and therefore, a *fokken* Boer. The next moment they pushed me to the floor and tied me to the bed with telephone cables.

It didn't help that Cara, in her innocence, suddenly piped up in Afrikaans: 'Skiet hulle, Pappa!' (Shoot them, daddy!)

My daughter's words sent the main attacker into a frenzied search for guns, but I didn't own a single gun. Yet they ransacked everything, even climbing into the roof. While their ranting got louder, Michelle calmly spoke up.

'If you kill him, you won't get any guns. If you *don't* kill him, you *still* won't get any guns.'

As soon as she said this, the main attacker lunged at her, pulled her out of the bed and slammed her into the wall. He held a knife at her throat.

'Fokkof, njakazi!' (Fuck off, bitch!) he screamed.

When he allowed her to sit on the bed again, she blandly asked him for a cigarette, which he begrudgingly put in her mouth.

'And now? How must I smoke this?' she said as he walked away.

The thug returned, loosened her hands and lit the cigarette, but I was still face down, tied to the bed. We're all dead anyway, I thought. At that moment, I realised that I had to calm myself down, so I started by breathing deeply. The less aggressive of the attackers came and stared at me in the half-light.

'Are you dying, heh? Fok jou, man! Why you breathe like that, heh?'

That was the moment the mad red-haired Irishman inside me came to life and started speaking – not in English or Afrikaans, but this time in Zulu. In a low, deep voice he said, 'Kepha nina ningazenzi kabi … ngoba thina singabantu abaziwayo la eMzantsi' (You guys must be careful what you do to us, because we are well known people in South Africa).

The main gun-wielding aggressor, who seemed to ooze nastiness, began screaming again.

'Voetsek, jou fokken Boer!' (Fuck off, you fucking Boer!)

But the Irishman kept talking. In a voice that was not mine, he spoke from a place beyond fear.

'Ngiyanichazele kahle, musa ukusenzela kabi' (I am telling you nicely, do not do bad things to us).

'Fokkof, jou fokken Boer! I will kill you!'

As the attacker tried to shout me into silence, I saw his finger on the trigger. An explosion would mean my end, but I did not care anymore. I was already emotionally dead, so I kept on going.

'We are very well-known actors in this country. If you hurt us, you will suffer the consequences if the police catch you. Hurt us at your peril.'

So continued the fearless Irishman until, eventually, the aggressor simply gave up. I suspect my droning voice might have unnerved him. They left us alone for longer and longer periods, and eventually they left with the stolen goods. They loaded my Land Rover station wagon with everything they could take, but then couldn't manage its old-fashioned 'crash' gearbox, so they left it standing in the middle of the road. The attackers made their escape in Michelle's Mini Minor, which could only carry them, our custom-made wedding rings, my German binoculars, a TV and a kettle.

The next morning, the cops were amazed that we were relatively unscathed. They said that, statistically, we had had a twenty-to-one chance of surviving the ordeal physically unharmed. It was a sad assumption on the part of our attackers that I was rich and owned guns, but, if that was how the world saw me, I was proud to be a 'fokken Boer'.

16

A can of the best

IN THE LATE 1980S. JOBURG was a great city to be in if you were an actor, as the arts were thriving. Apart from opportunities in television and film productions, advertisements for television also paid well. There was also a system whereby royalties had to be paid to actors if the ad was so successful that it kept running for a second season.

In 1988, Castrol decided to set aside a big budget to make an innovative television advertisement for a new motor oil. At the time there was a sort of creative flush in the air, and I could almost feel it as I made my way to the auditions for the Castrol ad in Rosebank.

Norman Anstey was auditioning for the character I eventually ended up playing, and I was auditioning for the role he was to play, that of a garage owner in the middle of the Kalahari. After the first run on camera, the director decided to swap the roles around, since he thought that would work best. He wasn't wrong.

Shortly after the audition, we set out for Bophuthatswana, one of the so-called homelands created for black South Africans by the apartheid government. Our location was to the north of Hotazel. There, in the sandy Kalahari, a large tented camp had been erected. There was a big catering tent, which had a well-stocked bar. On the night of our arrival, there was one hell of a party.

It was booze, *boom* and lots of cocaine on that dark night. People who were mostly suburban operators now found themselves way out there in a strange Kalahari world. No traffic, no nothing – just thorn trees and fresh air. Nobody back home would know what was going down around the fires among the camelthorn trees, because the closest phone was 80 kilometres away.

During that night of wild abandon, I was offered numerous lines of cocaine, but I turned down all of them. The idea of sniffing anything else than that wondrous fresh air seemed gratuitous to me. Many bright-eyed, overenergised people told me how much I was missing out, but I felt very happy and free.

We had the luxury of three whole days to shoot the ad. So, on the first day, a rehearsal was called to prepare for the first day of shooting, which would take place the following day. Most people were nursing a hangover as we convened in the sandy track in front of the set – an imaginatively constructed roadside garage, cleverly named the Horingboom Oasis, created by set designer Marlene Ming. The garage stood in the shade of a giant camelthorn tree on the edge of the track. The Horingboom Oasis was a garage-cum-trading-store-cum-bar where the traveller could find diesel, petrol and human company, and, more importantly, oil. The goal of the ad was to launch Castrol's new GTX2 motor oil.

The director was Jonathan Taylor, a cool dude with blue eyes and blond hair and a good sense of humour. 'Good morning, guys. So, tomorrow we're gonna start shooting this baby. Beautiful set, hey?'

Norman and I nodded in appreciation. Jonathan was handed a much-needed coffee before he proceeded to ask us what we thought of the script. I had been mulling over the two pages for some days. 'I think the script is good,' I said. 'But there's just one thing that is bothering me.'

'Yeah? What's that?'

'Well, in all the English adverts that I've watched over the years that had to do with people who live on the platteland, the actors always talk in a dumb English kind of way, with a heavy Afrikaans accent.'

By way of example, I said a few lines in the accent.

'Yes, I get it. So?' Jonathan asked.

'I come from the platteland myself. I grew up on a farm and my father is a citrus farmer. What I can tell you is that nobody in the rural parts of the country, Afrikaans or English, is dumb. On the contrary.'

Jonathan looked rather perplexed. 'So?' he asked again.

'I think we should place the English accent in this ad.'

'Place it? Like how?'

'Where I come from in the Eastern Cape there's a way of speaking English that's called the Lower Albany accent. I think we should try that.'

'Let me hear it,' Norman chipped in. 'Give us an example.'

'A can of the best': Filming the famous Castrol advertisements with
Fats Bookholane (Mogae) and Norman Anstey (Swaer).

'Jaaaa, Swaer, y'knauw, this bletty drowt is so bed, y'knauw, it's so damn draaai, I saw the black bass in the little pool of water below mah weir and you won't believe what they was doing …

'Ja? What's thet, Boet?'

'Them fishes were giving each other myouwth to myouwth resussita-a-a-yshun. Swaer, 's true, the Virgin Mary!'

I spoke the words naturally, with a speed of delivery that I had often heard in places like the men's bar at the Two Trees Hotel in Kenton-on-Sea, or the Pig and Whistle in Bathurst, which gave the impression that even though the speaker might be abusing the English language, he was none the less quick of mind.

'That sounds really cool,' said Jonathan enthusiastically. 'What do you think, Norman?'

I had done voice-overs with Norman and, in my view, he was always brilliant in the way he could magically adapt his voice and delivery of a line to satisfy even the most moronic of directors – and of those there were many. I knew that, for Norman, the Lower Albany accent would be easy to do.

'I think it's great. Let's give it a go. Why not?'

In that moment, under the blistering sun on a sandy track out in the Kalahari, the style of the characters in the Castrol advertisement was born. Norman's character became Swaer ('brother-in-law' in Afrikaans) and my character became Boet (Brother). We made a few changes in the dialogue to make it more Lower Albany.

As we started shooting the next day, I found myself giving Boet a kind of speedy, busybody type of energy, both in the way I walked and in the way I spoke. I also drove my bakkie at high speed over the rough sandy track.

Norman played Swaer, the owner of the Horingboom Oasis, with his own kind of energy. His character was a more sedentary man who would watch the world go by, wise to the foibles of mankind. This offset my performance perfectly. With Norman and me both having loads of experience acting in theatre productions, we had the suss to ensure that I never picked up on his energy and he never on mine.

Jonathan Taylor just worked at getting the shots right. He was a calm, confident director.

The basic storyline of the ad was that Boet arrives at Horingboom Oasis asking for motor oil. He insists on Castrol GTX2 ('a can of the best') for his bakkie, which he calls Sarie, but Swaer tells him they have run out. 'When will the oil lorry come?' Boet asks Swaer, who tells him it will be in about a month's time. Boet decides to stay and wait for the oil and makes himself comfortable.

The next scene shows that it's one month later. A beautiful blonde woman, played by Claudia Turgas, drives up the sandy track in her larney Range Rover.

'Hello, Hennie [Swaer's real name], hot today … isn't it?' she says.

At that moment, Boet is in an open-air camp shower next to the garage, showering with his pipe in his mouth (which I thought showed that he had become a bit dilly after waiting so long for the 'oil lorry'). He sees how Swaer eagerly takes out a can of the best from a stash hidden in a container by the petrol pump. He is so shocked that his pipe falls out of his mouth.

'Hey, Swaer, what's going on here? I've been waiting a whole month!' he says as he wraps a towel around his waist and hurriedly walks over to the pump. To which Swaer replies laughingly, 'All right, all right, man, I just wanted a bit of company, Boet!'

Boet then chases Swaer down the sandy road, flanked by the dark green of the camelthorn trees and with only a towel to conceal his family jewels.

It was a classic, very tightly constructed short story – that first advertisement was a complete hit. In a short while, men were ordering a can of the best in bars around the country. And the rest, as they say, is history. Castrol's ad campaign continued for the next 17 years. Each ad was a short vignette based on things that happened in and round the Horingboom Oasis.

It also ensured a steady income for me. With the money I made from the ads, I bought a second-hand turbo-diesel Land Rover (1989 model) and decided to call it Cecil, after my grandfather Cecil McWilliams. It is now approaching the million-kilometre mark, but it's still going. Cecil has been to far-flung places where I doubt any other vehicle has ever been – places where only drones will go today. It has pulled a good few Toyotas out of the mud and once crossed a flooded river in Mozambique while other marooned 4×4 drivers looked on in trepidation. They were

My beloved Land Rover.

sitting in their larney Land Cruisers, their V8 Range Rovers and their Mitsubishi Dakar Rally winners.

And, over all those thousands of kilometres, both on and off road, Cecil the Land Rover used only one type of oil – Castrol.

As the campaign continued, we worked with different directors. Jonathan Taylor moved to Los Angeles and various other directors took over the reins. Some were good, others not so much. There was always the expectation to come up with something equal to, or better than, the first ad. Make no mistake: the pressure on the director was great.

At one point, we shot two ads in one go. One was when we buried 'Skattie', the engine that had given such long and faithful service that Boet and Swaer thought she deserved a 'state burial'. In the ad, they toss a can of the best into Skattie's grave for the life hereafter. This ad was shot in both English and Afrikaans – the only Castrol ad we ever did in Afrikaans. The other ad was the story of Swaer's new 4×4, which he claimed didn't need a can of the best. And, he told an unbelieving Boet, it even came when he called it. Martha – the new 4×4 – was in fact a thoroughbred Kalahari donkey. While we were busy shooting, she merely cast a patient yet knowing glance at all the humans, a look of ancient wisdom and superiority in her eyes.

Over all those years, we only ever threw out one storyline: I had objected because it involved Boet getting stuck in his bakkie. In my experience, Kalahari farmers never get stuck in the sand. They might get stuck in a bar, in the bank or even in church, but never in the sand.

Castrol promptly threw out the proposal.

Over the 17 years we worked on the campaign, we actors were always guided by one principle: 'We do not find *ourselves* funny – it is up to the audience to decide whether we are funny or not.' Over and over, we had to remind ourselves of this golden principle.

It has been said that it is the responsibility of artists to hold up a mirror to society. The hope is that this will give people cause to reflect on themselves. Whether the responsibility for this task also falls on actors and scriptwriters working in advertising is open to discussion. I believe it does.

As the years rolled by, the Castrol ads also started to reflect the political changes that were happening in South Africa. When the first ad aired, in 1988, the National Party still ruled the country, but by the time of the last ad, in 2005, the African National Congress had been elected to power in the first democratic elections. Sometime in the 1990s, we were joined on the stoep of the Horingboom Oasis by the black actor Fats Bookholane. As I recall, the scriptwriters didn't give him a name, but when I wrote scripts for corporates and for the later M-Net series *Kalahari Oasis*, I decided to call his character Mogae, the Tswana name of the Chief Justice of Botswana at the time.

The most telling way in which the new political dispensation was reflected in the Castrol ads was in the dwindling budgets. We shot the first three or four ads far out in the Kalahari, but after 1994 the production team tried to find locations that were cheaper to get to. We began shooting on a vast lime mine near the small town of Pienaarsrivier, about a hundred kilometres north of Pretoria. On this land, a nature reserve surrounding the mine, there were a few camelthorn trees, but they weren't as big as the original one out at the first Horingboom Oasis. We shot the 'French rally driver', 'They all look the same to me' and 'I suppose not everybody's parts need oiling' ads at this location. For these shoots, we stayed at the nearby Carousel Casino, but it just wasn't the same as living in a tented camp in the Kalahari.

In the 'French rally driver' ad a distraught rally driver in a red racing outfit comes walking down the dirt road to the Horingboom Oasis, his racing helmet in his hand. He can only speak French and struggles to explain to Boet and Swaer that he needs a big container of Castrol GTX2.

During the filming, I was offered a spin with national rally champion Serge Damseaux in his rally car. He had been hired for the day in case the production needed to show the rally driver's car in action. We raced around at incredibly high speeds over the sandy track, my heart skipping a few beats. I was so relieved to still be alive when I got out of his car, and the experience completely cured me of my curiosity about rally driving.

Eventually, we had to recreate the look and atmosphere of the Kalahari in a film studio. That was for the 'My China' and the 'Tokolosh' ads. These ads were excellently conceived and scripted by the advertising agency and they worked well. Still, I feel the ads would have benefited immensely if we had been given the chance to go out into the Kalahari to shoot them.

With the immense success of the Castrol ad campaign and the popularity of the characters, we were often approached to do other work as the characters in the Castrol ads. A few years after the first ad aired, Fats, Claudia and I did a corporate shoot at an upmarket bush lodge in the Lowveld. The lodge had recently been built on a rocky ridge and we were shooting a promotional video for it. Its shaded verandahs looked out over the wild bush of the Kruger National Park. One late morning, a few of us were taking a break from shooting at the catering table that was set up behind the main lodge, where there was still some shade.

At some point, Claudia stepped directly into an uncovered drain. As she put weight on her foot, it slid down into the bend in the drain that acts as an odour trap and became stuck. Members of the film crew, conscious that it would cost a lot to reschedule the shoot, tried to pull her out, but they made no headway, even after pulling so hard that she screamed with pain. I tried to break the concrete with hammers and other implements, but it was fresh and very tough.

Eventually, in desperation, they found a company in Nelspruit that would drive out with a jackhammer. However, it would take them three hours to get to the lodge. That was that: Claudia was made as comfortable as possible because the sun was now blazing down on that part of the lodge. Someone put an umbrella over her but it was still a bad situation.

Then, as happens when nothing can be done about a bad situation for a while, people started to move off. I decided not to leave her alone and sat to one side in the scrappy shade of a thorn tree. To me, Claudia was such an innocent soul, who would never under any circumstances hurt anything or anybody. I was mulling over the cruel ironies of life and the fact that such a horrible thing could happen to her. Soon my anger began to grow.

As happened so often in past challenging situations, the crazy red-haired Irishman made an appearance and chose to speak. 'Don't worry, Claudia. I am not going to let you roast in this damn sun for four hours with your foot stuck in a bloody drainpipe!'

Claudia looked up at me, tears welling in her big eyes.

'Oh Ian, there's nothing you can do. We've tried everything!' she said and started to cry quietly.

'I am going to get your foot out of there, I promise!'

The crazy bastard had spoken.

I wandered into the back of the lodge and happened to notice a bottle of green dishwashing liquid standing by a large sink. I picked it up and the bells of genius began ringing in my head. I remembered that an acquaintance from the Transkei coast once told me that if your wedding ring won't come off, because your fingers have swelled or gotten too fat, simply pour dishwashing liquid over your hand and the ring will come off.

I picked up the bottle and walked outside to see someone dabbing Claudia's forehead with a wet cloth.

'Now Claudia, listen to me. I'm going to pour this stuff over your leg. Tell me when you can feel it with your toes.'

'I don't know if I can still feel my toes,' Claudia said despondently.

I squirted the dishwashing liquid down the hole. It seeped away slowly. People came over and walked away again, shaking their heads.

Eventually, Claudia said, 'I can feel it! Yes, it's at my toes.'

Now I knew that the liquid had gone past the bend at the bottom of the pipe, which meant that her entire foot was covered by it.

'We've only got one chance at this, Claudia. Now I am going to wrap my arms around you from under your armpits and pull you upwards. Okay?'

'Yes,' said Claudia, sounding rather unconvinced.

I put my arms around her and grabbed my left wrist with my right hand. The grip of my right hand has always been exceptionally powerful. In the bars of the Eastern Cape of my youth, I was never defeated by anybody at arm wrestling. I straightened my back and set my legs firmly, then I counted: 'One … two … three!'

I exploded backwards, my arms ripping upwards above Claudia's perfect boobs. I felt the resistance of the foot still curved into the drain, but then with a loud 'thwack!' the foot came out. Claudia was free! She turned round and collapsed into my embrace, weeping freely with relief and joy.

In 2000, Castrol was bought out by BP and it wasn't long before BP's advertising agency apparently advised them against carrying on with the 'Can of the Best' campaign. We were told that Swaer, Boet and Mogae had become more popular than the brand.

So, one day in 2005, we were invited to a larney restaurant north of Joburg, where we were treated to a farewell dinner – the same type of farewell given to long-serving staff members of a company. We had gotten to know each other well over the years and I had often visited the Castrol head offices. This was a wonderful gesture on Castrol's part and showed once again, and maybe for the last time, the swashbuckling 'we will do things our way' attitude of the company under their inspirational CEO, Deryck Spence. From a strictly business point of view, the dinner was quite fitting because the campaign had grown Castrol's countrywide sales of oil from 17 per cent to about 34 per cent over the 17 years of the campaign. As I have it, it was (and might possibly still be) the longest-running ad campaign ever in South Africa.

While the campaign might have come to an end, it wasn't the end of the road for Swaer, Boet and Mogae. Since Castrol had no copyright on the characters we played in their ads, we were free to exploit them commercially. By then I had gained good experience directing three television series, and I had also written plays for theatre, so it followed naturally to write corporate theatrical pieces that came the way of the three Can of the Best *outjies* (guys).

That was how I ended up directing a piece of corporate theatre for a company called Mr Video. It was to be a grand awards ceremony at Sun City, although not so grandly paid (if I remember correctly, I eventually had to go in person to their offices in Cape Town to extract the final payment). So now Norman Anstey, Fats Bookholane and I were deep into rehearsing for the show at Sun City, but dear Fats was having a real problem remembering his lines. After three days and nights (lines sink in while you sleep), he still couldn't remember more than three lines in a row. This meant the rehearsals were not progressing fast enough.

Now, an actor always has a clear deadline: the show is going to happen at 7 pm on a certain day, and when the lights come up or the curtain rises, that's it. Norman, kind soul that he is, was being *very* kind to Fats. He assisted him with all kinds of tricks and university techniques to help him remember his lines. I was being far less considerate, and at one point I remonstrated rudely and loudly at Fats.

What happened next shocked me: Fats basically broke down in front of me. Tears came to his eyes and, in a soft voice, he said he had to speak with me. Because Fats was a Sotho whose father had taken his family to Port Elizabeth in the late 1940s, he could speak Xhosa fluently. He now spoke to me in Xhosa.

'Hey, mfondini, mamela, kukho izintho kufuneka uzazi' (My friend, there are some things you need to know).

I listened carefully to what he told me then. It basically went like this: 'Look, my friend, you must go easy on me, because ever since I was first confronted by the security police for being non-white and a rebel, and then after that, when I was in Italy, their police insulted me and beat me in their jail, I can't deal with it when people raise their voices to me or shout at me. Then I just lose my senses and the last thing I will be able to do when that happens, is to remember these lines.'

Fats started telling me his life story – how he was christened Malefatse and that this was how he got his nickname. He told me about bad encounters with the police as a youth and the time when a bad-tempered farmer in the Free State had falsely accused him of theft. He also told me how, after he had acted in protest theatre in Port Elizabeth with Athol Fugard and Winston Ntshona, he was hounded by the security police. He then decided it would be better for him to leave the country and joined the merchant navy. He ended up in some Italian harbour, where, rabble-rouser that he was, he managed to get himself incarcerated. The (white) Italian cops had dealt out some heavy treatment as well.

I felt bad for being so rough with him. I calmed down and rehearsals went much more smoothly after that. With intense focus and hard work, we managed to put the show together and made our way to Sun City.

The arrangements for the event were quite chaotic. Rehearsals for the awards were running late, while the three of us were desperately trying to get in at least one rehearsal on the stage. In between everything, I also had to see to the building of a ramp: after entering the venue pushing a wheelbarrow through the audience, Fats was supposed to push it up the ramp and onto the stage at a crucial point in the play. In the end, we only just managed a single rehearsal for what was actually a complex piece of theatre. We finished mere seconds before the doors opened.

Apart from doing the show, I was also master of ceremonies. I rushed backstage to put on my penguin suit and got the show underway. Throughout the proceedings, I would often hurry backstage to see how things were with my two fellow actors. Norman was practising quietly, while Fats had ensconced himself in a chair in a dark corner.

As often happens, things were running late. The organisers had hopelessly underestimated the time it would take to get through all the awards and speeches. Meanwhile, every time I went backstage to check on Norman and Fats, things looked worse. When he wasn't out on the town, Mr Bookholane's normal bedtime was around 8 pm and it was now dangerously past that hour. Fats had begun nodding off in his chair, and that was not a good thing. I quickly got him up and ushered him and his wheelbarrow to the kitchen, which was situated off a wide service passage about halfway down the auditorium.

I asked the young chefs to please try and keep Fats awake, and then to usher him through the entrance to the venue with his wheelbarrow when they heard gunshots from the stage. The dear fellows, busy as they were, saw my desperation and promised to help.

At last, the time came for our show. I hurried backstage to change into Boet's 'Castrol wardrobe' – short pants, golfing shirt, velskoens and floppy hat. Norman and I got the show going and we were getting good laughs, but all the time I was wondering how things were going in the kitchen.

In the script, Swaer starts to lose it because he has been drinking too much brandy. Suddenly, he sees elephants in the surrounding bush and shoots into the air. (I had secured a starter pistol for this purpose.) This was the point when Fats was supposed to arrive. Right on cue, I saw the guys from the kitchen pushing him through the door. Bra Fats, squeaking wheelbarrow and all, staggered inexorably forwards. The audience loved it – Fats was always a big hit.

'Wow! He's actually coming and he's headed in the right direction!' Norman said out of the side of his mouth.

Fats pushed the wheelbarrow up the ramp. When he paused at the top, Norman was to fire another shot, which he did on cue. On hearing the shot ring out, the unsuspecting Mogae was supposed to get such a fright that he would fall over in shock. The rest of the show depended fully on this taking place.

But what happened after the shot was fired? Nothing!

Fats was frozen like an ancient stone statue at the oracle of Delphi. He stood dead still. I gawked at Norman, who raised his eyebrows and shrugged his shoulders. The audience watched us in anticipation, not knowing if this was part of the plot or not. Norman fired the next shot, even though it was only needed a bit further on in the plot. Still nothing. Fats just stood there, not even twitching. 'Maybe he's dead' flashed through my mind. Out of curiosity, I crossed the stage to take a closer look. The man was still breathing but his eyes were closed.

Then it hit me: Fats Bookholane was fast asleep on his feet! Thanks to the upward angle of the ramp (which, like most hastily contracted theatrical ramps, had no railings) and his leaning forward to push the wheelbarrow, Fats was perfectly balanced. With his legs resting against the back of the wheelbarrow, he had miraculously relaxed enough to fall into a deep sleep.

I clapped my hands right next to Mogae's ear and shouted loudly. Professional that Fats was, he responded immediately, his eyes flying open and stretching wi-i-i-i-ide to the limits of their sockets with genuine shock, before crashing unceremoniously to the floor. In that moment, I could have kissed the man, for this was exactly what we needed. Now we could actually continue with the show.

This is another important insight for actors: you must never drop your fellow actors. On stage there should be a feeling of impregnable solidarity. The show must go on, regardless of any on-stage drama, personal feelings or other problems. Norman, Bra Fats and I saw the production through, and afterwards none of us said anything about the snoozing.

A few years after we stopped doing the ads, producer/director FC Hamman and I started talking about making a TV series based on the comical happenings at the Horingboom Oasis. With much luck and help from the management team at Mabalingwe, a game reserve outside Bela-Bela, we finally got to a stage where we could begin shooting the 13 episodes.

We tried upfront to get the blessing of Castrol but were shoved from pillar to post by middle management, so we just went ahead and started shooting. BP, which had acquired Castrol, then threatened to shut us down. FC Hamman's lawyer established that, in media law, characters belong in fact to the actors who create them. Things got bad when M-Net, on hearing of our battle with BP, threatened to pull out of their offer to broadcast the series. Then FC invited the CEO of BP and his head of corporate communications and advertising to come and watch the first episode that had been edited. They liked it so much that they not only gave us the go-ahead but put a large amount of money into the project as well.

South African actors are so used to drawing the short end of the stick in any confrontation with producers that this news took some time to sink in. We continued shooting and eventually the show aired weekly on M-Net under the title *Kalahari Oasis*.

Sadly, it wasn't a great success. I believe the main reason for this was because the broadcaster asked for the episodes to be trimmed to 22 minutes from the original 25-minute timing we shot. This was the *coup de grâce* for any well-planned timing around the funny moments in each episode. In the Kalahari, things generally don't happen quickly, and therefore the lead-in to a funny moment ceased to be authentic or true when it had to be trimmed to allow the broadcaster to squeeze in another advert during the ad break.

It was such a sad irony that a comedy series that was a spinoff from an ad campaign was severely compromised, buggered up in fact, to create more time for adverts. Such is the tightrope that creative people have to walk when dealing with broadcasters. We had gone full circle from a Can of the Best to a Can of Worms.

17

Radio Kalahari Orkes

IN 1991. MICHELLE AND I moved from the farm at Honeydew, north of Joburg, and bought a house in 6th Avenue in Melville, a suburb where many other actors and artists lived. We were only able to do this with very generous help from my father. We were happy there and it was while we were living in Melville that our son Daniel was born.

If Cara's birth was strange, with Camel Filters replacing an epidural, then Daniel's was even stranger. Two weeks before Daniel was due, Michelle told me she wanted to go body-surfing. I phoned my father for advice: 'Body-surfing. Well, Ian, I really don't know what to say.' Neither did I, but happy wife, happy life …

This was why we were in a chalet at the camping grounds at Cape Vidal, on the KwaZulu-Natal North Coast, when Michelle's waters broke at 11 pm on a Saturday night. I loaded her and four-year-old Cara into the Kombi and turned the key, but nothing happened. I tried again and again, but the battery was dead. I went knocking at the other chalets and miraculously found an old Rhodes University acquaintance in one of them.

I explained to him that I had to get to Johannesburg General Hospital as a matter of urgency. He helped me tow the Kombi round and round the parking lot of the resort until about 2 am, when it finally started. Our first stop was Richards Bay, but the R4 000 deposit the hospital required meant that it was not an option for us. Thankfully, a sister checked out Michelle on the side and told us the cervix was still not dilated, so we still had a bit of time. It was Joburg or bust.

We got to Ermelo at around 6.30 am, and then I started nodding off. Brave Michelle calmly coiled a bath towel on the driver's seat for the broken waters and took over the driving. That Sunday afternoon at 5 pm, Daniel was born in Joburg Gen's water birth unit. As he entered the water, he raised his little hand up in jubilation. He grew into a quiet and sensitive little boy, and I never raised a hand to him, just like my father never raised a hand to me.

One day in 1995, we were sitting around the breakfast table in our Melville home shortly after we had realised that we would have to put it up for sale. We couldn't manage the bond repayments. I am sure many South African actors have had to face potential bankruptcy, and we have become very adept at survival. However, at this point we didn't have much choice, so I told Michelle I would go and find us an estate agent to sell the place.

Then the doorbell rang. Michelle looked up at me and frowned. 'Who the heck can that be?'

When I opened the front door, I found a well-built young man in a dark suit smiling up at me. 'Meneer Ian Roberts – is dit jy?' ('Mr Ian Roberts – is that you?')

Could the bank already have sent out one of their people to kick us out, I thought.

'Ja, dis ek, hoe kan ek jou help?' ('Yes, that's me, how can I help you?')

'Ek is Willem Moerdyk van *Rapport* en ek het goeie nuus vir jou. Jy is in *Rapport* se groot kompetisie aangewys as die mees gewilde kunstenaar in Afrikaans in 'n advertensie. Daar's binnekort 'n funskie en die prysgeld is R10 000 – baie geluk, meneer Roberts!' (I am Willem Moerdyk from *Rapport* and I have good news for you. You have been voted the most popular artist in Afrikaans in an advertisement in *Rapport*'s big competition. There's a function soon and the prize money is R10 000. Congratulations, Mr Roberts!)

In those days R10 000 was a lot of money. Our Melville house was safe.

In 1999, I received the bombshell that Michelle had grown apart from me and wanted a divorce. It was like an unexpected punch that left me reeling … The words of the Portuguese travelling salesman on the night of my bachelor party in Fort Beaufort ten years earlier came echoing back at me: 'And just remember, there are women and there are mothers.' I had always said that if a woman didn't want me around, I wouldn't try to charm her with a bigger diamond ring. I would leave. I told Michelle that if she got all the papers together, I would sign them.

It is suggested by astrologers that Cancerians like me are carers and home-builders. So divorce did not sit well with me. I know my children did not like it. Michelle probably didn't like it either. Yes, people grow apart, but I also believe they can grow together again. For quite a while, I wasn't in a good way. Bob Dylan's line about the little boy lost, who 'takes himself so seriously', came to haunt me, but I had to keep working to provide for the home, broken as it was.

In the months after Michelle and I divorced, I lived on my own in a cottage on a farm about five kilometres north of Lanseria Airport. I had been cast in the leading role in the Afrikaans TV series *Arsenaal*, written and directed by the talented Jan Scholtz. At a certain point, I had only one night to learn a long monologue written in a kind of high Afrikaans, the kind spoken by my character, Jack Degenaar. It was midwinter and bitterly cold, and so Ole Lonesome climbed into the steaming waters of the cottage's Jacuzzi-like bath and began learning his lines.

By 4 am I felt I had finally mastered the long speech. I slept for two hours and then drove to the set, which was on the rugby field of a school in Weltevreden Park. The call time was 7 am. I arrived to find the crew putting up a crane on tracks on the rugby field. From experience, I knew the crane meant that Jan Scholtz wanted to shoot the scene in one take, and I thanked my lucky stars that I'd learnt my monologue so well.

Jan came up to me just as I had finished my make-up, greeting me in his warm way. Then he said, 'Listen, I have looked at that monologue for the scene. Really, I don't know what possessed me – it's too damn long. Let's cut it quickly.'

He seemed startled when he saw the look of murder in my eyes.

'What? Cutting the text needn't take long – we'll get a cup of cof–'

'Jan! Listen, I have worked on that text the whole night. If you change one damn word of my monologue, I'll kill you!'

Jan was a very diplomatic man, so he apologised. We shot the entire monologue in one take – dolly-tracking camera up on the crane and all – and Jan was happy. Sometimes it is essential for an actor to focus and prepare well for a scene when faced with a long monologue. Maybe if I hadn't been asked to leave my home, I wouldn't have been able to focus

With Michelle and our daughter, Cara, and son, Daniel.

Taking Cara and Daniel on an outing.

and prepare to the extent that I did. In retrospect, I could say that a sense of rejection and a broken heart can be seen as a very creative thing. Over time, I have come to add: it *should* be seen as such. The poet Rilke said that 'the exposed heart is richest in suffering'. I believe that actors with a broken heart may be closer to achieving that special quality.

When I realised that my marriage was on the rocks, I remembered that I had become an actor in the first place because I had been rejected by my first love many years earlier. Looking back, I can say that getting divorced perhaps also led to my greatest act of self-preservation yet: I quit drinking. I had become bored with the cycle of party and *babelas* (hangover), and I knew I had to start searching for something else. There was a good health shop at Fourways where I used to stop on my way out to the farm after visiting my children. One day I bought a set of ten CDs made by a South African who had travelled to India as a young man and found a guru who had taught him many ways of meditation. I used to play the CDs and do the meditations.

As when I suffered serious depression as a student at Rhodes University, I was beginning to become more and more aware of the world of small things again. Alcohol was the catalyst for many a good time, but the habit did nothing more for me than get in the way of my experiencing the world in all its fine detail. I began taking longer and longer walks into the deserted farmland in the hills to the north of Lanseria Airport almost every afternoon, sometimes returning after dark. When I have become stuck in claustrophobic suburban situations, I have always found the nearest bush to disappear into.

To this day, I am thankful that I avoided becoming one of those sad men one can see hanging around in bars at closing time, hoping one more *loopdop* will ease their aching heart. I gave up alcohol with conviction. Nowadays I use it when I feel like it, which is not often, and certainly not as a habit.

In the 1960s and 1970s, there was a proliferation of music groups in the Eastern Cape, even in our little farming community of Fort Beaufort, which had four different bands. Every Friday night a session would be held at the parish hall, where bands would play and the young folks would come in for a small fee at the door. The girls sat on chairs and benches against one wall and the boys hung out along the other wall, and the band would take the stage. Any *vlerksleper* (would-be suitor) would have to cross the floor and ask a girl for a dance. If she rejected you, the walk back across the floor felt like you had just had apricot jam smeared on your face.

I would sometimes go up on stage and sing a song, but only if I had stopped at the coloured township on the way into town and bought a half-jack of brandy from the shebeen. After I downed it, I would have the courage to go on stage.

In the early 2000s, my cousin Dan, the writer and musician Rian Malan, fine artist (and friend from Rhodes University) Carl Becker, former PE photography lecturer Ian Difford and I formed a band in Joburg. However, we struggled to come up with a name. We considered anything from The Tepid Toppies to The Crying Shames. Four of us were divorced and the fifth had never been married. Each of us brought our own musical style to the band: Rian had avoided compulsory national military service by going overseas, where he had encountered many famous bands, including the Rolling Stones, whom he met face to face. Dan had had his own rock 'n' roll band at St Andrew's College that performed wild underground numbers by artists like Jimi Hendrix and Frank Zappa.

For us, it was an exceedingly creative time. One day, Irving Schlosberg – who headed the record company EMI – saw us performing Dan's song 'The Crying Shame'. He was so intrigued that he asked for a video to be made of it. The popular Castrol advertising campaign had recently been terminated and cousin Dan, ever astute in business, thought that me, Norman and Fats would make a great cast for the video. Apart from being a great actor, Norman had a musical background and was a very good singer. So, Norman and I became the singers, while Fats played a fly-whisk made out of an ox-tail and sang a chorus line when it suited him.

When Eric Gallo opened the first recording studio in the southern hemisphere in Joburg in 1934, it had only a single microphone. If you look at the videos of our songs 'Suikerbos' and 'Skeeloog Daisy', you will see that they are shot with this in mind. This style emanated from the fact that Dan, Rian and I shared a nostalgic curiosity about the way things used to be from a music-production point of view in South Africa – and the rest of the world, for that matter – in those early sound recording studios. For instance, in our videos we would incorporate the way in which a musician would play directly into the microphone when their turn came and then move back when the singers took over, and so on.

Soon a whole album followed, entitled *Stoom Radio*, containing songs written by Rian, Dan and me, and performed by Norman, Fats and me.

People often ask me how we came upon the name Die Radio Kalahari Orkes. While we were dealing with EMI and recording the video, we were also pitching a TV show to local broadcasters. Our idea was to make a comedy show around the goings-on at a ramshackle trading store at an oasis called Slangfontein, out in the Kalahari. No broadcaster had yet bitten on the proposal, so when EMI suggested we call ourselves Die Kalahari Boys, I suggested that we should rather change the setting from a trading store to a radio station so that, if a broadcaster decided to proceed with the show, our band could be the official orchestra of the Slangfontein radio station.

Whenever I think about Die Radio Kalahari Orkes, I find myself thinking in Afrikaans. In 2005, we played some concerts at Kaktus op die Vlaktes, the music segment of the Klein Karoo Nasionale Kunstefees, probably the biggest Afrikaans arts festival in the country. It was there, in Oudtshoorn, that Die Radio Kalahari Orkes started to gain momentum. Today, almost twenty years later, I am the only person in the band who has been on stage for every single performance.

There have been occasions when I've wanted to stop performing with the Orkes. My worst experience was at Ladybrand, in the eastern Free State, where we were booked to play at the local rugby club on a weekend afternoon when icy winds blew off the snow on the nearby Maluti Mountains. We had to set up on a narrow stage on the field. By some moronic oversight, the show was scheduled to begin at the same time as the Cheetahs kicked off against the Blue Bulls in a major rugby clash, so everyone was in the clubhouse!

On top of this, we were doing new material that had been difficult to master. As usual, we had our 37 loyal and enthusiastic *andersdenkende* (alternative or nonconformist) supporters who didn't give a damn about rugby or the icy wind, and I was grateful to them. At this point I was properly *gatvol* (pissed off) for a number of reasons.

I've been playing the guitar ever since I was a child. In the early 2000s
I was a co-founder of the band Die Radio Kalahari Orkes (bottom image).

By then, Norman had left the Orkes and I hesitantly became the lead singer. Sure, I loved being on the road, but was I really a singer? Was I a musician? Or was I just an imposter? I couldn't help but remember my primary-school music teacher, who kicked me out of the choir for 'dragging' notes. I often wondered whether I was good enough, but violinist Wynand Davel assured me, 'Sing jy maar net, Oom, en fok hulle almal!' (You just sing, Uncle, and fuck the rest!)

Afterwards, driving into the night, I also couldn't help but think how much work it was for so little financial reward. And to play for such a small audience was very discouraging. Unlike other band members, I didn't get drunk to soften the reality: I was an actor who had become used to getting paid good money.

I discussed the matter with a good friend and eventually realised that it wasn't all that bad. The one great thing was that the Orkes frequently took me away from the big city, something that was precious and very important to me. I believe that my voice has also become better over the years. So I kept on going and Die Radio Kalahari Orkes keeps broadcasting to this day, from Durbanville in the Western Cape to Kaapschehoop in Mpumalanga and Louis Trichardt in the north.

One year, we were set to play at the Aardklop Arts Festival in Potchefstroom and something happened that illuminated an important reality about the performing arts: perfection is not necessarily a good thing. In fact, it is impossible. Whatever kind of 'star' you might have become, and no matter how many months you may have rehearsed your piece, you are still a glitch-prone, emotionally variable human being. Like I said before: racehorses are skittish.

During the festival, I had an incredibly heavy workload: I had to perform the leading role in Rian Malan's *Die Nagloper*, a new play about Dawie 'Dave' de Lange, the first rebel in Afrikaans music. The rehearsals had been extremely challenging and I was struggling to pull the performance together. Rian was in the audience the night it opened and, as it turned out, he wasn't very impressed.

After opening night, Die Radio Kalahari Orkes was supposed to play a concert on the main stage of the festival, featuring a lot of new material that I hadn't had enough time to properly prepare for. The

Orkes delivered a pretty standard performance that evening, but there wasn't anything special about it and a few mistakes were made.

The next morning, to enjoy my first day off in four weeks, I drove out to a large dam near Potchefstroom, parked my Land Rover on the dam wall and fell into a glorious sun-warmed snooze, lying on the bonnet with my back against the windshield. A couple of honeybees were buzzing round when my phone rang suddenly. It was the convenor of the band and he explained that Rian was very unhappy with the Orkes's performance the previous night and so he had called for a rehearsal in Potchefstroom at 11 am.

My hard-earned peace destroyed, I drove back into town to the rehearsal venue, a garden cottage where some of the band members were staying. As I walked in the door carrying my guitar, I found Rian standing in the middle of the lounge, practising some guitar licks, his eyes smarting from the smoke of a cigarette dangling from his mouth. The great concertina player Manie Bodenstein and banjo player Frans 'Wille Hond' Steinhobel stood joking against the far wall.

I put my guitar down and walked up to greet Rian.

'Hello, Rian,' I said.

'Howzit,' he mumbled past the cigarette butt, but without stopping the riff on his guitar. I could barely hear him. The mad red-haired Irishman inside me became livid in an instant.

'Rian, you better listen and listen to me good, because I am not going to say this again.'

Something in my voice made him stop playing. For the first time he looked directly at me.

'Ja?'

What the man wouldn't, couldn't know is that, in the world of the theatre, the day after opening night is sort of sacred to actors. It is a break from the intense activity of rehearsal that cannot come soon enough. It is the actors' hard-earned freedom from each other. On top of that, actors are often nursing hangovers from opening-night parties. They have learnt that it is better to let sleeping dogs lie, and that things that weren't right on opening night will come out in the wash in following performances. It was from this pressure that my harsh words came.

'Rian, I will suffer your paranoia for imperfection once more in my life. That is today. If you ever lay it on me again, I will fuck you up, okay?'

Rian's eyes narrowed as he took in my tirade. He is a sensitive, highly intelligent, very talented man, and I have often gone so far as to say he is a genius, but I felt he had overstepped the mark with me and my long journey of intense labour in the world of the performing arts. He didn't say anything in response.

We did the rehearsals and that evening I was back on stage for the performance of *Die Nagloper*, which wasn't all that good because of what actors call the 'second night blues'. The concert after that went well, maybe as a result of Rian's rehearsal. The following day cousin Dan phoned me from Joburg.

'I have just had Rian here at my place. He is very disturbed. Says you threatened him with physical violence.'

'Ja, I did. So, what did you say?'

'I told him that if Ian threatened you with physical violence, then he must have had a very good reason to do so. I advised him to be careful.'

What I have learnt over the years, and what I had tried to convey to Rian that day, is that there is not and can never be such a thing as a perfect performance. Should it ever occur, such a performance will likely be predictable and even stale. The true art of acting is to deliver a performance in which there is enough breathing room for something indescribable – some inexplicable magic – to come to the fore. This something is beyond words; it is that certain *je ne sais quoi.* I have always loved the interaction between performers on stage, in plays or in music and on movie sets. Although I have tried solo performances, I have never really enjoyed them. In fact, I have always ended up avoiding them.

Achieving this magic has always been my quest, from my days roaming the veld with the Hunter-Gatherers to portraying whatever role on stage or screen, sixty-odd years later. This is what my quest will continue to be.

I have no idea why I took to the bush whenever I could as a boy, but it certainly had a lot to do with my friendship with the other Hunter-Gatherers: Djonni Kieghlaar, Pieter Trompetter and Pese and Kununu Piet. Truth is, we all loved escaping the normal order of things. Out in the bush no one told us what to do and no one admonished us for doing the wrong thing because nobody knew what we were up to. We were a law unto ourselves.

I suppose there must have been a few squabbles, but generally we never fought among ourselves. At school, when we read William Golding's classic *Lord of the Flies*, I could never understand what drove the boys on the island to turn on each other and form different tribes. In my social anthropology lectures at Rhodes University, I learnt from studies done in the Kalahari by Monica Wilson that the Masarwa (the Tswana name for the San people or Bushmen) never fought among themselves, for the simple reason that they couldn't afford to do so. Eking out a living in the semi-desert meant that everybody was needed to help the group survive.

In my other life at St Andrew's College, competition was the name of the game. Your status depended on whether you were playing for the first team, the second or the third. Everything centred around the results of inter-house competitions, from theatre competitions to boxing matches. I became a committed part of that world as well. I even became captain of some sports teams.

Still, I never yearned to be part of big, organised groups. For example, even though I love my Land Rover, I would never think of joining a 4x4 club. I would rather vanish into the desert or the mountains on my own. Why this unwillingness to join the herd? I'm not sure. I think the red-haired Irishman would have the answer, but I'm scared to ask him.

When I think back to my unconventional youth, I realise it was the start of a lifetime of being different to the norm. An incident at Rhodes University highlighted my apartness: I stayed in digs with three other students and in the lunch breaks we would get together and compete for money in a game of darts. One Friday, three of my digs mates started verbally attacking me, telling me of things I had done that pissed them off and saying how I had a devious personality. It seemed to be a premeditated attack.

I was devastated. I left the digs and walked to the road that led to Fort Beaufort, my home town, 80 kilometres away. It was a cold winter's day but eventually I got a lift to my parents' farm. Lunch was being served when I unexpectedly walked through the door, and I got a gloriously warm greeting. I was back among my own people. I walked into the mountains of my hunter-gathering days trying to figure out what had triggered the attack on me. I got no answer.

When I got back to Grahamstown I went to visit a friend, fine art student, David Newman, a quiet, unusual young man who spoke very softly yet had survived terrible things in the Rhodesian bush war. I explained to him what had happened and how I struggled to understand what I had done wrong. I didn't get very far into my story when he held up his hand to stop me.

'You don't have to go any further, Ian. I know what it is – jealousy. They can't get a handle on you, so they have to attack you.'

Over the years, I have come to realise that I have always been an outsider and I will continue to be one. I also seek out similarly spirited people. There have been times when this aspect of my personality has made life difficult for me, but mostly it has been of huge benefit, most definitely in my acting career.

Sometime in 2003, after more than 25 years on the stage and screen, I received a strange request from my parents. Please could I come and visit them at their retirement home in Greyton: they wanted to talk with me. In 48 years this had never happened, and I was curious what could be so important that they needed to have a face-to-face with me. So I drove the thousand kilometres to the Cape.

After the usual greetings and chit-chat, my mother poured us some Ceylon tea and took the lead in the 'talk'.

'Your father and I have been thinking that we need to apologise to you.'

'Apologise? Crikey, what for?' I replied.

'Because we feel we never looked after you properly when you were growing up as a boy.'

I stared, surprised, at these two extraordinary, lovely people, my parents. True to their emotionally reticent Englishness, they were struggling to express what was essentially a highly emotional issue. They had failed me as parents, they felt. Of course, I knew the truth was exactly the opposite: they had brought me up the only way they could have.

It was my father's turn.

'Your mother and I think we never gave you enough *love*.'

The word came awkwardly from his mouth. It had never been easy to express emotion in our family and the word was only used in statements like 'I love it when it rains' or 'It's been a lovely day/holiday/dinner. I love it by the sea.'

The Roberts family.

'Yes, we feel we never gave you enough love, when you were growing up,' said my mother now that the shackles had been broken. I smiled at them. I was astounded that they had felt it important enough to bring me all that way just so that they could apologise face to face for what they felt was a major shortcoming in their duty as parents.

'Well, what do you think about that, Ian?'

'Me? I say thank you for that!' I said emphatically. Not sure what to make of my response, they looked at each other. Then they both looked at me with surprise.

'Gawd mawd, Ian. You say thank you?' my mother asked.

'Yes! In that case I can only thank you for not giving me enough love, because you brought me up absolutely perfectly. I wouldn't have wished it another way and I will be eternally grateful to you for that.'

We didn't stand up to give each other a group hug. We simply continued to sit quietly, sipping our cups of tea. I felt eternity flit through the room like a soft, warm wind. I was in the company of two very special people. I was a happy man.

Epilogue

IT IS THE YEAR 1992 and in the little town of Warden in the Free State the funeral of a grandfather is taking place. The grandchildren have all been placed in a room, out of the way of the mourning grownups. There is a TV set but only one young girl is watching the episode of *Arende* that is being shown. This eight-year-old girl is lying on her back, with her head over the end of the bed, so she is watching the programme upside down. She calls out to her mother in the room next door, asking her to come over.

'Mamma, wie is hierdie man?' (Mom, who is this man?)

She points to the character Sloet Steenkamp. Her mother explains that, in real life, he is an actor.

'Hoekom vra jy, my kind?' (Why are you asking?) the mother says.

'Ek hou van hom. Ek wil eendag met hom trou.' (I like him. One day I want to marry him.)

'Genade, kind! Trou?' (Goodness gracious, child! Marry?)

In 2013, I travelled with Die Radio Kalahari Orkes to an arts festival in Lydenburg that was being organised by De Ark Guesthouse. That was the first time I saw Francoinette le Roux. She was the daughter of the woman running the arts festival and I was struck by her unique look and manner.

As I drove out of town the next morning, heading back to Joburg, I noticed a piece of paper under the windscreen wiper blade, flapping in the wind. I stopped and took it out. The note was written in the most beautiful cursive handwriting (I have to say, very much like my mother's): 'Ek hou van jou kar. Ek hoop ons kan eendag saam in hom op 'n road trip gaan.' (I like your car. I hope one day we can go on a road trip together in it.)

It was signed by Francoinette. I realised then that I hadn't had the grace to say goodbye to her, so I drove back into Lydenburg and did just that. Back then, I was in a ten-year relationship and I put Francoinette out of my mind.

A year later, in 2014, I was driving to Lydenburg again for the same festival. I had time to waste, so I climbed to the top of the Trout River Falls and swam in the pools up there. As I floated in a pool with the sun in my eyes, I suddenly remembered that Lydenburg was where that lovely, unusual woman lived ...

When we met again late that afternoon at the top of the long stairway that led up to the rooftop venue of the hotel, the magic was again there. When we shook hands, I held on to her hand for an unnaturally long time, indeed for all the time it took for us to reach the bottom of the long stairway again.

The little girl who had been so intrigued by Sloet Steenkamp more than 25 years ago was now 31 and I was sixty-something. She later told me that, as a child, when she'd seen Sloet in close-up looking into the camera, it was if he had looked into her soul. 'Maar toe het ek van hom vergeet' (But then I forget about him).

Francoinette ran her own hair salon at the hotel premises, and over many months we became closer and closer to each other. Eventually, I did take her away in my Land Rover and we went wild camping in the Tsitsikamma on the farm of a friend. There were no amenities whatsoever. For me, it was a return to my hunter-gathering days, and Francoinette somehow managed to enjoy it too. Any refined woman who can survive that kind of camping with her grace intact can survive anything.

Perhaps it is as simple as this: my long and sometimes difficult journey to becoming an actor, which eventually led to my being given the opportunity to play the character of Sloet Steenkamp in *Arende*, may also have been intended to get me to this point of meeting true love.

In 2019, when I was 67, Francoinette and I became parents to twins, Ian-Keith and Lynn-Sophie, who keep us on our toes every single day. I have noted, over the years of being a parent, that the people who give you the most advice on bringing up children usually don't have any children themselves. You can only have the temerity to comment on the incomprehensible if you don't have any experience of it. All I can say is that I now have newfound respect for my grandparents Scotty and Daniel Roberts, who brought up my father and uncle, who were identical twins.

Bringing up our twins has meant giving up four years of what you thought used to be your life. However, the rewards are indescribable. It is like that feeling I got when, many years ago, I went to pick up Cara and Daniel from Michelle's house and saw her new boyfriend's car in what used to be my driveway. All my sadness disappeared when I saw the utter joy with which my two children came running up towards me, carrying their little holiday bags and shouting with absolute abandon as only a child can: 'Daddy! Daddy! Daddyyyy!' My downturned mouth would immediately break into a smile.

As an older man now with four-year-old twins, that smile returns every time I watch their interactions with their extraordinary mother. Amid all the usual nonsense that happens in life and in relationships, with age I have thankfully become aware what a special privilege this is. x

Ever since I wrote my first theatrical play, at the age of ten at St Andrew's Preparatory School, writing has been a constant part of my life. I feel like I have always been writing and that is what I will continue to do. I have written many poems, most of which are flapping about somewhere in the wind on a piece of paper. Some I have kept.

The biggest challenge to me now is to become adept – might I go so far as to say good – at writing movie screenplays. I have been at it for nearly twenty years and I hope that I am getting better. Then, once I have managed to get a script financed, I would like to direct it. I feel this is the way in which I could give back the most to an industry that has given me so much over the years.

Things have changed substantially since the heyday of the performing arts in the 1980s and 1990s. Sadly, the structures to support the arts that were built up by the previous government are mostly non-existent. These days, as an actor you need a lot of luck to keep going. But, as I tend to say, 'Luck seems to like hard work.'

The beauty of Die Radio Kalahari Orkes is that we don't belong to anybody and don't have to answer to anybody. We don't have to be politically correct and can simply be ourselves, and that feels really good. People often come up to us after a show, a light of positivity

With Francoinette and our twins, Ian Keith and Lynn-Sophie, and my step-daughter Ava (far right).

shining in their eyes, thanking us for what we are doing and asking us never to stop making music. Looking at my grey hairs, some of them let slip: 'Haai jinne, hoe lank kan julle nog aanhou?' (Gosh, how long can you still keep going?)

My answer would be like Michelangelo's response to the Pope after he'd asked the artist how long it would be before he completed painting the ceiling of the Sistine Chapel. 'It will be finished when it is finished,' he said.

Retirement has always seemed a strange concept to me. You surely have to keep working at whatever you're doing to get better at it. Or, as we say in Die Radio Kalahari Orkes, 'Hoe kan jy dit ooit opneuk as jy dit nooit eers in die eerste plek reggekry het nie?' (How can you screw up something if you never even got it right in the first place?)

www.ingramcontent.com/pod-product-compliance
Lightning Source LLC
Chambersburg PA
CBHW062056080426
42734CB00012B/2665